# THE ORIGINS OF THE KOREAN WAR

ORIGINS OF MODERN WARS
General editor: *Harry Hearder*

*Titles already published:*

THE ORIGINS OF THE FIRST WORLD WAR
  *James Joll*
THE ORIGINS OF THE ARAB-ISRAELI WARS
  *Ritchie Ovendale*
THE ORIGINS OF THE RUSSO-JAPANESE WAR
  *Ian Nish*
THE ORIGINS OF THE FRENCH REVOLUTIONARY WARS
  *T. C. W. Blanning*
THE ORIGINS OF THE SECOND WORLD WAR IN EUROPE
  *P. M. H. Bell*
THE ORIGINS OF THE KOREAN WAR
  *Peter Lowe*
THE ORIGINS OF THE SECOND WORLD WAR IN ASIA AND THE PACIFIC
  *Akira Iriye*
THE ORIGINS OF THE VIETNAM WAR
  *Anthony Short*

# THE ORIGINS OF THE KOREAN WAR

*Peter Lowe*

**LONGMAN**
London and New York

**Longman Group UK Limited**
Longman House, Burnt Mill, Harlow
Essex CM20 2JE, England
*and Associated Companies throughout the world*

*Published in the United States of America
by Longman Inc., New York*

*First published 1986
Fourth impression 1989*

**British Library Cataloguing in Publication Data**

Lowe, Peter, 1941 —
  The origins of the Korean War. — (Origins of
  modern wars)
  1. Korean War, 1950–1953—Causes
  I. Title    II. Series
  951.9′042    DS918
  ISBN 0-582-49278-5

**Library of Congress Cataloging in Publication Data**

Lowe, Peter.
  The origins of the Korean War.

  (Origins of modern wars)
  Bibliography: p.
  Includes index.
  1. Korean War, 1950–1953.    2. Korea–History–Allied
  occupation–1945–1948.    3. World politics–1945–1955.
  I. Title.    II. Series.
  DS918.L68    1986    951.9′042    85-23056
  ISBN 0-582-49278-5

Produced by Longman Group (FE) Limited
Printed in Hong Kong

# CONTENTS

List of maps                                                        vi
Editor's foreword                                                   vii
Preface                                                             x
Acknowledgements                                                    xiii
Abbreviations                                                       xv

1.  Korea, the Japanese empire, and the Pacific War                 1

2.  The establishment of two Koreas                                 19

3.  The approach of confrontation in Korea                          43

4.  General MacArthur and the recovery of Japan                     72

5.  The demise of the Kuomintang and the triumph
    of Chinese communism                                            98

6.  The Cold War in Europe                                          126

7.  The outbreak of the Korean War                                  150

8.  Rollback and Chinese intervention in Korea                      175

Conclusion                                                          206

Appendix                                                            217
Select bibliography                                                 219
Maps                                                                225
Index                                                               230

# LIST OF MAPS

1. Korea and neighbouring areas     226
2. Korea, the 38th Parallel, and the Demarcation Line, 1953     227
3. The North Korean advance, July to September 1950     228
4. The UN Command's counter-attack, September to November 1950     229

# EDITOR'S FOREWORD

The war with whose origins Dr Peter Lowe is concerned in the present volume differs from wars previously considered in the series in that one – but only one – great power was fully engaged in it in a military sense. Communist China, so recently emerging from a hard-fought civil war, was not yet a great power. Only the American government among major powers believed that the war required the employment of very considerable armed forces. Dr Lowe therefore concentrates much of his analysis on American policy, and his dissection of the disagreements between American military men and diplomats, the Pentagon and the State Department, MacArthur and Truman, and finally between Washington and London, makes fascinating reading. But he sets the study of American policy firmly within the context of a divided Korea and of the Cold War in the world at large.

One factor in the present volume reflects an identical one in Ritchie Ovendale's *Origins of the Arab–Israeli Wars*: the electoral pre-occupations of the American President. But there is a difference. In Dr Ovendale's story an appreciable section of the American public – the Jews and especially the Jews of New York – felt directly involved in the Middle Eastern crises. In Dr Lowe's account there is no similar specific group in the USA directly concerned, but Harry Truman was obviously aware that to involve a considerable number of American servicemen in a war so soon after the Second World War was a heavy responsibility which would be assessed with absorbing interest by the public. On the other hand the Republican opposition would be ready to charge the administration with failing to resist communism if they had the chance so to do, and there was the added complication that General MacArthur was himself considering accepting nomination for the presidency in the next elections. Public opinion was thus playing a very strong role in influencing American policy, but unfortunately, if inevitably, the American public was even more naïve and green in its understanding of world politics than were its political and military leaders. The point brings with it the reminder that public opinion, usually because of the aggressive and myopic nature of the media, is often more belligerent than the political government, although in the case of American policy since 1945 the *Washington Post* and the *New York Times* have been honourable exceptions to the rule.

That the basic motives of political leaders are rarely those which they proclaim was suggested by James Joll in *The Origins of the First World War*. In the case of Korea the real motives sometimes coincided with the professed ones, but were sometimes more mixed. Kim Il Sung was probably sincere in claiming that his main aim was to unite his country, a country which, as Dr Lowe points out, had been united for centuries. But Kim also wanted to advance the cause of communism in Asia, even if he was not the puppet of Stalin that the West believed him to be. MacArthur's main motive was the defence of Japan against communism, and his occasional praise of the corrupt and incompetent Syngman Rhee could hardly have been sincere.

Then there is again the question of miscalculations. As Dr Blanning has shown in his *Origins of the French Revolutionary Wars*, the Prussian monarchy and revolutionary France both grossly miscalculated their chances of a quick victory in 1792, and as Professor Nish has shown in his *Origins of the Russo-Japanese War*, the Tsar and most of his ministers absurdly expected a rapid defeat of Japan in 1904, so did the North Koreans underestimate the likelihood of a determined resistance by the Americans, and MacArthur underestimated the possibility of a North Korean attack and subsequently of a Chinese attack. MacArthur's mingling of optimism with loose talk of using the atom bomb, should his optimism prove unjustified, was surely the height of irresponsibility.

In Korea the United Nations played a bigger role than it had done in any war since its foundation. Lowe reminds us that before the USA had utilised favourable votes in the UN as a cover for American military action in Korea, the UN was already deeply involved. It was perhaps sad that it was not even more deeply involved in that initial stage. Dr Lowe cites Evan Luard's point of the contrast between the UN supervising force of 30 for the elections of 1948 in South Korea with the League of Nation's supervising force of 1,000 in the Saar for the plebiscite of 1935. The UN has always suffered from the parsimony of the great powers, and not least the parsimony of Soviet Russia. Lowe's account of the role of the UN in Korea before the fighting started is extremely valuable, and shows that, while the Russians believed that the organisation was dominated by the Americans, the Americans themselves were often critical of UN moves. Once the fighting had started there was clearly a strong element of deceit in the American use of the UN umbrella, but it is surely better for a superpower to work through the UN, on those occasions when it can do so, than to take nakedly unilateral action.

It is difficult, however, not to accept the conclusion which Peter Lowe's interpretation implies: that both American and Chinese intervention were dangerous to world peace, and could have been avoided. Of May 1950, he writes (p. 68): 'The situation in the Korean peninsula was one of civil war. As in other civil wars the big question mark was the approaches to be adopted by the great powers.' The principle which has from time to time been recommended by the British Foreign Office – the principle of non-intervention by great powers in the affairs of smaller countries – still deserves respect. It is unlikely that a united Korea under Kim Il Sung would have endangered the security of MacArthur's Japan, or that it would have been a tool either of Moscow or Peking. It might very well have brought greater stability to the area.

But Chinese intervention was not an inevitable result of American intervention. As Dr Lowe tells us, 'Chinese participation could have been averted by the adoption of more sensitive, realistic policies.' (p. 201). Such realistic policies would have included an American diplomatic recognition of Mao's China, following the British recognition, and the admission of Communist China to the UN. Even as late as October 1950 large-scale Chinese action could have been avoided through appreciating the perils of crossing the 38th parallel and of advancing to the Yalu. Perhaps the final message to be received from Peter Lowe's analysis is that courageous political leaders with closed minds are more dangerous than cautious ones with open minds.

HARRY HEARDER

# PREFACE

It is the contention of this study that the origins of the Korean War are best understood in the light of developments in the Korean peninsula, in China, Japan and in Europe. Hence the approach adopted of examining the origins under these chapter headings. This in turn means that there are essentially two themes – the nature of the political and social evolution of Korea between 1945 and 1950 and the place of Korea within the emerging Cold War with the United States and the Soviet Union as the two central powers. The two Korean states, the Republic of Korea (South Korea) and the Democratic People's Republic of Korea (North Korea) came into existence formally in 1948 but in effect they had already appeared in 1945–46. Following the lengthy period of colonial occupation by Japan, Korea was seized in 1945 with fierce patriotism and the ardent desire for the country to be unified once more. The running was made by the forces of the left, untainted by collaboration with Japan, as were so many on the right, and anxious to direct and to channel the spontaneous revolutionary manifestations in much of Korea. The American military government in south Korea, headed by General John R. Hodge, was determined to thwart communism and proceeded to oppose the original wish of the administration in Washington to see trusteeship provide the solution to Korea's problems through cooperation between the United States and the Soviet Union. The Russians were determined to see a communist government established in Korea and believed that developments pointed to this as the likely outcome. Before they emerged formally the two regimes hostile towards one another had already appeared; each was spurred on by burning zeal to unite Korea and to liquidate the other. The leaders of the two states, Syngman Rhee and Kim Il Sung, personified the confrontation. American policy regarding Korea vacillated: put succinctly Korea was not important enough to warrant a deep American commitment but was too important to be allowed to go communist. This dilemma was resolved by Harry Truman on June 25 to 27 1950.

Events in neighbouring parts of East Asia and in Europe profoundly affected perceptions of Korea. A protracted civil war in China culminated in the triumph of Mao Tse-tung's movement and the defeat of the Kuomintang regime headed by Chiang Kai-shek. American policy-makers were divided as to whether Chinese communism operated independently of Moscow or as part of a monolithic world communist movement directed by Stalin. The trend in thinking in 1949–50 pointed to the latter conclusion. Much American opinion, especially on the right, was outraged at the 'loss' of China to communism and the pressures experienced by the Truman administration intensified. The fate of the island of Taiwan loomed large in the spring of 1950 and it was held in Washington before the start of the Korean War that Taiwan must be denied to the Chinese communists, which was *not* synonymous with supporting the Kuomintang regime in politically bankrupt Taiwan. In Japan General Douglas MacArthur presided over the transition from the abject surrender of Japan to the reforms of Japanese government and society, at first envisaged as radical and then tempered by expediency under the impact of the Cold War. Japan was recognised as fundamental to the maintenance of American interests in East Asia: accordingly American initiatives had to be moderated so as to achieve stability in Japan and friendship between Washington and Tokyo. The 'reverse course' from 1948 connoted the revival of the Japanese economy and the beginnings of the integration of Japan into the American-dominated defence of the island chain in which Japan and the Philippines were basic constituents. To the Soviet Union, China and North Korea, the recovery of Japan threatened their interests and arguably rendered it wise to incorporate the whole of Korea under the authority of a communist government sooner rather than later. Similarly a North Korean attempt to unify Korea by force would be a major threat to Japan, since most observers in the West discounted the idea that Kim Il Sung might act independently of Stalin. The situation in Europe, with the rapid growth of mutual suspicion and acrimony exemplified most starkly in the clash over the blockade of Berlin, brought the classic era of the Cold War to a climax. Soviet control of central and eastern Europe and the construction of the NATO alliance marked ominous stages in the fears and tensions of the communist and western worlds in which both sides were prepared for a crisis in a particular region or country that might be transformed swiftly into a third world war.

The first six chapters consider the origins of the conflict in fulfilment of this approach. With the outbreak of any war it is essential to examine the particular circumstances in which it began and the immediate aftermath. Chapter 7 explores the sequence of events in June and July 1950. An investigation of the origins would not be complete without explaining why China decided, in October–November 1950, to participate in the war with such dramatic repercussions; this is pursued in Chapter 8. It might be thought that some discussion of developments in South-East Asia and in the Middle East is required. The communist insurgency in Malaya from 1948 and the serious challenge to French authority in Indo-China, not to mention the absence of stability in Burma and in the Philippines, were certainly significant and worried officials in Washington and London. The British and the French popularised the 'domino' theory before American politicians revealed the obsessions that preoccupied them in the 1950s and 1960s. American anxiety about Indo-China in particular is relevant in accounting for the belief of Harry Truman and Dean Acheson that the western world was faced with the menace of a situation analogous to Munich in 1938; increased American aid to the French in Indo-China was approved in May 1950. Alarm over the Middle East centred upon Iran and the possibility of Soviet intervention leading to a confrontation similar to that seen in Berlin in 1948–49. However, the problems in South-East Asia and the Middle East were secondary in importance; the close relationship between Korea, China, Japan and Europe in terms of the formulation of the crisis leading to the Korean War necessitates concentration upon these areas.

This study considers the attitudes and motivating influences of each of the countries most deeply involved. The availability of sources means inevitably that it is far more feasible to assess the role of the United States and to some extent of South Korea than it is of the Soviet Union, China and North Korea. The precise position of the Soviet Union in particular is obscure. Some aspects should become more comprehensible when the North Korean records captured during the drive north in October 1950 have been fully assessed but even then it is improbable that more than a partial clarification will be possible. Compared perhaps with most other wars being examined in this series, the Korean War leaves more room for speculation concerning the intentions of those contributing crucially to the start of the war. Lastly it should be emphasised that for the inhabitants of Korea developments in June 1950 did not constitute the beginning of a war but rather the continuation of a civil war that had started in 1945 and which has not ended yet.

# ACKNOWLEDGEMENTS

The research for this volume was generously assisted by the Nuffield Foundation through its Social Sciences Small Grants Scheme and by the British Academy. I am extremely grateful to both bodies. It is a most pleasant task for me to thank the staffs of the various libraries and institutions in which I have worked: in Britain, the Public Record Office, Kew, the British Library of Political and Economic Science, the Bodleian Library, Oxford, Churchill College, Cambridge, the John Rylands University Library of Manchester, the Library of University College, Cardiff, the Library of the School of Oriental and African Studies, London University, and the Institute of Historical Research; and in the United States, the National Archives, Washington, DC, the Harry S. Truman Library, Independence, Missouri, and the MacArthur Memorial, Norfolk, Virginia. It is invidious to name some individuals rather than others but my work in American archives was cheerfully and efficiently advanced by Mr John E. Taylor of the Modern Military Branch, Military Archives Division, National Archives, Washington; Dr Benedict K. Zobrist and Messrs Dennis Bilger and Warren Ohrvall of the Harry S. Truman Library; and Mr Edward J. Boone, Jr of the MacArthur Memorial.

I have derived much encouragement from discussing various aspects of this subject with the following: Mr Chris Alcock, Dr Roger Buckley, Professor Bruce Cumings, Dr Gordon Daniels, Professor Roger Dingman, Dr Reinhard Drifte, Professor Ian Nish, Professor Geoffrey Warner and Professor William W. Stueck Jr. While I was in Washington Mr Richard D. Finn kindly assisted me and introduced me to Mr John J. Muccio, formerly United States ambassador to the Republic of Korea: I am most grateful to Mr Muccio for agreeing to see me.

I should like to thank the following and, where appropriate, acknowledge permission to quote from collections in their custody: the Harry S. Truman Library for the Acheson, Elsey, Truman, and Webb Papers; the MacArthur Memorial for the MacArthur Papers; Sir George Kenyon and the estate of Sir Raymond Streat for the diaries of Sir

## Acknowledgements

Raymond Streat, which are being prepared and edited for publication by the Manchester University Press in the near future. Public Record Office documents cited in this work are British Crown copyright and are reprinted by permission of The Controller of Her Majesty's Stationery Office.

I acknowledge the assistance of the University of Manchester granting me study leave for two terms during the academic session 1981–82, which enabled me to make considerable progress.

Professor Harry Hearder first suggested that I contribute to this series and has given me every encouragement in the course of fulfilling his editorial responsibilities.

Finally I wish to thank most warmly Mrs Tina Reid and Miss Gillian Edge, who have typed the final draft with efficiency and good humour.

PETER LOWE

# ABBREVIATIONS

| | |
|---|---|
| ACJ | Allied Council for Japan |
| Cab | Cabinet Office Papers, Public Record Office, Kew |
| CC | Left–Right Coalition Committee |
| CCP | Chinese Communist Party |
| CIA | Central Intelligence Agency (United States) |
| CPKI | Committee for the Preparation of Korean Independence |
| DEFE | Defence Papers, Public Record Office, Kew |
| DFUF | Democratic Front for the Unification of the Fatherland |
| DNF | Democratic National Front |
| DPRK | Democratic People's Republic of Korea (North Korea) |
| ECA | Economic Cooperation Administration |
| FEC | Far Eastern Commission |
| FO | Foreign Office Papers, Public Record Office, Kew |
| *FRUS* | *Foreign Relations of the United States* |
| IMTFE | International Military Tribunal for the Far East |
| KDP | Korean Democratic Party |
| KMAG | Korean Military Advisory Group |
| KPR | Korean People's Republic |
| NATO | North Atlantic Treaty Organisation |
| NKIPC | North Korean Interim People's Committee |
| NKLP | North Korean Labour Party |
| NSC | National Security Council |
| NSRRKI | National Society for the Rapid Realization of Korean Independence |
| OEEC | Organisation for European Economic Cooperation |
| OSS | Office of Strategic Services |
| POWs | Prisoners of war |
| Prem | Prime Minister's Office Papers, Public Record Office, Kew |
| RDC | Representative Democratic Council |
| ROK | Republic of Korea (South Korea) |
| SCAP | Supreme Commander for the Allied Powers, Japan |

*Abbreviations*

| | |
|---|---|
| SKLP | South Korean Labour Party |
| UN | United Nations |
| UNCOK | United Nations Commission on Korea |
| UNCURK | United Nations Commission for the Unification and Rehabilitation of Korea |
| UNTCOK | United Nations Temporary Commission on Korea |
| WEU | Western European Union |

# Chapter 1

# KOREA, THE JAPANESE EMPIRE, AND THE PACIFIC WAR

The outbreak of the Korean War in June 1950 focused world attention on a remote peninsula in East Asia, which had never previously been the centre of a crisis of such dimensions as to threaten the possibility of a world war. To elderly people with long memories Korea connoted a localised crisis at the end of the nineteenth and beginning of the twentieth centuries resulting from the decline of the Ch'ing dynasty in China, the landward expansion of the Russian empire, and the beginning of the Japanese colonial empire in the Far East. The Sino-Japanese War of 1894–95 occurred because of the Japanese desire to establish a presence in the kingdom of Korea and the Chinese attempt to thwart this ambition. The close geographical proximity between the Japanese home islands and Korea resulted in Japanese determination to assert herself in Korea so as to ensure the more effective defence of Japan herself; in addition, it was hoped to exploit Korea economically.[1] The Russo-Japanese War of 1904–05 occurred because the partially concealed rivalry of a decade before was now overt. Japan did not want war against Tsarist Russia but was determined to fight unless positive assurances were forthcoming that Russia would cease to meddle in Korean affairs. Russia blundered into a conflict that was to have such serious consequences for the future of the Tsarist state and for an Asian challenge to occidental dominance.[2] However, the Sino-Japanese and Russo-Japanese wars, while significant struggles and in the case of the latter conflict involving savage warfare in Manchuria anticipating the kind of warfare to be seen in Europe between 1914 and 1918, did not constitute a confrontation between two superpowers set against a background of vitriolic suspicion and rivalry, as happened in 1950.

What was the nature of Korean society and how had Korea been affected by the experience of having been ruled as an integral part of the Japanese colonial empire for almost half a century before the defeat of Japan in 1945? Korea is an ancient country with a very lengthy period of having been governed as a unified area (from AD 668 to 1945). The Yi dynasty presided over Korean affairs from 1392 to 1910 but the dynasty

1

was in decline from the seventeenth century onwards; and Yi ascendancy was distinguished by a combination of exploitation, corruption and brutality in which endemic factionalism predominated. As Gregory Henderson has observed, there were close parallels between the political strategies and tactics during the Yi dynasty and the political developments in both north and south Korea after 1945.[3] In geographical terms Korea extends from the long frontier with Manchuria along the Yalu and Tumen rivers to the short border area with Russian territory in the north-east. The southernmost part of Korea was a mere 90 miles (145 km) from Japan; Korea resembled Japan in having a large number of islands but only one is politically significant – Cheju-do, to the south-west of the peninsula.[4] Korea extends for approximately 600 miles (965 km) from the north-east to the south-west and is about 150 miles (240 km) wide, although narrowing in the northern part of the peninsula to less than 100 miles (160 km). The population of Korea averaged around eight million during the Yi era but increased rapidly in the twentieth century growing from approximately ten million in 1900 to about thirty million in 1949. In economic terms, in the twentieth century industry was concentrated in the north and the south was principally concerned with agriculture, particularly rice. The arbitrary division of Korea at the 38th parallel in 1945 was absurd economically, creating two areas which could not function efficiently in terms of what they possessed. The Korean language was comprehensible throughout the country with major differences only in Cheju island.[5]

Korean government was dominated by court circles and the greater landowners until the demise of the Yi dynasty. Chinese cultural influence was important and was most clearly seen in the impact of Confucianism. China regarded Korea as a vassal state of the Ch'ing empire and Chinese policy was implemented through her representative in Peking. Between 1882 and 1894 China was represented by an ambitious, astute official, Yuan Shih-k'ai, who worked to postpone the rise of Japanese authority in Korea.[6] However, the swift rout of China in 1894–95 was followed by a period of tense rivalry between Russia and Japan culminating in the war of 1904–05. Japanese authority over Korea was confirmed by the settlement of the conflict in 1905 but Japan did not immediately annex Korea; instead the Korean monarchy was retained and a Japanese resident-general was appointed in Seoul. Prince Ito Hirobumi, a distinguished *genro* (elder statesman) and a former Prime Minister, was the first resident-general. Ito was subtle, shrewd and slightly more liberally inclined than the other *genro*. In 1909 Ito was assassinated at Harbin in Manchuria by a Korean nationalist. An act designed to register Korean antagonism to the consolidation of Japanese dominance in Korea undertaken by Ito ironically led to the imposition of full Japanese rule in 1910. Korean independence was thus liquidated and Korea was rendered an integral part of the Japanese empire.

The character of the Japanese colonial empire has not as yet been investigated with the thoroughness revealed in the analyses of the British, French and Dutch colonial territories. An important contribution to an assessment of Japanese policy is contained in a collection of papers edited by Ramon H. Myers and Mark R. Peattie.[7] Japanese colonial possessions comprised Taiwan (Formosa) acquired in 1895; the Kwantung Leased Territory of southern Manchuria secured in 1905; Korea, annexed in 1910; and Micronesia (the Marshalls, Carolines and Marianas excluding Guam), the former German island territories in the western Pacific, obtained as League of Nations 'C' mandates in 1919 after the earlier Japanese capture of the islands from Germany in 1914. Korea was the most important of the colonial possessions for strategic and economic reasons. Japanese rule was competent and effective yet harsh. Japan wished to eliminate the vestiges of Korean autonomy and to establish Japanese military control in the interests of extending the security of Japan herself. The Korean monarchy was terminated and the Japanese administration was headed by a governor-general, subject to the somewhat remote control of Tokyo. The office of governor-general was recognised to be a major one carrying much prestige and authority; the incumbent enjoyed substantial initiative in the formulation of policy. The early governors-general were military men, distinguished by their narrow, intolerant attitude to their subjects. Field Marshal Terauchi Masatake, the first governor-general, believed that rebellious manifestations, of which there were many between 1908 and 1910, should be suppressed ruthlessly: he was alleged to have said, 'I will whip you with scorpions' and this conformed with his approach.[8] The calibre of Japanese colonial officials was competent in the main and was explicable through the transfer of bureaucrats from Japanese ministries to the colonies.[9] They worked diligently and enthusiastically but tended to be aloof from the local inhabitants. Japanese rule in Korea was always controlled by the military: each governor-general was a general or an admiral. The Japanese interpreted their responsibilities seriously but, as in other colonial empires, stressed the obligations of the people rather than their rights.[10] There was no sympathy with the national aspirations of the inhabitants; Japanese administrators were determined to eradicate nationalism and to inculcate loyalty to the Japanese emperor in accordance with the state Shintoism fostered in Japan after the Meiji restoration. This objective could be reached through blatantly coercive methods or by those less obviously repressive. The first decade of annexation (1910–20) witnessed the most rigorous phase in which draconic punishments were enforced for resistance to Japan. Discontent simmered and then exploded in the nationalist protests against Japanese rule in 1919. These were put down ferociously but were followed by the application of a more enlightened policy. This coincided with the formation of the Hara government in Tokyo and the development of the so-called liberal era in Japan before the ascendancy of the military from

1931 onwards. An attempt was made in the 1920s and 1930s to pursue Japanese aims more skilfully and to enlist the cooperation of the Korean people. Collaboration was accomplished with certain segments of society, notably with landowners and the wealthy élite, but in total Japan did not succeed in reconciling the most articulate in Korea to the continuance of the Japanese presence. Administratively Korea was dealt with by the Colonial Ministry until 1942 when the Home Ministry assumed responsibility.[11] After some uncertainty as to whether the Meiji constitution applied to Japan's colonial possessions, it was decided that it did apply to Korea and Taiwan.[12] Almost all Japanese believed that colonial rule in Korea should be extended for a very lengthy period, if not permanently. Yanaihara Tadao was one of the few who courageously advocated home rule for Korea and even, if necessary, independence.[13]

Economic motivation was important in explaining the original drive for establishing Japanese power in Korea but it was subordinate to political and strategic arguments. As Peter Duus has observed, between 1895 and 1910 Japanese leaders contemplated the future of Korea in terms of helping to fulfil Japan's expanding market in East Asia; there was less concern with investment in manufacturing or in non-agricultural aspects.[14] After annexation Korea was seen as crucial in providing support for the Japanese economy and four times as much long-term capital was invested in Korea than in Taiwan. This stimulated the swift growth of industrialisation during the 1930s.[15] The infra-structure was encouraged with the development of railways, ports and roads: the preoccupation with railway construction reflected military concern and, as Bruce Cumings has remarked, helped to put Korea in a far more favourable situation *vis-à-vis* other developing countries in 1945.[16] Rice production was encouraged with significant investment in the sugar and rice processing industries.[17] Modern industrial enterprises were started by Mitsui, Mitsubishi, Sumitomo and Yasuda from the late 1920s onwards.[18] Japanese economic policy in Korea was governed by the motive of strengthening the economic and strategic situation of Japan but the basis for the subsequent development in the Korean economy had been laid.

In the educational sphere Japanese rule aimed to achieve a level that would improve literacy but which would keep the Korean people in a subordinate position.[19] The school system was expanded more rapidly under the more liberal regime of the governor-general, Admiral Saito Makoto, in the 1920s. Amendments in the curriculum to placate opinion through offering teaching of Korean history and geography were introduced. Approximately 20 per cent of elementary school age children were attending 2,000 ordinary schools by 1933.[20] Schools in urban areas were predictably more numerous and efficacious but the gap between urban and rural areas narrowed. About half of all children of school age were in attendance at elementary schools by 1940.[21] Beyond the elementary stage private schools managed by Koreans or by

foreign missionaries were prevalent. As Patricia Tsurumi has commented, the evidence indicates that Koreans embraced the educational
opportunities afforded by the Japanese as a means of aiding the future
development of their country in the hope that the shackles imposed by
Japan could later be discarded: it was a more subtle way of manifesting
Korean nationalism.[22] The high literacy rates attained in Korea
encouraged a sustained expansion in publications. This was steady, if
less marked in the early years of Japanese rule, but in the 1920s a large
increase in the number of publication permits issued by the authorities
occurred. The number of Korean language publication permits granted
rose from 409 in 1920 to 1,466 in 1926, to 2,383 in 1937 and to 2,749 in
1939.[23] Confrontations took place between newspapers and Japanese
censors and Japanese publication policy possessed an erratic quality; in
the 1930s the number of confiscations and suspensions diminished.

Japanese living and working in Korea increased steadily in number
after 1905. In 1910 Japanese living in Korea totalled 171,500; by 1942
this had risen to 752,823 out of a population of over 26 million (2.9 per
cent of the population).[24] The police force in Korea was controlled by
Japanese at the higher levels but included appreciable numbers of
Koreans: in 1930 Korean police officers represented approximately 40
per cent of the total force of 18,811.[25] Koreans serving in the police force
were often extremely brutal in their conduct and it is hardly surprising
that they were a target for revenge after the termination of Japanese
rule; many of them served under the American occupation and in South
Korea from 1948 and vengeance continued to be taken at periodic
intervals for years to come. Summing up the Japanese impact on Korea,
it may be said that efficient but harsh administration was provided;
economic progress was promoted yet in a distorted way, designed to
benefit the colonial master. The military illustrated, as in South-East
Asia, the effect upon future developments after 1945; the Japanese
stimulated the growth of the military in South Korea in later years. The
leadership of the army was heavily influenced for a generation to come
by those who had served in the ranks of the Imperial Japanese army; five
of the first seven chiefs of staff and three of the ministers of defence
between 1948 and 1961 were officers trained at the Imperial Defence
College in Tokyo.[26] The Manchurian Academy trained others who were
to be prominent after 1945.

There was always trenchant opposition to Japanese annexation of
Korea and this was revealed on the left and the right of the political
spectrum. From the end of the First World War a body claiming to be
the Korean government in exile functioned at Shanghai and afterwards,
during the Sino-Japanese War of 1937–45, at Chungking. This
conformed to the usual character of *émigré* groups in being extremely
quarrelsome and factionalised. For the greater part of this period it was
controlled by Kim Ku, a conservative nationalist vehemently opposed
to the Japanese occupation of his country. Kim encouraged terrorist

activities and one of his followers was responsible for the bomb incident in Shanghai in 1932, which caused Admiral Nomura Kichisaburo to lose an eye and Shigemitsu Mamoru a leg.[27] Kim and his associates were closely identified with the Kuomintang government in China led by Chiang Kai-shek. The most famous opponent of the Japanese and their most implacable critic from the standpoint of conservative nationalism was Dr Syngman Rhee. In 1945 Rhee possessed moral authority and commanded deep respect, even among those antagonistic to his conservatism. Unlike so many conservatives he had not compromised his position and was consistent throughout in his condemnation of Japan. Syngman Rhee was born in 1875 into a branch of the royal family but one lacking in wealth. Rhee became involved in political agitation in the 1890s at an early age during the period of squabbling between court factions supporting Russia or Japan respectively. Rhee joined the Independence Club soon after his conversion to Christianity; he was arrested and spent seven years in prison.[28] Aferwards he went to the United States and obtained three degrees, the most prestigious being a doctorate from Princeton awarded in 1910. For most of the period from 1912 to 1945 Rhee lived in the United States where he was eventually to build up support from American friends, who assisted in financing his activities. He was chosen as president of the provisional government, based in Shanghai in 1919, but visited Shanghai only in 1920–21 for a limited period. From the 1920s to the 1940s he acted as the principal representative of the provisional administration in Washington, having given up the presidency.

Rhee was a formidable politician and often an underrated one. He had a clear vision of the kind of Korea he wished to see created, which would be based on the repudiation of Japan and vehement antagonism to communism. As a tactician Rhee was subtle and ruthless. He was driven on by a potent sense of mission and a deep faith in his own ability to secure what he wanted.[29] Rhee knew that little could be accomplished until Japan was embroiled with the United States. After Pearl Harbor Rhee felt that it was simply a question of time before Korea regained her independence and he could assume power. He badgered the State Department in an attempt to gain recognition but he was regarded as a tiresome person of no real importance by the bureaucrats in the Roosevelt administration. Rhee's American associates included a lawyer and a journalist, respectively John Staggers and Jay Jerome Williams. In addition, he became acquainted with Preston Goodfellow, who at this time worked for the Office of Strategic Services (OSS); Goodfellow played an important if opaque role in advancing Rhee's career in 1945–46. The official American view was reflected in a report compiled for the American Navy Department that Rhee and his Korean colleagues were 'frustrated and unemployed men'.[30]

The left-wing campaign against Japanese rule in Korea was conducted by the several varieties of Korean communism. The story of the communist movement in Korea is a singularly tortuous one.[31] It was bedevilled by factional rivalries and suspicions generated by the origins of the particular faction and the loyalties within it. As a generalisation Korean communism may be divided into Koreans living in the Soviet Union and loyal to Moscow; Koreans working with the Chinese Communist Party (CCP); Koreans operating as guerrillas in Manchuria and pursuing forays against the Japanese; and Korean communists working secretly in Korea. In no sense whatever was Korean communism a monolithic movement; it was riddled with internal divisions and did not become relatively unified until Kim Il Sung purged his opponents in the 1950s after the Korean War. As part of the background it has to be understood that large numbers of Koreans lived outside their own country and emigration was encouraged by the Japanese, at any rate to Manchuria. In 1919 there were approximately 200,000 Koreans living in Siberia and 430,000 living in Manchuria.[32] Fierce rivalry existed between the early communist factions, based respectively in Irkutsk and Shanghai. The communists in Shanghai were influenced more by nationalism and were prepared to cooperate with the provisional government, nominally presided over by Rhee. Factional hostility was so great in 1921 as to produce full-scale conflict between the Irkutsk faction and its opponents; Russian forces intervened to support the Irkutsk group and hundreds of Koreans were killed or wounded.[33] The Comintern worked predictably but with difficulty to establish control over the recalcitrant comrades in both factions but was faced with firm opposition from those who did not wish to see Korean communism become a minor branch of the world communist movement directed by Moscow.[34] The policies of the Korean Communist Party emphasised the overthrow of Japanese imperialism as axiomatic and this must be followed by policies to foster mass education, liberation of women, and the elimination of religion. Korean gentry and bourgeoisie could only be dealt with after the Japanese had been removed.[35] The indigenous party was formed in Seoul in 1925 when fifteen members were present.[36] The Japanese police proved as zealous as they were in Japan in investigating communist activities and in rounding up suspects. Torture was used as a matter of course and some suspects died or became insane as a result of the methods employed.[37] Dae-sook Suh has remarked that there is truth in the saying that the Japanese police created more communists by their draconian methods than did the Comintern by its intrigues.[38] The crucial weaknesses of Korean communism in the 1920s and 1930s were caused by the inadequate leadership, jealousies and animosities, the poor response among the proletariat and peasantry to communist propaganda, and the rigorous behaviour of the Japanese police.[39]

A growing proportion of the leadership became more closely associated with the Chinese communists in the later 1920s and in the 1930s. The CCP encouraged guerrilla actions in Manchuria against the

Japanese but the complete take-over of Manchuria by the Japanese army with the creation of the 'state' of Manchukuo in 1932 rendered such activity more difficult.[40] The CCP itself was experiencing a traumatic period in its development between the break in cooperation with the Kuomintang in 1927 to the retreat from Kiangsi in 1934–35 in the 'Long March' when Mao Tse-tung assumed the leadership of the CCP. The trend towards a more nationalistic variety of communism, independent of Moscow and resting on the approach of mass mobilisation advocated by Mao, inspired those Korean communists who felt that this approach could prove valuable for their own party in the future. The indigenous communists in Korea were led by Pak Hon-yong, who emerged as one of the principal contenders for power in Korean communism. Pak was imprisoned by the Japanese but was released early in 1939. He then endeavoured to coordinate activities through an underground body called the Communist Group. Progress was unavoidably slow but they set up and directed most of the subversive organisations. The police, usually well informed, arrested most of them in 1941 but Pak managed to escape to a brick factory in the guise of a common labourer.[41] Pak's power base was in south Korea and he was to re-establish the Korean Communist Party on 12 September 1945. Pak was then to be outmanoeuvred by Kim Il Sung with the merger of the South Korean Workers Party with the North Korean Workers Party between June and August 1949. Although Pak was Foreign Minister of North Korea, his position was weak and he was purged immediately after the Korean War ended.[42]

Kim Il Sung was not to emerge as a major personality until after 1945. There is much obscurity over his early career and indeed it is hard to state positively and with conviction what Kim did before the end of the Pacific War. His real name was Kim Song-ju but he adopted the alias of Kim Il Sung, derived from a courageous but possibly mythical guerrilla fighter against the Japanese between 1910 and 1930.[43] He came from a peasant family and was born near the city of Pyongyang in 1912. It would appear that he attended Chinese schools in Manchuria in an area densely populated by Koreans. Japanese records suggest that Kim was opposing them in May 1929.[44] Kim obtained experience in his formative years in cooperating with the Chinese and with the Russians; it is relevant to note he had no experience of working with the communists in Korea.[45] Kim was a fervent nationalist of eclectic, pragmatic outlook. He was willing to take from the divergent policies of the Chinese and Russian parties whatever he deemed appropriate for success; he was inspired by Mao's mass mobilisation but equally impressed by the authority and ruthless direction shown by Stalin. Kim had no intention of being anyone's puppet but this did not become clear until the later 1950s and 1960s. It is likely that Kim moved from Manchuria to Khabarovsk in January 1941. Kim probably then fought with the Soviet forces but there is no evidence to substantiate the grandiose claims

Kim was later to make concerning his contributions to the Second World War.[46]

In 1945 Korean communism was divided into those loyal to Moscow, Yenan, indigenous communists led by Pak Hon-yong, plus those identified with Kim Il Sung. Despite the divisions the omens were encouraging, for the communists of all factions had striven to undermine Japanese rule and had not compromised with Japan, as had so many of the conservative nationalists with the exception of Syngman Rhee and Kim Ku. The Soviet Union was clearly about to play a major and perhaps decisive part in Korean affairs. In such a situation communism should flourish: the uncertainty surrounded personnel and attitudes. Who would emerge as the key personality and how far would Korean communism be controlled by Moscow? Such matters remained a subject for speculation in August 1945.

The prospect for Korea regaining independence lay in the defeat of Japan: only two powers could achieve this, the United States and the Soviet Union. The Americans were engaged in bloody battle against the Japanese empire from December 1941 but the Soviet Union had concluded a neutrality pact with Japan in April 1941 and, given the gigantic struggle against Nazi Germany, had no intention of becoming involved in the Far East before the European War had been successfully concluded. It was unclear as to what the fate of Korea would be at the end of the Pacific War, since Korean affairs would be subsumed in the profound questions involving the future of Japan and the eventual intervention of the Soviet Union with much depending on the character of the American–Soviet relationship at that time. In the American government more consideration was devoted to Korea between 1943 and 1945 than might have been anticipated, although without an outcome that gave rise to a smooth and considered implementation of policy at the end of the Pacific War.[47] In the State, Navy and War departments, officials contemplated Korean capacity for self-government and the certain resurgence of Soviet power in East Asia including Korea. It was widely held that the Koreans would not be ready for independence when the war ended: memories of the closing phase of the Yi dynasty did not inspire confidence in Korean ability for effective government and the era of Japanese dominance had been so repressive as to necessitate a period of readjustment. The Navy Department considered in 1943 that Korea was bereft of leadership and feared Korea could fall into a vacuum similar to that which would exist in Poland and the Balkans when the European War terminated.[48] The Secretary of State, Cordell Hull, believed that the application of trusteeship offered the most satisfactory solution, in part because he held that the Soviet Union and Kuomintang China would not work together after the Pacific War and that an American role in trusteeship with the Soviet Union, China and Great Britain would be indispensable.[49] President Roosevelt broadly favoured trusteeship for dealing with the former western colonial territories in South-East Asia occupied by Japan in 1941–42. He disliked occidental empires and wished to see them ended as soon as practicable. This was a contentious issue, since the British, French and the Dutch had every intention of returning to their former territories, not comprehending the extent to which the Japanese had forced the pace of change. Winston Churchill was proud of the British empire and was determined to reverse the harm done by the grossly humiliating surrender at Singapore in February 1942; he was not willing to accept Roosevelt's advice on the treatment of India or Hong Kong.[50] Roosevelt thought that Korea would be suited to trusteeship for an undefined period, which could perhaps last for as long as forty years.[51]

The Cairo conference, which met in November–December 1943 and was attended by Roosevelt, Churchill and Chiang Kai-shek, agreed that the Pacific War must conclude with the expulsion of Japan from all parts of the empire she had accumulated since 1895. Taiwan should revert to China and Korea should at some point receive independence. The first draft of a document prepared by Roosevelt's aide, Harry Hopkins, referred to Korean independence being secured 'at the earliest possible moment'.[52] At the Tehran conference in December 1943, from which Chiang was excluded, Stalin confirmed that Russia would participate in the war against Japan three months after the European War had been won. Discussion took place over Korea and it was agreed that trusteeship was the appropriate policy to adopt. Position papers continued to be drafted in the State Department in 1944–45 with preference being expressed for a unified administration in Korea as part of the trusteeship rather than the creation of military zones.[53] The Yalta conference in February 1945 considered the future of the Far East in the light of the entry of the Soviet Union into the Pacific War. The European struggle was drawing to a close but in the Pacific and Far East the savage struggle continued. The Japanese were obviously being defeated but it was far from certain when this would finally be accomplished. The likelihood was that Japanese resistance would become more ferocious as the battles approached the home islands with heavy casualties being incurred if Japan was invaded. The Americans were anxious to see the Russians engaged in the Far East as soon as possible so as to minimise American losses. Roosevelt was aware of the dangers of the United States and the Soviet Union drifting apart once the common cement of the war against Germany was removed. The President was perturbed at the signs of Russian obduracy over Poland but felt that cooperation with Moscow could be preserved if the correct blend of firmness and concession was applied. Roosevelt was a dying man at Yalta and it is a matter for speculation as to how far his judgements were influenced by his health.[54] It was recognised that Russia should obtain the Kuril islands and Sakhalin from Japan and that she should regain the naval base at Port Arthur forfeited at the end of the Russo-Japanese War in 1905. In addition, the Soviet Union would secure railway concessions in

Manchuria with the creation of a joint Soviet–Chinese company to operate the railways.

Earlier statements that Japan must surrender all colonial possessions were reiterated but the precise fate of Korea was not clarified: Korea was to become independent at a future date but what would happen in the interim period remained to be decided. Soviet views over Korea were not easy to assess. It is likely that Stalin was confident that the situation would evolve in Russia's favour, for it appeared improbable that the United States would pursue an active policy of intervention in the Asian continent and the left would possess the initiative in decision-making within Korean politics, since much of the right was discredited through collaboration with the Japanese. Stalin was usually cautious and calculating in his foreign policy and if he bided his time, Korea would almost certainly fall into the Soviet orbit. However, as Michael Sandusky has remarked, the United States and Russia were not too far apart in their ideas on the future of Korea in the spring and summer of 1945.[55]

American military planners were preoccupied in May–June 1945 with devising the strategy that would envelop and ultimately throttle Japan. A full-scale invasion of the southern island of Kyushu was envisaged with the resigned acceptance that the scale of casualties would be high, bearing in mind the larger casualties sustained in recent battles.[56] The possibility of attacking Korea as part of this process was considered in May but it was decided that the Kyushu operation should be sufficient. Korea was referred to more frequently than might have been expected in the summer of 1945 and the new President, Harry S. Truman, displayed some concern over Korea. Truman had been propelled into the presidency through the sudden death of Franklin Roosevelt on 12 April 1945. He disarmingly admitted his lack of preparation for the huge range of problems with which he had to grapple. He had achieved a position of some prominence in the Senate between 1942 and 1944 but his choice as Roosevelt's vice-presidential running mate at the Democratic convention in July 1944 had come as a surprise. Truman's career had developed wholly in the domestic context where he had shown considerable guile and courage. His knowledge of foreign issues was limited and Roosevelt had not consulted him in the brief period that Truman held the vice-presidency. Truman had to learn through experience in office without a period of gradually accumulating knowledge in a subordinate position.

The differences between Roosevelt and Truman have sometimes been exaggerated where their attitudes to Russia were concerned. There was no sudden, sharp break in policy when Truman entered the White House. Rather there was a gradual change in tone and emphasis but one that should not be exaggerated. Truman's character and method of operating were different from his predecessor's. Truman was blunt and straightforward where Roosevelt had been subtle and evasive. Truman had a trenchant dislike for communism and was certainly more critical of the Soviet Union than Roosevelt. Yet he realised how important it was to work with the Russians and he had no intention of disrupting the wartime alliance. It has been suggested by revisionist historians that Truman's policy in the Far East in the summer of 1945 was governed by his hostility to Russia and that the atomic bomb was deployed against Japan in part at least to persuade the Soviet Union to follow a less abrasive policy in eastern Europe.[57] It has also been suggested that the use of the atomic bomb was authorised by Truman in order to influence developments in Korea.[58] The atomic weapon had been developed in the expectation that it would be used if necessary; this was made explicit in the Hyde Park agreement signed by Roosevelt and Churchill in September 1944.[59] It was not until the bomb was tested that a definite decision could be reached on its use. The Potsdam conference, attended by Truman, Stalin and Churchill (until the latter was replaced by Attlee as a result of the British general election) met in July 1945: while the conference deliberated the atomic tests were completed successfully in the United States.

American contemplation of Korea intensified in the course of July 1945 amid the deeper considerations of the most effective method of terminating the Pacific War. General Marshall and his colleagues in the joint chiefs of staff believed the United States must occupy at least part of Korea in order to increase American power in the postwar balance between American and Soviet interests in the Far East. This was not made explicit to the Russians, since more attention had to be devoted to the logistics of deploying American forces in Japan and Korea when the war ended.[60] The 38th parallel was already being envisaged as a possible division but no decision was taken in July to propose it formally. The joint chiefs held that General MacArthur should have sufficient resources to provide for the occupation of part of Korea in addition to his principal task of occupying Japan. Marshall pondered the feasibility of implementing an alternative strategy for the occupation of Japan through the utilisation of naval and air forces with troops being transported by air to assume control of vital areas. However, MacArthur was adamantly committed to the existing plan for a full-scale military invasion of Kyushu, employing large numbers of troops and was uninterested in alternatives. Indeed MacArthur was concerned almost wholly with the culmination to his four-year struggle against the Japanese and was determined to accept the formal surrender himself as a prelude to his new role as the reformer of Japanese society.[61] In Washington more interest was being shown in the broad range of problems in East Asia in the concluding phase of the war. President Truman and his advisers were anxious over Sino-Soviet relations and wondered whether American forces could take the port of Dairen and thus prevent the Soviet Union from occupying the Liaotung peninsula of south Manchuria. Truman's thoughts in this direction were stimulated by advice from Edwin Pauley, then in Moscow on a special mission', that the United States should occupy as much of Korea and Manchuria as possible in the immediate future.[62] It was assumed by most American policy-makers that the Soviet Union possessed the forces to fulfil a *rapid* occupation of Manchuria and Korea but this was not borne out by the course of events.

The successful testing of the atomic bomb in New Mexico in July 1945 transformed the challenge of terminating the war against Japan. Truman received the news during the Potsdam conference and was elated: the atomic weapon's potential greatly increased the authority of the United States. The President informed Stalin in casual manner; Stalin, who must have been well informed through his network of spies, showed no emotion. Opinion in Washington had slowly been moving, during the previous three months, to the conclusion that it was not essential for the Soviet Union to participate in the final stages of the Pacific conflict. The principal argument for Soviet involvement was the apprehension at the scale of casualties envisaged in an invasion of the Japanese home islands. The cogency of this factor was underlined by the far higher casualties involved in the capture of Okinawa, completed shortly before the Potsdam conference assembled.[63] Much controversy has surrounded Truman's decision to use the atomic bomb. It was clear that the Japanese war effort could not be extended for an appreciable period in the light of the allied command of the sea and air and the nature of the crippling conventional bombing by American planes. The Potsdam declaration by the allies – to which the Soviet Union was not a signatory – had warned Japan to accept unconditional surrender but without stating frankly enough how terrible was the new weapon about to be deployed against Japan. More could have been done to allay Japanese fears regarding the survival of the imperial institution in a new constitutional form; this was not achieved because Truman and his Secretary of State, James F. Byrnes, wished to permit the Japanese no room to cause difficulty over the surrender terms. It has been suggested that Truman was influenced more by a determination to warn the Soviet Union and to compel cooperation in eastern Europe rather than to procure Japanese surrender in itself. The most convincing answer is that Truman was intent primarily upon terminating the Pacific conflict speedily so as to save American lives but that he was interested simultaneously in strengthening American interests *vis-à-vis* Russia, which included restricting the amount of territory to be occupied by the Soviet Union. Russia declared war on Japan on 8 August but, as the Japanese military reported, the Soviet forces did not appear fully prepared for conflict extending throughout Manchuria and Korea:[64] while much of Manchuria was captured, significant parts of southern Manchuria had not been taken when Japan surrendered on 15 August. In Korea Soviet forces had crossed the Siberian border but had not advanced beyond Chongjin in the extreme north-east.[65]

American planning for the occupation of Korea dveloped after the dropping of the second atomic bomb on Nagasaki on 9 August. James Dunn, an official in the State Department who acted as chairman of the State–War–Navy Coordinating Committee, informed Brigadier-General George Lincoln of the Operations Division that it was desirable that as much of Korea as possible be occupied. According to Lincoln's recollection subsequently, he glanced at a map in his office and decided within ten seconds that the 38th parallel was the correct demarcation line between the zones of American and Soviet occupation.[66] Lincoln referred the proposal to Colonels Charles Bonesteel and Dean Rusk for consideration. They reflected as to whether division at the top of the Korean peninsula might not be preferable but believed that the 38th parallel could be accepted if the Russians insisted on moving into the northern part of the peninsula.[67] Truman indicated on 11 August that American forces should if possible occupy Dairen and a port in Korea as soon as Japan surrendered without awaiting the formal surrender of Japan: the latter could not occur until approximately a fortnight after surrender.[68] The Joint War Plans Committee took the President's wishes into account and thought that the 40th parallel would be a suitable line of division, since Dairen and Port Arthur would then come into the American sphere.[69] Michael Sandusky has argued that United States troops could have assumed control of the greater part of Korea had Korea been identified as a priority and had MacArthur been willing to modify his decision to concentrate American forces in Japan prior to the official surrender on 2 September at the ceremony planned by MacArthur.[70] This may be correct, but it would be misleading not to give full recognition to the fact that the priority was the occupation of Japan and ensuring that the Soviet Union was not directly involved in the administration of Japan.

The United States aimed to prevent the Russians from occupying the whole of Korea through reaching a diplomatic agreement with Moscow to restrict Soviet occupation to the northern part of the peninsula. Colonel Bonesteel believed the 38th parallel was the most satisfactory line in dividing Soviet and American spheres that could be arrived at; this would place Seoul, the Korean capital, in the American sphere.[71] Precedents for dividing Korea included Japanese plans following the invasion of 1592 for having the south controlled by Japan and the north under the king of Korea.[72] Japanese leaders had thought of a similar division after the Sino-Japanese War of 1894–95. The 38th parallel was not an ideal boundary and in economic terms was absurd; the 39th parallel would have been preferable.[73] However, in favour of the 38th parallel was the fact that it appeared a rough and ready division, which might satisfy the Russians and give Seoul to the south.

The Soviet Union accepted division at the 38th parallel. Stalin was satisfied with this agreement and was not tempted to violate it. General MacArthur did not regard the deployment of American troops in Korea as a priority and it was not until 8 September that the forces led by General John R. Hodge began the task of occupation. Despite the preparation of various position papers between 1943 and 1945 the United States was not organised for the task of governing Korea. American bureaucrats did not comprehend the speed of change in Korea and that a potent sense of nationalism with a corresponding ardent wish for the unification and independence of the country existed in August 1945. It was assumed that the Korean people would docilely accept trusteeship with decisions being taken for them by their American and Soviet masters. American policy was already characterised by the traits that existed to 25 June 1950: it was felt to be undesirable that the Soviet Union should incorporate Korea within her sphere of interest yet there was little inclination in Washington to commit the United States deeply to supporting whatever kind of government emerged in the south.

In August to September 1945 Korea was in a ferment of revolutionary upheaval. The pent-up tensions and emotions of colonial servitude had been cast off, even though many Japanese were still in posts in south Korea at the request of the incoming American military administration. Political and social revolution was in the air and Koreans of all political persuasions longed for unity. To a combustible internal situation in August 1945 was added the beginnings of great power rivalry and animosity, which would ensure that the deadly hatreds within Korean society would be resolved amid a framework of hostility between superpowers that would have profound repercussions for Korea.

# REFERENCES

1. For an account of Japanese aims in external policy after the Meiji restoration of 1868, see Ian Nish, *Japan's Foreign Policy, 1869–1942* (London 1977), chs 1 and 2.

2. For a thorough assessment of the events leading to the conflict of 1904–05, see Ian Nish, *The Origins of the Russo-Japanese War* (London 1985).

3. See Gregory Henderson, *Korea: The Politics of the Vortex* (Cambridge, Mass. 1968) for an extremely stimulating, wide-ranging examination of Korean society over many centuries.

4. For a discussion of Korean geography and of the economy, see A. J. Grajdanzev, *Modern Korea* (New York 1944) pp. 8ff.

5. Henderson, op. cit., p. 16.

6. On Yuan's actions in Korea, see Jerome Ch'en, *Yuan Shik-k'ai, 1859–1916* (London 1961), pp. 21–45.

7. R. H. Myers and M. R. Peattie (eds), *The Japanese Colonial Empire, 1895–1945* (Guildford 1984).

8. Peattie, 'Introduction', in Myers and Peattie (eds), p. 18.

9. Ibid., p. 26.
10. Ibid., p. 29.
11. M. B. Jansen, 'Japanese imperialism: late Meiji perspectives', in Myers and Peattie (eds), p. 77.
12. E.I-te Chen, 'The attempt to integrate the Empire: legal perspectives', in Myers and Peattie (eds), p. 242.
13. Peattie, 'Japanese attitudes toward colonialism, 1895–1945', in Myers and Peattie (eds), pp. 116–18.
14. Peter Duus 'Economic dimensions of Meiji imperialism: the case of Korea, 1895–1910', in Myers and Peattie (eds), p. 161.
15. Mizoguchi Toshiyuki and Yamamoto Yuzo, 'Capital formation in Taiwan and Korea' in Myers and Peattie (eds), p. 411.
16. Bruce Cumings, 'The legacy of Japanese colonialism in Korea', in Myers and Peattie (eds), p. 487.
17. Myers, 'Post World War II Japanese colonialism in Korea', in Myers and Peattie (eds), p. 466.
18. Grajdanzev, op. cit., p. 152.
19. E. P. Tsurumi, 'Colonial education in Korea and Taiwan', in Myers and Peattie (eds), p. 300.
20. Ibid., p. 305.
21. Ibid.
22. Ibid., p. 306.
23. M. E. Robinson, 'Colonial publication policy and the Korean nationalist movement', in Myers and Peattie (eds), p. 325.
24. Grajdanzev, op. cit., p. 75 and Myers and Peattie (eds), p. 271.
25. Ching-chih Chen, 'Police and community control systems in the Empire', in Myers and Peattie (eds), p. 225.
26. For a comparative account of the Japanese impact upon the military in the areas they occupied, see Joyce Lebra, *Japanese-Trained Armies in South-East Asia* (Hong Kong 1977). For Korean developments, see Henderson, op. cit., pp. 336–7.
27. Nomura was later Japanese ambassador in Washington and conducted the protracted talks with Cordell Hull, the American Secretary of State, the breakdown of which precipitated the outbreak of the Pacific War in December 1941. Shigemitsu served as Japanese ambassador in London from 1938 to 1941 and as Foreign Minister from 1942 to 1945; he again served as Foreign Minister in the mid 1950s.
28. Henderson, op. cit., pp. 423–4, n. 11.
29. For biographies of Rhee, see R. T. Oliver, *Syngman Rhee: The Man Behind the Myth* (New York 1955) and *Syngman Rhee and American Involvement in Korea, 1942–1960* (Seoul 1979).
30. M. C. Sandusky, *America's Parallel* (Alexandria, Va. 1983), p. 90.
31. For the most exhaustive treatment, see R. A. Scalapino and Chong-sik Lee, *Communism in Korea*, Parts I and II (London 1972). See also Dae-sook Suh, *The Korean Communist Movement, 1918–1948* (Princeton, NJ 1967) and Suh (ed.), *Documents of Korean Communism, 1918–1948* (Princeton, NJ 1970).
32. Scalapino and Lee, op. cit., I, pp. 4–5.
33. Ibid., pp. 32–3.
34. Ibid., pp. 35–7.

35. Suh, *Korean Communist Movement*, pp. 16, 28.
36. Scalapino and Lee, op. cit., I, pp. 58–9.
37. Suh, *Korean Communist Movement*, p. 112.
38. Ibid., p. 164.
39. Ibid., pp. 180–1.
40. Ibid., p. 187.
41. Ibid., pp. 192–3.
42. Scalapino and Lee, op. cit., I, p. 386.
43. Suh, *Korean Communist Movement*, p. 260.
44. Ibid., p. 267.
45. Ibid., p. 293.
46. Ibid.
47. See Bruce Cumings, 'Introduction', in Cumings (ed.), *Child of Conflict: American–Korean Relations, 1943–1953* (London 1983), pp. 12–14.
48. Sandusky, op. cit., p. 90.
49. Ibid., p. 96.
50. For an admirably thorough examination of Anglo–American relations during the Pacific War with incisive assessments of Roosevelt and Churchill, see Christopher Thorne, *Allies of a Kind* (London 1978). See also Thorne, *The Issue of War: States, Societies, and the Far Eastern Conflict of 1941–1945* (London 1985).
51. Soon Sung Cho, *Korea in World Politics, 1940–1950* (Berkeley and Los Angeles 1967), pp. 22–3.
52. Ibid., pp. 19–20.
53. Ibid., p. 30–1.
54. For a lucid assessment of the Yalta conference, see D. S. Clemens, *Yalta*, (New York 1970).
55. Sandusky, op. cit., p. 150.
56. See *FRUS, 1945: Conference of Berlin (Potsdam)* (1), pp. 903–10, memorandum.
57. See Gar Alperovitz, *Atomic Diplomacy: Hiroshima and Potsdam* (New York 1965), for a statement of the revisionist case.
58. For a discussion of the issues involved in terminating the Pacific War, see Mark Paul, 'Diplomacy delayed: the atomic bomb and the division of Korea, 1945', in Cumings (ed), pp. 67–91, and B. J. Bernstein, 'The perils and politics of surrender: ending the war with Japan', *Pacific Historical Review*, **46** (Feb. 1977), 1–28.
59. See *FRUS 1945, Potsdam*, (1), p. 1371, *aide-mémoire* of conversation between Roosevelt and Churchill at Hyde Park, 18 Sept. 1944.
60. Sandusky, op. cit., p. 194.
61. Ibid., pp. 187–90.
62. Ibid., p. 225.
63. Ibid., p. 248.
64. Ibid., p. 205.
65. Ibid., p. 252.
66. Ibid., p. 226.
67. Ibid., p. 227. See also Paul in Cumings (ed).
68. Sandusky, op. cit., p. 232.
69. Ibid., p. 237.
70. Ibid., pp. 239, 245.

71. Ibid., pp. 227–8.
72. Cho, op. cit., p. 47.
73. Ibid.

*Chapter 2*

# THE ESTABLISHMENT OF TWO KOREAS

In August 1945 Korea, as with the other parts of the Japanese colonial empire, faced turmoil and uncertainty on a massive scale. The vacuum created by the sudden termination of the Pacific War raised enormous questions on the combustible internal situation in the territories affected, on allied policies, and on the relationship that would exist between local representatives of the allied powers and their home governments. American officials had shown greater interest in Korea from 1943 onwards as part of the State Department's preparations for handling the consequences of Japan's defeat. The assumption was that Korea would require a period of trusteeship in which the United States and the Soviet Union would play the principal roles, before Korea became independent as a unitary state. Concern was felt over ambitions that might be stimulated in Moscow with the result that Korea could become a focal point of tension. The Soviet Union entered the Pacific War in its dying moments in August 1945 to fulfil Stalin's wish that the Russian voice should be raised to influence postwar developments in East Asia. Decisions on the administration of Korea had to be reached swiftly and the United States would be dependent on Soviet goodwill at first, since American forces were not immediately available to occupy south Korea. American–Soviet agreement on respective zones in Korea was attained through acceptance of the 38th parallel as the dividing line between the Soviet-controlled area to the north and the American-controlled area to the south.[1]

There was nothing magical about the choice. The 38th parallel was an obvious line to adopt and had the merit from the American viewpoint of placing the border north of Seoul; this maximised the territory under American direction. Korea south of the 38th parallel included the bulk of the population and was predominantly rural; north Korea contained most of the industry, previously linked with the Japanese economic interests in Manchuria. Soviet troops advanced into Korea to accept the surrender of Japanese forces; Stalin kept his word and when American troops arrived on 8 September, they assumed responsibility to the 38th

19

parallel. Stalin adhered to the agreement because he wished to maintain satisfactory relations with the United States if possible and perhaps because he felt that sooner or later Korea would fall into the Soviet sphere in any case.

Within Korea in 1945–46 a revolutionary situation and spirit existed. This has been thoroughly assessed by Bruce Cumings in the first volume of his study of the antecedents of the Korean War.[2] Fundamental to everything was the bitter experience of Japanese colonialism and the determination to eliminate the legacy of that experience together with those who had collaborated with the Japanese. Much of the old Korean élite had worked with the Japanese for the material rewards and defence of their interests; the police force was the most hated feature of the colonial era and the vengeance taken on police guilty of torture, extortion and corruption was savage. The collapse of Japanese authority was followed by the emergence throughout Korea of 'people's committees'; they appeared at various levels – province, city, county and village. The committees functioned effectively in north Korea in the initial stage of communist rule before their independent characteristics were curbed as the northern regime consolidated itself. In the south the people's committees operated in over half the counties. Cumings has remarked, 'These people's committees are examples of that rarest of Korean political forms, locally rooted and responsive organization.'[3] The emergence of the people's committees was promoted by the significant improvement in the communications network in Korea during the Japanese era and through the population growth and mobility of the population under colonialism.[4] The people's committees connoted a manifestation of profound discontent against deprivation and oppression: high rents, interest rates, large grain collections, the exactions and interventions of landowners and police contributed to a spontaneous revolutionary environment. The people's committees were of radical outlook in the main, representing the aspirations of the 'have-nots' of Korean rural society. However, the most vital feature in eligibility for participation in the committees was the attitude or relationship previously adopted to the Japanese: if village elders had shunned the colonial regime, they could be chosen to play a leading part in the work of the committees.[5] The American occupation misunderstood the nature of the unrest in south Korea and attributed it to the machinations of the communists. In fact the people's committees were a genuinely spontaneous growth in which communist agitation was involved only to a minor extent. The existence of the committees posed problems for both the American and the Soviet occupations in the sense that any vigorous, independent organization represents a latent challenge to outside authority. However, the challenge was bound to be more difficult for the Americans to handle, since they opposed drastic change while the Russians desired it.

The most important individual for deciding the direction of United

States policy in Korea was the head of the military occupation, from 1945 to 1948, General John Reed Hodge. Hodge was frequently criticised by contemporaries for his inability to grasp the finer points of the problems confronting him and for reacting in too blunt a manner. Much of the criticism was justified but to be fair to Hodge, he had been placed in an invidious position and, blinkered as he was, in some respects, he was correct in appreciating that a rebuilding of the Korean right offered the only means of preventing communist success in south Korea. Hodge came from rural Illinois and had climbed the military hierarchy without the prestige of having served at West Point. He served with distinction in the Pacific theatre and had commanded troops in some of the worst fighting, including the battle for Okinawa.[6] General MacArthur appointed Hodge to Korea with Hodge responsible to MacArthur in Tokyo. Hodge's merits were that he was honest, courageous, forthright, without arrogance or pretension. His defects were that he lacked subtlety, was vehemently anti-communist to the point where any unrest or dissent might be regarded as a sign of communist activity, and that he lacked preparation for the tasks he faced.[7] Such a situation was not unusual amid the vicissitudes of war and of the United States being propelled at speed into undertaking vast global responsibilities. One of Hodge's advisers was George Z. Williams, born in Korea and the son of a missionary; Williams was strongly anti-communist and well connected with the rightists in Korea. From the moment he arrived in Korea, Hodge was concerned with the maintenance of order and of developing quickly a viable framework of control. Circumstances in Korea, as in China and South-East Asia, pressured the Americans into relying on Japanese administrators and police in the early months of the occupation. Whilst to begin with inevitable, Hodge and his colleagues need not have relied so heavily or for so long on Japanese personnel. Many Koreans were affronted at the liberation of August 1945 being followed by the continued presence of Japanese and of the odious methods they had employed to suppress dissent. The Korean police, as reorganised under the occupation, included numerous former collaborators, operating as in the past but serving different masters.[8] Ordinary Koreans wishing to see their country independent, unified and tackling its social and economic problems radically felt betrayed at the deep conservatism that distinguished the occupation.

The political situation in south Korea in August–September 1945 was largely dominated by the Committee for the Preparation of Korean Independence (CPKI), founded by Yo Un-hyong and his supporters. Yo was left of centre but not militant; in the dying moments of the Japanese administration he was invited to form a transitional administration and agreed to do so, on the basis of the release of political prisoners and of no interference with the organisation of workers, peasants, students and youths.[9] Yo regarded the CPKI as a temporary, transitional, administration pending the arrival of the allies and the formulation of more permanent plans.[10] Political debate soon raged at different levels throughout Korean society; an intoxicating sense of freedom prevailed. Workers and peasants meetings developed spontaneously in August and September; later from November to December 1945, the new mass organisations came to be more tightly controlled from above.[11] The CPKI was a typical umbrella nationalist movement characteristic of the struggle for independence before divergent ideological approaches had shattered the organisation. The CPKI was broadly divided into a faction supporting Yo Un-hyong, which was leftist but not communist, and a faction that consisted chiefly of communists. The CPKI issued a statement on 28 August advocating radical reform and 'mass struggle against the anti-democratic and reactionary forces' which had collaborated with Japan 'and committed crimes against the nation'.[12] The leading personality in the growth of communism in south Korea was Pak Hon-yong, who established the reconstructed Korean Communist Party on 8 September.[13] Two days earlier a CPKI meeting in Seoul proclaimed the establishment of the Korean People's Republic (KPR). The action demonstrated the belief that Korea was ready for independence and was intended to forestall a lengthy American occupation or the Americans advancing Koreans of their own choice. The danger of internal dispute was recognised and the KPR strove to achieve coalescence of all elements whether right or left, that had been opposed to the Japanese. This was illustrated in the list of cabinet members, which included Syngman Rhee, Kim Ku, Ho Hon and Kim Kyu-sik.[14] The statement of KPR policy objectives included the elimination of feudalism, imperialism, the implementation of radical land policies, the nationalisation of major industries, and the encouragement of industrialisation.[15] Civil liberties were guaranteed, the franchise was extended to all over the age of eighteen, and an enlightened approach was urged for the industrial and education spheres. The KPR was unduly idealistic in aspirations and it proclaimed a programme that was too grandiose. The communists within the CPKI moved to take over as much power as they could for themselves in August–September and this, too, weakened the KPR.[16]

The Korean right was weak, despondent and lacking in effective leadership. Many rightists had worked closely with the Japanese and had so discredited themselves. The two most prominent rightists were Kim Ku and Syngman Rhee. Both had been associated with the exiled 'government' based at Chungking from 1938 to 1945. This was a shadowy body with few supporters but at least it represented definite opposition to the Japanese presence. Kim Ku and Syngman Rhee had been active in politics since the closing years of the Yi dynasty and were driven by a potent sense of mission. Rhee had been expelled from the exiled 'government' because of his maverick qualities in 1925 and he had then functioned as an independent, although claiming still to be the authentic voice of the government. Rhee never doubted that he was destined to lead Korea and acted with a strange mixture of arrogance, duplicity, cunning and tenacity to establish his power. It took him a considerable time to do so but he succeeded and left a deep mark on Korea only equalled or exceeded by his arch-rival, Kim Il Sung in north Korea. Rhee had persistently sought recognition during the Second World War and badgered the American State Department frequently. Rhee hoped the United States and Britain would recognise his provisional government; a British Foreign Office minute from March 1945 reads, 'These people cannot in any true sense be said to represent Korea and Anglo-US recognition of them might well lead to those [problems] we have experienced over the "London Poles".'[17] General Hodge and his advisers saw the rightists as the most reliable supporters of the American presence and regarded the left as dangerous or communist-dominated. Benninghoff, a political adviser to Hodge, reported in October 1945 that Korea was divided into two groups – the Radical/Communist and Conservative/Democratic. Benninghoff stated that the KPR had been organised by 'The Communist or Radical Group in Seoul'.[18] Hodge and those around him believed Syngman Rhee should be encouraged and believed he could be controlled; they were later to regret having aided Rhee's ambitions to the extent that they had done when they found themselves exposed to Rhee's mordant censure.

In Washington attention was focused on the application of trusteeship to Korea. The difficulty lay in the vague nature of trusteeship as a concept and its uncertain duration. It was clear that Korea was in political turmoil and that securing stability in south Korea and then unity with north Korea would be hard to accomplish.[19] James F. Byrnes, the American Secretary of State, visited London in November 1945 and told the British Prime Minister it was imperative to reach a decision rapidly on the future of Korea. If the allies wasted time, the Soviet Union would establish effective control. Byrnes advocated a quadripartite trusteeship comprising the Soviet Union, the United States, Great Britain and China.[20] At this stage the State Department was contemplating a neutral high commissioner, possibly Dutch or Swiss, supported by an advisory council including representatives of the trusteeship powers. The administration would be conducted by Koreans under the guidance of foreign advisers. Occupation troops would be withdrawn and the Korean police force streamlined. Byrnes indicated the American anxiety at the position in south Korea and the wish to withdraw American troops.[21] Hodge and the top circles of the occupation ironically were moving firmly against trusteeship as a result of developing opposition throughout south Korea to trusteeship itself and, more importantly, because of their belief that trusteeship would assist communism. William Langdon, Hodge's political adviser, told Byrnes on 20 November that the Korean people had always been a distinct nation except for the short colonial period and possessed high literacy, cultural and living standards, when judged by Asiatic or Middle Eastern standards: if trusteeship was approved, it would have to be supported by force.[22] Langdon believed Kim Ku was the most obvious candidate for leading the first independent government. Langdon went on to outline a scheme whereby Kim Ku could set up a governing commission, which would subsequently take over from the military government. Britain, the Soviet Union and China could provide supervisors and advisers so as to reduce the American composition of the governing commission. Ultimately the latter would choose a head of state and a government would be formed, which would be admitted to the UN. In addition, arrangements should be reached at an earlier juncture for withdrawal of Russian troops and for representatives from the Russian zone to join the governing commission. As Cumings has pointed out, the importance of this paper is that it foreshadowed with considerable accuracy the sequence of events over the next three years, culminating in the formal establishment of the Republic of Korea in 1948.[23] The major difference was that north Korea evolved along wholly different lines and that Korea was divided into two states.

The Moscow conference of American, British and Russian foreign ministers met in December 1945 against a sombre background of anxiety at the deterioration of relations between the powers since the end of the European War. The conference was misleadingly regarded as a success and as reversing the trend in relations. Korea was fully discussed at the conference and agreement was secured, which later ran into the sands. The United States advocated trusteeship. The Soviet Union submitted a scheme envisaging the establishment of a joint commission by the Soviet and American military commands in Korea, which would advise on the formation of a provisional Korean government. The powers approved the Soviet scheme with slight amendments.[24] The outcome was that the concept of trusteeship was played down: the agreement concentrated on the creation of a provisional government. Trusteeship would not be considered until after a government had been established and after the Joint Commission had been approached. As Cumings observes, this was open to the interpretation that trusteeship might not be proceeded with at the end of the day.[25] The Moscow agreement could have offered the basis for a settlement had the United States and the Soviet Union cooperated and had the bulk of opinion in Korea accepted it. Instead the United States was soon to swing against it with General Hodge undermining it, and most opinion in south Korea was hostile to it. Hodge had fostered relations with the Korean Democratic Party (KDP), which at the time took a pro-American stance and preferred a continuance of the American occupation to any suggestion of trusteeship. Hodge had pursued policies from his arrival in Korea designed to strengthen the opposition to communism and to move away from rather than towards cooperation with the Soviet Union. He firmly believed this was the only sensible course to pursue. Byrnes and the State Department lived in a world of their own or, at any rate, a world that did not include the realities with which he grappled in Seoul.

Kim Ku was ambitious for power and discerned the opportunities created by the controversy over trusteeship. Unfortunately from his viewpoint he lacked the skill to handle the matter and the result was a catastrophic decline in his reputation. His rival, Syngman Rhee, gained instead. Kim Ku inspired a series of strikes at the end of December 1945 and issued statements of a Napoleonic character calling for the dissolution of political parties and the recognition of a new government. On 31 December he challenged Hodge directly. The military government suppressed the coup easily: Hodge, now regarding Kim with contempt, summoned him and threatened to 'kill him if he double-crossed me again'.[26] Kim's ludicrous failure punctured his stature and he declined to be replaced by Rhee. The trusteeship crisis enabled the KDP to take the initiative in gaining popular support over a subject on which public opinion in Korea for once sided with the right. The Korean left had opposed trusteeship down to December 1945 and the communists changed policy only when Stalin did so. However, the communists were now defending an unpopular cause and an impetus had been given to the creation of a south Korean state.[27] A British report on the American occupation written at this time commented scathingly that the Koreans employed by the military government were 'almost hopelessly incompetent'.[28] It was reassuringly added that the Americans were well aware of the shortcomings and had no intention of pushing Korea into premature independence. This was a fair appraisal, for Hodge was conversant with the deficiencies of the rightists and did not consider Korea fit for independence.

The United States moved steadily away from the Moscow agreement in the first half of 1946. The worsening of relations with the Soviet Union in Europe meant that Hodge's policy of constructing a viable right–centre opposition to left communism won growing support in Washington. The next significant development occurred with the formation of the Representative Democratic Council (RDC) as the nucleus of a south Korean administration. The body emerged in February 1946 and resulted from the actions of Hodge, Rhee and the mysterious M. Preston Goodfellow. Goodfellow had worked in American intelligence during the Pacific War and became deputy director of the OSS.[29] Rhee met Goodfellow during the war and they assisted each other's interests from then onwards. Goodfellow went to Korea in November 1945 and remained there until the following summer. He worked to achieve a coalition of right–centre political groups under Rhee's leadership. Hodge worked to advance the RDC as the coalition of rightist elements that would strengthen the American hand in the impending negotiations with the Soviet Union in the Joint Commission. The RDC comprised twenty-eight political leaders, almost all rightists.[30] Rhee stated that the RDC would 'represent the Korean people in its dealings with General Hodge and the Military Government'.[31] The deliberations of the RDC revealed that it was intended to pave the way for the establishment of a provisional government. Hodge supported and utilised the RDC until November 1946 when the Interim Legislature came into existence.[32] The polarisation in south Korea was underlined with the formation of the Democratic National Front (DNF) as a coalition of left–centre groups embracing moderate leftists and communists. It included Yo Un-hyong, who had refused to attend the RDC, and Pak Hon-yong. Bruce Cumings has shown that the DNF was not run by communists trained by the Soviet Union, as Hodge alleged, but was designed as an authentic voice of independent leftist opinion. While most obviously a reaction to the coalescence of the right, it was also a reaction against the establishment in north Korea on 14 February of the Interim People's Committee under the leadership of Kim Il Sung.[33]

The talks between the United States and the Soviet Union, provided for in the Moscow agreement, preoccupied the State Department and General Hodge in 1946. A Joint Conference was held from 16 January to 5 February as a prelude to the Joint Commission with the purpose of settling certain economic and administrative issues. A few extremely minor matters were resolved but conflict arose because of American failure to send rice supplies to north Korea. Grave food shortages in the north led the principal Soviet representative, General Shtikov, to request rice in return for coal being supplied to the south. However, the American occupation had changed rice policy fundamentally through the introduction of a 'free market' policy in rice. The consequence was that there were no rice surpluses to use. The Soviet Union regarded the American refusal critically and predictably withdrew the offer of coal to the south, which instead had to be supplied from Japan.[34] The Joint Commission began on 20 March in Seoul with five American and five Soviet members of the respective military commands assembling. The delegations were headed by Major-General Arnold and Colonel-General Shtikov. The conference debated the identification of the various groups of Koreans to be approached in the eventual formation of a provisional government. The Soviet view was that those Koreans who had condemned the Moscow agreement should not be consulted, since they did not accept the premises on which decisions were being reached. The Russians stuck firmly to the Moscow terminology of December 1945, including the reference to trusteeship, the reason being that they wished to prevent the Americans from going back on their past support for trusteeship. This was strengthened by the American admission during the exchanges that they proposed to recognise the RDC as the official consultative body in the south. Since the RDC was vehemently critical of trusteeship, the attitude of the American military government was clear.[35] The Soviet position was that consultation should take place with 'democratic parties and organizations'.[36] After much argument it was agreed on 6 April that the two sides would prepare lists of groups to be approached. After appearing close to agreement they diverged on 8 April when the Americans proposed further change to permit more flexibility in consultation. The Soviet side then reiterated adherence to the Moscow agreement. The disagreement could not be remedied because of the American commitment to the rightists controlling the RDC, who were hostile to trusteeship. On 16 May the Joint Commission was adjourned to resume its exchanges in 1947.

The British view of developments in Korea, upon which Britain was rarely approached by the United States – and this had been true since the Yalta conference – was that American policy was blundering and General Hodge inept. Arthur de la Mare observed on 29 June 1946 that a situation had arisen which could, without exaggeration, be regarded as a menace to world peace. Complete deadlock existed after the inability to resolve the intransigence in the Joint Commission.[37] Esler Dening commented that he had always suspected that the Americans had not appreciated the full significance of what they had taken on in Korea; it appeared that they were unwilling to accept the consequences of being located in an area of Soviet predominance and it would be regrettable in its implications elsewhere if the United States retreated.[38] In early September de la Mare minuted that the American military government was patently incapable of coping with Korean problems. He recalled General Hodge's unfortunate remark on his arrival in Korea that the Japanese and Koreans were 'all the same breed of cats'.[39] The Americans had been handicapped through inexperience, changes in personnel, and the corruption and lethargy in Korea. The American reaction in Seoul was to emphasise to Washington the dangers of south Korea following a path already being trodden in eastern Europe. William Langdon reported to secretary of state Byrnes on 24 May:

It is now all too clear that despite US occupation of Southern Korea the Russians have intended to impose a united front policy throughout the country. ... Such a policy if we could be forced to accept it would doubtless hasten and simplify Soviet control over the entire Peninsula. It is therefore entirely possible that the Kremlin will delay a resumption of negotiations and wait for our natural impatience, our demobilization problems, declining American interest in Korean affairs and local dissatisfaction with the division of the country to oblige us to supply speedy solution of these terms, i.e. a united front which excluding [excludes] all but elements controlled by the Communist Party. On the other hand, if we stand firm, it is not unlikely that Russia will find her long range interests best served by reaching a compromise solution on a government acceptable to us, thereby accelerating our departure from Korea and thus, in her estimate, leaving the Soviets a free hand to pursue their political aims here.[40]

Langdon believed that American determination to resist Soviet expansion in Korea had to be demonstrated and that the current unpopularity of communists in the south should be used to encourage the moderates in north Korea. Within south Korea policy should be aimed at consolidating democratic groups and drawing them into the military administration. Langdon stated that all groups should be represented except the DNF, which in his view was communist dominated.[41] The DNF contained patriotic leftist Koreans led astray by communist propaganda; it was important to persuade such people to support moderation and democracy. Langdon indicated that Hodge intended to establish a Korean Non-administrative Cabinet and Legislative Body which, under his supreme authority, would enact requisitions and laws in the period before the setting up of a unified provisional government. Kim Ku was no longer of any real importance but Rhee had proved himself a formidable politician; he had rallied moderate opinion, curbed the exuberance of his more militant supporters, and made conciliatory moves towards the Russians. Hodge did not deem Rhee essential to a future government but so long as he remained one of the few nationally known leaders, his cooperation was required.[42] Hodge hoped that the Joint Commission would resume its work and he did not wish to convey the impression to Koreans that it was American policy to prevent unification. Before very long the view of Rhee's helpful conduct was to undergo radical revision.

Rhee felt he must maximise his support. He now worked through the National Society for the Rapid Realisation of Korean Independence (NSRRKI) and in May 1946 embarked on a provincial tour to strengthen his position further. Interestingly, in a speech delivered at Chongup, Rhee urged a separate government for south Korea. This followed fierce anti-communist demonstrations by Rhee's supporters in Seoul, which had included protesting outside the Soviet consulate. Hodge castigated Rhee's statement and the actions of his supporters. Goodfellow, who had played an opaque and evidently important role in advising Rhee in 1945–46, left Korea in May.[43] General Hodge thus had the first of the many tempestuous scenes in which he was to be involved with Rhee over the next two years. Hodge commented in a letter to Goodfellow, 'The old man has made a lot of unfortunate statements ... he wants to set up separate government now and *drive* Russians out. ... I've had a couple of stormy sessions with the old rascal trying to keep him on the beam.'[44]

A new attempt was made by Hodge to promote cooperation between the right, centre and non-communist left in June and July 1946 with the establishment of the Left–Right Coalition Committee (CC), which met on 22 July. It was attended by rightist leaders such as Kim Kyu-sik and Won Se-Hun and leftist leaders like Yo Un-hyong and Ho Hon. The plan was that the CC should meet twice a week to devise a joint programme acceptable to left and right. Political leaders omitted from the charmed circle worked to frustrate the CC. Pak Hon-yong torpedoed compromise through engineering leftist proposals unacceptable to the right, who reciprocated predictably.[45] The CC failed, despite attempts to revive it. In October 1946 elections were held for the Interim Legislature. The military government believed elections were imperative to accentuate consolidation of the rightists and that the elections should be followed by the extension of Koreanisation. The elections conformed to the pattern seen under the Japanese. In numerous areas voting was restricted to taxpayers and landlords. Village elders voted at the lowest level instead of constituents and determined representatives to vote at the next highest level. At the county level representatives from lower levels were permitted to vote for candidates; the secret ballot obtained only at this level. The elections were held against the background of the serious and savage autumn harvest uprisings in October 1946 and were characterised by various grave deficiencies: some electors were not notified of the election, votes were cast by others in the names of genuine electors. The elections were dominated and won by the rightists. The most disputed regional elections were cancelled by Hodge but the new elections again led to rightist triumph. The membership of the Interim Legislature comprised ninety, half elected and half appointed. The right swept the election but most of the appointed members were moderates and leftists so as to redress the balance.[46]

At the end of 1946 and beginning of 1947 speculation centred on the prospects of a south Korea split by bitter political and social tensions. The suppression of the autumn harvest uprisings dealt a fatal blow to the 'people's committees' in many areas; the right was strengthened further. Rhee became more vocal and extreme in advancing his ambition. The Americans endeavoured to persuade the Russians to reconvene the Joint Commission but without success. Inflation had become a particularly serious and contentious subject. Two leading State Department officials took part in a radio broadcast on Korea aimed at engendering public debate before a large appropriation for Korea was included in the War Department's next vote. Arthur de la Mare of the British Foreign Office remarked that one of the most noteworthy features of the broadcast by Hugh Borton and Edwin Martin was Borton's admission that the failure of the Joint Commission was not entirely an American responsibility, 'nor was it entirely the Russians'.[47] American official policy was to promote self-government in south Korea as a prelude to unification but de la Mare observed that the long delay in accomplishing unification made this unlikely. Rhee intensified his pressure in the early months of 1947 and became more outspoken in criticising the military government. The British consul-general in Seoul, D. W. Kermode, informed London on 8 February that Rhee intended sending Byung Chic Limb on a 'goodwill visit' to Britain and that Rhee hoped Limb could be received at the Foreign Office. Kermode felt Limb would have to be greeted but recommended a low-key approach. De la

Mare felt Limb could not be received because it was British policy to sustain the Moscow agreement and it would be difficult to see the representative of a leading opponent of the government.[48] Kermode summarised Rhee's position vividly:

> Although Rhee poses plausibly as champion of Corean independence and has made a deep impression on sentimental audiences in United States, his admittedly genuine desire for the country's independence is really the desire of a megalomaniac. An extremist of the Right he is interested in the welfare of the people only in so far as some concession to their welfare is necessary to enable him to gain and retain dictatorial leadership. His aim is to be the first President of Corea and since he is 72 and has few more years left in which to realise his ambition he will use any means to hand including, if time presses, the blood of his deluded followers. Unable to hold the stage in any other way he set out to organise a 'popular demand' for immediate independence without trusteeship, and having succeeded beyond his expectations now finds himself in the position of having to deliver the goods or recede from the front of the political stage and lose all hope of fulfilling his personal ambitions. His present campaign of eloquent pleading for Corea is a manœuvre by which he hopes to ride to power as a national hero. If it fails, he may as a last resort fling his band of 'patriotic' assassins into general action.[49]

At the same time in February 1947 American intelligence spokesmen told the assistant military adviser at the British mission in Tokyo that the communist threat had subsided since November and that the main threat to public order came from rightists. The extreme right had adopted a bellicose attitude and had denounced the Americans; they had no faith in the Joint Commission and were opposed to any form of trusteeship. The rightists might orchestrate a demand for withdrawal of American troops.[50]

B. C. Limb called at the Foreign Office, having obtained a visa while in the United States, and gave an extremely misleading account of developments in Korea. Limb proposed abandonment of trusteeship, withdrawal of foreign forces from Korea, and Korean independence as a unitary state with membership of the United Nations (UN). Limb was told that Britain was watching developments in Korea with interest.[51] Hodge departed from Seoul on 13 February for a holiday in the United States. In his absence Major-General Albert Brown, head of the American delegation to the Joint Commission, would replace Hodge. Kermode, the British consul-general, wrote that Brown was free from political bias, unlike Hodge. He added, 'The United States Consul General and Dr Bunce, head of the State Department's economic mission, consider that it was largely Hodge's convention-rooted antagonism toward the left during the early stages of the occupation that led Korea into the impasse in which it stands today.'[52] R. A. Butler, one of the Conservative Party's chief spokesmen on foreign affairs, stated in the House of Commons on 27 February 1947 that he had for some time regarded Korea 'as perhaps the greatest danger spot for peace in the Far East'.[53] The Soviet journal, *Trud*, discussed Korean developments in an article published on 25 February 1947. It declared that 'no tricks and manœuvres of the corrupt Korean reactionaries who are the bosses of S. Korea will distract the Korean people from setting up a single democratic Korea'.[54] The interim legislative body was condemned as phoney, membership having been determined by the Americans; it contained no representatives of workers or peasants but instead represented the sordid interests of Korean capitalism. Rhee was stated to have adopted 'A more cunning policy for deceiving the Korean people'; Rhee's diverse tactics were all designed to enhance his ambition to be dictator of Korea.

Much more attention was being devoted to Korea in Washington in March 1947 at a time when the Truman administration was deeply involved in the complex issues inherent in taking over from Britain in handling aid to Greece. A small committee of State and Treasury Department officials plus General Arnold was set up to advise on Korean policy. Hodge was recalled to give evidence. It was envisaged that Congress be requested to approve a grant-in-aid of 600 million US dollars, to be spread over three years. A sum of 250 million dollars would cover the launching of the programme in the first year; part of the costs of administering the occupation would be incorporated in the 600 million dollars. The committee believed it would be appropriate for President Truman to speak to Congress in a manner analogous to that adopted for aid to Greece and Turkey.[55] The funds would be devoted to agricultural improvement, the revival of industry, and social and educational reforms. The aim was to put south Korea on a viable footing in case unification of the peninsula was postponed for some years. The committee held that a direct approach should be made to Moscow to try and secure progress in the Joint Committee. The State Department would select an able adviser to assist General Hodge: this official would gradually assume direction of political affairs and would act as a 'tutor' to the Interim Legislative Assembly. Dean Acheson was actively involved as Under-Secretary of State in dealing with the subject and believed that the United States must do what was feasible to sustain south Korea. Acheson met the Senate Foreign Relations Committee on 24 March to discuss the proposals for Greece and Turkey and to answer questions on Korea. The British ambassador in Washington, Lord Inverchapel, fittingly commented on the hearing, 'I draw your attention to Mr Acheson's denial that the programmes for aid to Greece, Turkey and Korea constitute an ideological crusade and to his following remarks which show that that is precisely what they are.'[56]

Acheson told the committee that aid would be required for Korea, probably for the next three years. He stated that the United States had attempted to secure the unification of Korea but without success. This was because of Soviet intransigence. Acheson would not commit himself on the sums of money involved and indicated that estimates had to be finalised.[57] The *Manchester Guardian* observed on 22 March that the situation in Korea was dangerous since 'Korea is one of the two parts of the world (Germany is the other) where the United States and the Soviet Union meet face to face in physical contact'.[58] It was most unlikely that an American–Soviet agreement would be forthcoming and this strengthened the case for broadening discussion on Korea. The Moscow agreement was effectively dead and the most sensible move would be for the UN to sponsor simultaneous withdrawal of American and Russian forces to be followed by the establishment of a unified Korean government – 'It might not be a very democratic or very efficient Government, but almost anything would be better than the present absurd and dangerous division.'[59]

The atmosphere in Seoul was extremely tense. The rightists, whipped up by Syngman Rhee and Kim Ku, organised demonstrations attacking the Soviet Union and the American military government. The Joint Commission reconvened in a final attempt to make some progress. In a speech in Seoul on 27 April Rhee cleverly sought to reconcile his own vigorous hostility to communism with the American approach to world problems. He welcomed the Truman Doctrine and claimed he had frequently predicted the development to Hodge:

> With the change of the international trends, not only have the gloomy prospects of the Korean people become bright, but also General Hodge's policy to South Korea will be changed in accordance with the policy of his country.
> The American authorities told me that I should make a general election law and arrange that the Korean people rule themselves. In view of this we must enact election laws as soon as possible. After this we must participate in the UNO and try to unify North and South Korea by negotiating with Russia from the standpoint of freedom. On the other hand I have considered the problem of supporting the Great Korean Provisional Government, but we must cooperate with the MG [military government] as much as possible and then talk about the provisional government. ...
> We must fulfil our task by ourselves and we must not create any cause for an American and Russian war. If a new war should occur no country will suffer as much as Korea would. ... [60]

The Joint Commission reconvened in late May. At first it appeared that some progress was being made. A joint bulletin issued on 7 June stated that agreement had been reached over methods of consulting Korean democratic parties and other relevant organisations on developments leading to the creation of a unified government and that the text of agreement would be issued shortly.[61] General Hodge reported that the reopening of the Joint Commission was a disappointment for Rhee and the extreme right in that they had campaigned vociferously for the past year against further American–Soviet discussion.[62] The Joint Commission soon became bogged down in renewed argument over the eligibility of various groups for consultation, with the Russians reiterating refusal to consult rightists currently denouncing the Soviet Union vehemently and demonstrating noisily in Seoul. On 23 June rightist demonstrations took place in Seoul and in other parts of south Korea; Hodge ordered American tanks on to the streets to disperse the crowds.[63] The exchanges in the Joint Commission again ended in deadlock and this marked the termination of the discussions set in train at the Moscow conference. The *Soviet Monitor*, circulated by the Tass agency, issued a special bulletin on 25 July expressing the Soviet view of the failure of the talks. The blame was placed squarely on the United States for having gone back on the Moscow agreement and on the basis worked out by Marshall and Molotov for renewing the meetings of the Joint Commission. The American delegation had submitted 'a long list of trading firms, educational institutions, research institutions, local and provincial organizations, each amounting to only a few people, and even street neighbour groups, and is insisting on consultations with them'.[64] Even non-existent bodies were allegedly included. On 21 July General Shtikov, head of the Soviet delegation, addressed a press conference and explained the Soviet position:

> The Soviet delegation strove and is striving to achieve on the basis of the Moscow decision, the speediest creation of a truly democratic Government in Korea expressing the will of the Korean people and capable of defending its interest. Consultation with Korean democratic parties and public organisations are an important means of ascertaining the opinion of the Korean people on the question of the formation of the Korean provisional democratic Government, and therefore the Soviet delegation attaches great importance to the consultations.[65]

Numerous defects were discovered in the list of organisations produced by the Americans through the inclusion of bodies not relevant to consultation or of organisations which did not exist. He gave as an example the 'Union of Building and Repair Workers of Korea' with an alleged membership of over one million, which was challenged by the Soviet delegation; subsequently the American delegation conceded it did not exist. Shtikov continued:

> The total number of members of parties and organisations of Southern Korea which made application for consultations is recorded in the list submitted by the American delegation as 70 million persons. This means that each adult Korean both male and female, must have been a member of eight organisations – which one must recognise as absurd.[66]

The Soviet Union was against consulting parties and organisations formed for the purpose of attacking the Moscow agreement. Bodies wishing to be consulted must leave the umbrella committee established to coordinate activity against the Moscow decision on trusteeship. The American delegation refused to accept the Soviet proposals and thus undermine the Moscow agreement to which the United States was a signatory. Problems could be surmounted but the American delegation would have to show a far more positive attitude than hitherto revealed.

Political unrest in south Korea increased appreciably in June and July 1947, stimulated by Rhee's intrigues. Hodge reported on 7 July that Rhee had issued a statement criticising the Americans for not supporting him; this was in keeping with Rhee's denunciation of the State Department and of an alleged plot to assassinate General Brown. Rhee was encouraged by certain people in Washington and Hodge named Oliver, Staggers and Jerome Williams; Staggers and Williams were respectively president and vice-president of the American World Trade Export-Import Company Inc.[67] Shortly afterwards Hodge described the political unrest as worsening with the anti-trusteeship campaign having become a campaign against the Joint Commission, the Soviet Union and the United States. The possibility existed of Rhee forming a government unilaterally. Hodge lamented the rift between the military government and the rightists after their earlier cooperation. It was, he sadly reflected, impossible to keep the Koreans away from factionalism and skulduggery.[68] The military government was in the position where it wished to sustain the south Korean rightists, who now repudiated it and pursued an independent path. The Truman administration recognised the catastrophic deterioration and determined at the beginning of August that action would have to be taken. It was decided that the Joint Commission should be required to submit a report by 15 August. It was anticipated that the Soviet Union would either oppose the suggestion or, if she agreed, that the report would be negative in approach. Whatever transpired, the United States would circulate identical notes to the Soviet Union, Britain and China proposing discussions on Korea. The American proposals would embrace holding of elections in north and south Korea through multi-party ballot based on universal suffrage; each legislature established in consequence would select representatives to meet representatives from the other to form a provisional government for a united Korea; the provisional government would meet representatives of the four powers to consider on a basis of equality the assistance required by Korea; the provisional government and the powers would agree on a date by which occupation forces would be withdrawn.[69] The British consul-general in Seoul thought that Soviet suspicion of the anti-trusteeship groups was understandable enough and that both sides in the Joint Commission were jockeying to gain the best tactical place before the breakdown of talks; neither wished to appear responsible for precipitating the collapse.[70] The Soviet Union supported the narrow definition of eligibility for consultation and the United States favoured too broad a definition of eligibility. The truth was that the controversy was symbolic of mutual suspicion and acrimony between the Russians and the Americans exacerbated by the consuming tensions of Korean politics.

An American note was sent to the Soviet Union on 11 August 1947 requesting a report from the Joint Commission by 21 August to enable the two governments to decide on the next step.[71] Four days later a statement emanating from the State Department expressed confidence in General Hodge and affirmed the American objective in Korea as the attainment of a free, united, sovereign nation with a democratic form of government reflecting the will of the Korean people.[72] Jacobs, the political adviser to Hodge, believed that steps must be taken leading to a permanent government in Korea: it would not be wise to accept a provisional government, since the Soviet Union had shown skill in eastern Europe in exploiting such a situation.[73] Jacobs felt that progress must be made through the four powers or the UN if the American position was to be viable. It would not be feasible to continue with the military government being assailed by left and right in south Korea. It would probably be necessary meantime to adopt a tougher line with the rightists: 'The only safe alternative would be to arrange with the Soviet Union for mutual withdrawal of troops and let nature take its course which will eventually mean another Soviet satellite state in Korea.'[74] The assistant chief of the Division of Eastern European Affairs in the State Department, Stevens, argued for rearming in Korea as a sign that the United States would resist communism:

Korea ... is a symbol to the watching world both of the East–West struggle for influence and power and of American sincerity in sponsoring the nationalistic aims of Asiatic peoples. If we allow Korea to go by default and to fall within the Soviet orbit, the world will feel that we have lost another round in our match with the Soviet Union, and our prestige and the hopes of those who place their faith in us will suffer accordingly. ... [75]

Clearly the point had arrived in September 1947 where fundamental decisions had to be taken on the American commitment to Korea. The vital questions were aptly summarised by Jacobs on 19 September. Was Korea of sufficient importance for the United States to accept a substantial financial and political involvement? If the answer was that American global strategy required an allocation of priorities in geographical terms could south Korea be abandoned in favour of a stand being made in Japan or elsewhere? These would be central to the arguments over defence policy that resounded or echoed through the State Department and Pentagon until the beginning of July 1950. If Korea was deemed vital, Jacobs recommended liquidation of the Moscow agreement as rapidly as possible and the full implications in cost and personnel worked out. If the United States decided to get out of south Korea, it should not be difficult to transfer the burden to the UN where an agreement could be reached: this would incorporate simultaneous withdrawal of American and Russian forces. Bloodshed would ensue as the rival sides fought each other, as had happened in

India after British withdrawal and as was happening in China. However, American involvement would be at an end.[76] The joint chiefs of staff assessed Korea in September and concluded that 'from the standpoint of military security, the United States has little strategic interest in maintaining the present troops and bases in Korea ... '.[77] If war broke out in the Far East 'our present forces in Korea would be a military liability and could not be maintained there without substantial reinforcement prior to the initiation of hostilities'.[78] Any offensive operations which the United States might have to conduct on the Asiatic continent would probably avoid the Korean peninsula. If an enemy developed powerful air and naval bases in Korea, American communications and operations in east China, Manchuria, the Yellow Sea, the Sea of Japan and contiguous areas could be adversely affected. Such enemy forces based in Korea could be neutralised through air action. The latter would be more feasible and less expensive than large-scale ground operations. Since the American army was under pressure with the impact of economy measures, the two divisions of approximately 45,000 men in south Korea could be deployed more profitably elsewhere. Withdrawal would not undermine the military position of the Far Eastern Command unless the Soviet Union built up military strength in south Korea sufficient to implement an attack on Japan.[79] As George Kennan has remarked, the heavy emphasis upon American air power was a characteristic error of the period; the extent of the misjudgment became abundantly clear in early July 1950.[80]

Opinion in Washington therefore moved to the conclusion that on balance it would be best to reduce American involvement in Korea and to request the UN to assist in achieving an acceptable solution. In the Joint Commission, which had reached the end of its futile labours, General Shtikov proposed in early October the withdrawal of foreign troops from Korea as a prelude to the various Korean factions agreeing on a provisional government to lead the peninsula to unified independence. Shtikov's proposal was warmly welcomed by the Korean left and viewed with alarm by the right. Although the right had advocated foreign withdrawal they were well aware that the retention of some American troops was needed to prevent communist domination – 'Under Shtikov's proposal, [a] strong Korean Communist Army in [the] North of Korea would be free to sweep down on the virtually unarmed south and quickly over-run it.'[81] Rhee reacted by toning down his recent criticisms of the Americans and he urged that a small force be left in south Korea until the south could defend itself effectively. The United States wished to secure a transitional period in which limited American military and economic aid would be extended to south Korea in the hope that the communists would be kept at bay, at least for a decent interval. The role of the UN would be to supervise elections, if possible throughout Korea but if not in south Korea alone, and to afford some measure of protection to the infant state as it moved to independence.

The United States began consultations with friendly powers in October letting it be understood that a UN temporary commission would be proposed, charged with supervising elections and reporting back to the UN Security Council and General Assembly at Lake Success. The British attitude was that American troops should remain pending the completion of the UN task in supervising elections; the change of policy away from the Moscow agreement, which Britain had so far supported, would be justified in the UN debate on the grounds that the assumptions on future developments at Moscow had proved erroneous and the only course of action now was to appoint a UN temporary commission. Britain doubted whether the UN could do more than to postpone the day when Soviet domination over Korea was established.[82] John Foster Dulles, a leading Republican spokesman on foreign affairs, was a member of the American delegation to the UN, and the State Department intended that Dulles should speak in conciliatory vein in the hope that the Soviet Union would accept the establishment of a temporary commission; the Truman administration was embarrassed but wished to advance non-communist prospects in Korea as far as was possible.[83]

The UN was a relatively small body in 1947 and effectively dominated by the United States. The Soviet Union possessed a veto in the Security Council but there was little doubt that the United States could convince the UN General Assembly to accept a proposal of reasonable character. The motion providing for the establishment of the UN Temporary Commission on Korea (UNTCOK) was carried easily against Soviet opposition on 14 November 1947. The members were India, Canada, Australia, France, China, El Salvador, the Philippines and Syria; the Ukrainian Soviet Socialist Republic declined to serve. The chairman was the Indian representative Kumara P. S. Menon. The successor body, UNCOK, had the same membership with the exception of Canada. It was established by a motion carried on 12 December 1948.

This chapter has so far focused mainly upon south Korea and on the American–Soviet deliberations upon producing a unified administration. This final section will look concisely at the construction of north Korea between 1945 and the beginning of 1948. It was widely believed in the western world that north Korea was simply created by the Soviet Union in a manner similar to that used by the Soviet Union in eastern Europe. There were some similarities but it would be wrong to consider north Korea as analogous to Bulgaria or Hungary. Stalin was less interested in Korea and the type of state that developed was of idiosyncratic character, in some respects resembling the Soviet Union and in others the kind of communist party devised by Mao Tse-tung during the Yenan era. Before 1945 Korean Marxists had cooperated with the Soviet Union from bases in Soviet far eastern territories and had worked with the Chinese communists at Yenan. Of Korean communists associated with Russia, the best known was Kim Il Sung but he had also been involved with the CCP. There is considerable difficulty in ascertaining precisely what was Kim's relationship with Moscow, since the accounts of Kim's early life and guerrilla activities contain wide variation, not to mention ideological 'realignment' to fit in with the nature of Kim's foreign policy in later years and the state of his current relations with Moscow and Peking. Bruce Cumings has examined the evidence as fairly as is feasible and has discounted the more grandiose claims, such as Kim's participation in the battle for Stalingrad.[84] Cumings concludes that Kim was probably based at Kharborovsk from 1941 to 1945 and conducted his guerrilla forays from there. Information from Soviet and Japanese military intelligence indicates that Kim organised several hundred guerrillas and fought against the Japanese in Korea and Manchuria. It is conceivable that Kim had spent a brief period with the CCP at Yenan in the later 1930s. Kim was frequently regarded in the West as a Soviet stooge but this was erroneous. Kim was a passionate nationalist imbued with determination to restore self-respect to Korea and to unify the peninsula, to liquidate feudalism and to remove foreign dominance – American or Russian – from Korea. Admittedly these characteristics became more obvious later on; Kim Il Sung was dependent on the Soviet Union for assistance in the early years in north Korea and had to tread warily. The Korean communists at Yenan probably numbered about 300, some of whom fought with the CCP. Naturally the Koreans in Yenan were deeply influenced by Mao Tse-tung's ideas for reorganising a party and for pursuing guerrilla warfare.[85] In the short term the Yenan Koreans were important in the development of the north Korean state but subsequently were to be liquidated by Kim Il Sung.

The Soviet Union had made few preparations for occupation of north Korea in August 1945. Improvisation was necessary in the haste of the Soviet attack on Japan. People's committees operated extensively, comprising progressive non-communists and communists; the Soviet task was helped by the will for reform and change. The initial behaviour of the Soviet forces was bad, including rape and plunder; this was explicable through the rawness of troops and inadequate provision for the occupation – some soldiers lacked proper uniform or shoes. They were permitted by their superiors to take personal booty back with them.[86] From the beginning of 1946 Soviet troops were efficient and well disciplined; they were not liked but were respected. In 1945–46 Soviet policy was to encourage cooperation between the moderate leftists and the communists until an administrative framework had been created. The independence of the people's committees was not ultimately compatible with communist rule in north Korea and problems occurred in the first few months of communist dominance.[87] The Russians were helped through the fleeing southwards of many of those who might have obstructed them. The coalition between moderate leftists and communists was shattered by the trusteeship crisis of January 1946. The beginning of the north Korean state dates from this period. Kim Il Sung soon established his authority. He became leader of the northern branch of the Communist Party in December 1945; there was always latent rivalry between Kim and Pak Hon-yong, the leader of the southern branch. It is likely that Pak would have been more amenable to the Russians than Kim but Kim was the tougher of the two and had the opportunities, which he fully exploited. Kim put forward a blend of Russian and Chinese approaches, which marked the beginning of the independent and sometimes eccentric path subsequently trodden by Kim. In a speech on 17 December 1945 Kim stressed the necessity for creating a wide range of party organisations in factories, enterprises and villages with the formulation of suitable criteria for party membership so as to eliminate some of the dubious elements which had recently joined the party. He emphasised the importance of a tightly organised centralised party on Leninist lines but also injected Mao Tse-tung's views with stress on working with the masses.[88]

The North Korean Interim People's Committee (NKIPC) developed in February 1946 as a reaction to the trend of events in the south; it was meant to assist in the process that would lead to a government for the whole of Korea. Kim Il Sung headed the NKIPC; the membership was disparate and it took some time for Kim to establish his control. Gradually autonomous organisations in north Korea were curbed by Kim and the Soviet forces.[89] The north Korean army originated in a coalescence of Kim's guerrilla supporters and the Yenan Koreans; it was only lightly armed prior to the departure of Soviet forces in 1948. Thereafter it evolved rapidly into a formidable force. Land reform policies were swiftly implemented on lines similar to China with the poor peasants and landless labourers constituting the spearhead. Landlords and rich peasants were identified as the enemy and their power broken.[90] The changes were carried through with relatively little bloodshed.

Kim Il Sung faced challenges from other communist and leftist leaders. The Yenan Koreans had formed a separate party, the New Democratic Party. Kim worked to bring this party into a merger with the North Korean Communist Party; this was accomplished in July 1946 with the formation of the North Korean Workers Party. The principal figures in the leadership were Kim Il Sung, Kim Tu-bong and Min Chong with the addition of Pak Hon-yong as leader of the South Korean Workers Party. Kim Tu-bong was a distinguished scholar, who had lived mainly in China; between 1942 and 1945 he worked in Yenan. Min Chong had also lived in China for many years and had taken part in the Long March. Pak Hon-yong was the most obvious choice in terms of political experience but his power base was in the south and he disliked Kim Il Sung, a feeling that was heartily reciprocated.[91] As it was, Kim Il Sung worked successfully to establish his authority. By the beginning of 1948 his position was strong but could still be challenged. The emerging north Korean state was solidly based and possessed much more cohesion than its counterpart in the south. The two leaders of Korea, Syngman Rhee and Kim Il Sung, confronted one another, both intensely nationalistic, ruthless, driven on by a sense of destiny and confidence that he – whether Rhee or Kim – would unite Korea and lead the nation to a glorious future.

# REFERENCES

1.  For a lucid examination of developments in 1945, see Michael Sandusky, *America's Parallel* (Alexandria, Va. 1983).
2.  Bruce Cumings, *The Origins of the Korean War: Liberation and the Emergence of Separate Regimes, 1945–1947* (Guildford 1981). This is an excellent, trenchant analysis, particularly concerning the social ferment within the Korean peninsula between 1945 and 1947. It has proved invaluable in the preparation of this chapter, as the references below indicate.
3.  Ibid., p. 267.
4.  Ibid., pp. 276–81.
5.  Ibid., p. 298.
6.  Ibid., p. 123.
7.  Ibid., p. 156.
8.  Ibid., p. 166. According to statistics cited here, a high proportion of the more senior ranks in the Korean National Police had served in the colonial police: 83 per cent of inspectors, 75 per cent of captains and 83 per cent of lieutenants in November 1946 had previously served in the colonial police.
9.  Ibid., p. 71.
10. Ibid., p. 72.
11. Ibid., p. 77.
12. Ibid., p. 83.
13. Ibid., p. 83.
14. Ibid., p. 87.
15. Ibid., p. 88.
16. Ibid., pp. 90–1.
17. Minute by Arthur de la Mare, 13 March 1945, on J. M. Allison (US embassy) to J. C. Sterndale Bennett, 28 Feb. 1945, F1394/1394/23, FO 371/46468.
18. *FRUS 1945* (6), p. 1070, Benninghoff to Atcheson (political adviser in Japan), 10 Oct. 1945.
19. Washington to FO, 14 Sept. 1945, F6911/2426/G23, FO 371/46476, reporting the views of John Carter Vincent in favour of four-power trusteeship as the most satisfactory method of surmounting current difficulties of ending the arbitrary division of Korea at the 38th parallel.
20. Washington to FO, 16 Nov. 1945, F10156/1394/23, FO 371/46469.
21. Ibid.

22. *FRUS 1945* (6), pp. 1130–1, Langdon to Byrnes, 20 Nov. 1945.
23. Cumings, op. cit., p. 186.
24. Ibid., pp. 216–17.
25. Ibid., p. 217.
26. Ibid., p. 221.
27. Ibid., pp. 221–2.
28. Tokyo to FO (from D. F. MacDermot), 29 Dec. 1945, F729/199/23, FO 371/54294.
29. Cumings, op. cit., p. 188.
30. Ibid., p. 235.
31. Cited ibid., p. 235.
32. Ibid.
33. Ibid., p. 237.
34. Ibid., p. 240.
35. Ibid., p. 241.
36. Cited ibid., p. 241.
37. Minute by de la Mare, 29 June 1946, F9219/199/23, FO 371/54250.
38. Minute by Dening, 28 June 1946, ibid.
39. Minute by de la Mare, 5 Sept. 1946, F12585/199/23, FO 371/54251.
40. *FRUS 1946* (8), pp. 685–6, Langdon to Byrnes, 24 May 1946.
41. Ibid., p. 687.
42. Ibid., pp. 688–9.
43. Cumings, op. cit., p. 250. Goodfellow was in part concerned with developing his own economic interests in Korea but it is possible that he was still fulfilling an intelligent role. For perceptive observations of an American journalist on developments in the American military administration, see Mark Gayn, *Japan Diary*, paperback edn (Tokyo 1981), pp. 349ff.
44. Cumings, op. cit., p. 250.
45. Ibid., pp. 256–7.
46. Ibid., p. 262.
47. Minute by de la Mare, 8 Jan. 1947, on Washington to FO, 3 Jan. 1947, F145/54/81, FO 371/63831. The text of the broadcast is in US Information Service handout in F54/54/81, ibid.
48. Seoul to FO, 8 Feb. 1947, F1712/54/81, ibid, with minute by de la Mare, 11 Feb. 1947.
49. Seoul to FO, 8 Feb. 1947, ibid.
50. Tokyo to FO, 7 Feb. 1947, F2017/54/81/G, ibid.
51. FO to Seoul, 28 Feb. 1947, F2095/54/81, ibid.
52. Seoul to FO, 18 Feb. 1947, F2207/54/23, ibid.
53. FO to Seoul, 28 Feb. 1947, F2944/54/81, ibid.
54. Cited in Moscow to FO, 27 Feb. 1947, F2695/54/81, ibid.
55. Washington to FO, 14 March 1947, F3550/54/81, FO 371/63832.
56. Washington to FO, 29 March 1947, F4751/54/81, ibid.
57. Extract from Senate hearing, 24 March 1947, enclosed, ibid.
58. *Manchester Guardian*, 22 March 1947, leading article.
59. Ibid.
60. *Han Sung Ilbo* ('Seoul Daily'), 30 April 1947, translated and enclosed in Seoul to FO, 6 May 1947, F7410/54/81, FO 371/63835.
61. Seoul to FO, 9 June 1947, F7731/54/81, ibid.

62.  *FRUS 1947* (6), p. 661, Hodge to MacArthur, 2 June 1947.
63.  Seoul to FO, 28 June 1947, F8715/54/81, FO 371/63835.
64.  *Soviet Monitor*, 25 July 1947.
65.  Ibid.
66.  Ibid.
67.  *FRUS 1947* (6), pp. 691–2, Hodge to Marshall, 7 July 1947.
68.  Ibid., pp. 696–7, MacArthur to Marshall, 9 July 1947, enclosing message from Hodge.
69.  Washington to FO, 4 Aug. 1947, F10470/54/81/G, FO 371/63836.
70.  Kermode to Bevin, 23 July 1947 (received 18 Aug.), F11315/54/81, ibid.
71.  *FRUS 1947* (6), pp. 748–9, Marshall to Bedell Smith, 11 Aug. 1947.
72.  Ibid., p. 754, Acheson to Jacobs (political adviser in Korea), 15 Aug. 1947.
73.  Ibid., pp. 760–1, Jacobs to Marshall, 21 Aug. 1947.
74.  Ibid., p. 783, Jacobs to Marshall, 8 Sept. 1947.
75.  Ibid., pp. 784–5, memorandum by Stevens, 9 Sept. 1947.
76.  Ibid., pp. 803–7, Jacobs to Marshall, 19 Sept. 1947.
77.  Ibid., p. 817, memorandum by Forrestal, 26 [29] Sept. 1947.
78.  Ibid.
79.  Ibid., p. 818.
80.  G. F. Kennan, *Memoirs, 1925–1950* (London 1968), p. 484.
81.  Seoul to FO, 5 Oct. 1947, F13473/54/81, FO 371/63829.
82.  FO to New York (UK delegation to UN), 21 Oct. 1947, F14064/54/81, ibid.
83.  Washington to FO, 24 Oct. 1947, F14328/54/81, FO 371/63840.
84.  Cumings, op. cit., pp. 398–401.
85.  Ibid., p. 399.
86.  Ibid., p. 388.
87.  Ibid., p. 405.
88.  Ibid., p. 404.
89.  Ibid., pp. 409–10.
90.  Ibid., p. 414.
91.  Ibid., p. 423.

# Chapter 3

# THE APPROACH OF
# CONFRONTATION IN KOREA

The UN became heavily involved in Korean affairs from the beginning of 1948 as a consequence of the acceptance by the UN General Assembly of the American proposal that elections should be held in both parts of Korea to achieve a national assembly and then a unified government for Korea. The United States had taken the initiative in this development, since it appeared the only means by which the Americans could disengage gradually from Korea with some hope that the UN could produce a solution that would sustain south Korea for at least a limited period. The Soviet Union made clear its firm opposition, maintaining that UN intervention was unnecessary and that Korea could advance to independence through the withdrawal of foreign forces and agreement reached among the Koreans themselves. There was no prospect of the UN securing consensus, since the terms of reference for UN involvement represented the position of the United States. It is possible but unlikely that progress might have been made had the UN adopted an investigative role instead of a course of action proposed by the United States. In the practical working out of UN policy the UN has to be regarded as a vehicle of American foreign policy; this was not always the case and the Americans criticised aspects of the functioning of the UN in Korea and especially the attitudes of individual members of UN commissions. Nevertheless in the main the UN fulfilled American desires and was condemned by the Soviet Union. There is strong continuity in the position of the UN over Korea from the end of 1947 to the termination of the Korean War in 1953.[1]

Direct UN activity in Korea began with the establishment of UNTCOK under the terms of the resolution proposed by the United States in October 1947: UNTCOK was to observe the holding and conduct of elections throughout Korea and to advise in the establishment of a unified, independent Korea. Elections were to take place no later than 31 March 1948 and UNTCOK would have the right to verify any aspects it wished. American and Russian armed forces would have to be withdrawn from Korea as soon as possible and within three months of a Korean government being formed.[2] The hostility of the Soviet bloc was pronounced from the outset and is illustrated in the refusal of Ukraine to participate in UNTCOK. The members of the commission met in Seoul on 12 January 1948. The challenges facing it were daunting: a considerable proportion of the UN was opposed to its existence; the predominant political forces in south Korea regarded it simply as providing a veneer of international respectability for the creation of a south Korean state; north Korea had no intention of helping it in any way and the United States believed the commission should complete its task swiftly and without asking awkward questions. It is hardly surprising that the members of UNTCOK felt exasperated and frustrated or that acrimony occurred between certain members and the American military government.

When UNTCOK began to assess the situation in January 1948 it was clear that it was impossible to fulfil the conditions of the UN resolution. The members of the commission could not gain entry to north Korea and could not observe the nature of elections there. In south Korea it could not determine the registration of voters, political parties or other electoral arrangements. There was division in UNTCOK whether it could accomplish anything in the circumstances; some members felt it should report the impossibility of proceeding but others believed that it could make limited progress. A majority believed that UNTCOK should supervise elections in the south but Australia, Canada and India were against doing so on the grounds that it would perpetuate and not eliminate the division in Korea. A report was made to the Interim Committee of the UN General Assembly, which operated when the General Assembly was not sitting. The Interim Committee reached the decision on 26 February 1948 that UNTCOK should adhere to the original intention in so far as this could be accomplished; elections would be supervised in the south but nothing could be done about the north.[3] Canada, Australia and eleven other members of the Interim Committee opposed the decision and a number of other countries abstained. American pressure ensured it was carried, however. On 28 February UNTCOK stated that elections would proceed no later than 10 May 1948. The American military government promptly announced that elections would be held on 9 May 1948, and UNTCOK undertook to observe the elections provided they were held 'in a free atmosphere, wherein the democratic rights of freedom of speech, press, and assembly would be recognized and accepted'.[4] Canada and Australia maintained it was unwise to observe elections only in south Korea; France and Syria abstained.

The American military government resented the presence of UNTCOK since it was bound to inquire into many features of the political scene, some of which were better not pursued from the American viewpoint. Jacobs, the political adviser to General Hodge, castigated members of UNTCOK for interfering in local politics. The

Chinese delegation had endeavoured to promote the ambition of Kim Ku, long a favourite of the Kuomintang; the Syrian was hostile to the military government. The French, Filipino and Salvadorean delegates were sympathetic to the United States. Jacobs placed the three remaining delegates, from Canada, Australia and India, in the category of being obstructive. The delegates concerned, Jackson (Australia), Patterson (Canada) and Menon (India), comprised a 'British bloc' or 'anti-American bloc'.[5] It would no doubt have upset Kumara Menon to be described as a member of the 'British bloc'; Jacobs could not decide whether Menon was a visionary or was persuaded by the arguments of Patterson, Jackson and Djabi (Syria). The principal obstacle was Jackson; as in Tokyo, Americans believed that Australian representatives were too radical in their political sympathies and that they worked against American policies. Jacobs described Jackson as clearly anti-American and anxious to find 'dirt' on the military government. Jackson had previously been in Japan and appeared to harbour ill will because Australia had not played a more prominent part in the allied occupation of Japan. Jackson was well disposed towards journalists of left-wing sympathies. Jacobs quoted the British consul-general as describing Jackson as a 'man of very strange and wild ideas, in many cases very radical'.[6] General Hodge met Jackson and deduced that he and some other members of UNTCOK would do all they could to sabotage American aims in south Korea. Jackson conveyed the impression of wishing to establish a permanent UN presence in Korea on the basis of always seeking to convince the Russians of the value of cooperation. Hodge believed that Jackson wanted American troops to remain in order to protect a long-term UN presence and this could frustrate the American wish to withdraw troops from Korea. Hodge contended that if the Interim Committee failed to reach a satisfactory conclusion that it would be preferable to terminate UNTCOK, withdraw American troops (even though the Soviet Union was demanding this), and press ahead with the establishment of a government in south Korea.[7]

The British consul-general in Seoul, D. W. Kermode, reported a view of Jackson different from that ascribed to him by Jacobs. When Kermode met Jackson in January 1948 he commented that he was able, responsible and steady. Jackson told him that General MacArthur had spoken to Jackson before he left Tokyo and had urged him to do all he could to assist Hodge and to prevent any dangerous developments.[8] The British Foreign Office held that the prestige of the UN must be preserved and that it would be foolish for the United States to treat the UN as a rubber stamp for decisions already taken in Washington. The British delegation to the UN informed London on 11 February that when UNTCOK reported to the Interim Committee the United States would advocate observing elections in the south despite the refusal of north Korea to cooperate. Seats in the new national assembly could be left vacant for north Korean representatives, should the latter subsequently be elected on an acceptable basis; the United States held that it was vitally important that the Soviet Union should not exercise a veto on the role of the UN in Korea.[9] D. F. MacDermot of the Foreign Office minuted that the report from UNTCOK must be considered before determining a course of action: to stipulate a detailed plan in advance would play into the hands of the Russians and of dissident political groups in south Korea.[10] This view was communicated to the United States embassy in London.[11] In the middle of February press reports indicated that the Soviet Union was advancing with the formation of a government in north Korea to be supported by a north Korean army. This pointed to the likelihood of the withdrawal of Soviet troops soon. The British assessment was that the United States had no long-term interest in Korea and had no scheme to extend sufficient economic or military aid to render a south Korean administration viable: 'It is probably therefore the American intention to pull out herself, as soon as she has found a face-saving formula for doing so.'[12]

The decision of the Interim Committee that supervision of elections should proceed left UNTCOK with the task of indicating basic guidelines to the military government. The members of UNTCOK met American and Korean officials and travelled throughout south Korea. However, the supervision was of an extremely cursory nature: there were only thirty non-Koreans involved in observation over an area of approximately 40,000 square miles (100,000 sq. km) with a population of twenty million.[13] As Evan Luard has remarked, this was in stark contrast to the thorough supervision provided by the League of Nations for the Saar plebiscite in 1935 when 1,000 neutral observers operated.[14] Meanwhile in the United States important decisions were being taken, which established the essentials of American policy in south Korea to the outbreak of the Korean War. The National Security Council (NSC) submitted a report to President Truman on 2 April 1948 reviewing the situation in Korea and recommending the principles that should govern future policy. The choices facing the administration were to acquiesce in Soviet domination of Korea, to provide aid for south Korea without assuming excessive commitments, or to provide a full guarantee of defence and support for south Korea. The first possibility was discounted:

> The extension of Soviet control over all of Korea would enhance the political and strategic position of the Soviet Union with respect to both China and Japan, and adversely affect the position of the US in those areas and throughout the Far East. Unless the US, upon withdrawal, left sufficient indigenous military strength to enable south Korea to defend itself against any but an overt act of aggression, US withdrawal could be interpreted as a betrayal by the US of its friends and allies in the Far East and might well lead to a fundamental realignment of forces in favour of the Soviet Union throughout that part of the world.[15]

Furthermore the authority of the UN was involved and this would be undermined by a Soviet-inspired invasion of south Korea. At the same time American global responsibilities were such that it was not feasible to give an unlimited guarantee to south Korea. The best policy would be a middle approach whereby economic and military aid was provided for south Korea in the hope that this could give sufficient strength for the regime to survive.[16] This demonstrated the uneasy nature of American policy from 1948 to 1950 – clear that south Korea was not essential to American strategy against the Soviet Union but equally unable to accept that south Korea might go communist. Most observers believed that south Korea would eventually be unified by north Korea with the support or at the instigation of the Soviet Union. While this deduction was logical, it ignored the repercussions for American prestige and for the authority for the UN for the unification of Korea on a communist basis. This dilemma was starkly perceived in June 1950 and answered in a way directly contrary to that anticipated so widely in the spring of 1948. Truman accepted the report's recommendations and instructed that withdrawal of American forces should commence.

In south Korea the preparations for the elections took place in a tempestuous, acrimonious atmosphere. Tension along the 38th parallel had been serious for some months: General Hodge informed the joint chiefs of staff in January 1948 that both the south Korean police and north Korean border guards were engaged in sporadic attacks on one another. Some of the Korean rightists provoked incidents and Hodge intended watching matters carefully:

> In view of the Korean love for fighting, although we have no proof it is safe to assume that some of the North Korean attacks are in retaliation of South Korean attacks. I am renewing my efforts to be sure that these incidents are not instigated by South Koreans.[17]

Political rivalry was intense in the south with Syngman Rhee making the running in censuring his rivals and in attacking the military government. Rhee condemned Hodge for not understanding the strength of the Korean wish for independence and for unity. Hodge recognised that his position had become untenable and wrote to MacArthur proposing that he be replaced within six to eight weeks. He explained that he was definitely *persona non grata* with Rhee and that the latter would bring in his 'carpetbaggers' if he won the election, meaning Rhee's supporters in the United States, Hawaii and China. Given Rhee's vindictiveness, it would be counter-productive for Hodge to remain.[18] Hodge was replaced by General John B. Coulter, the next most senior officer in Korea. W. Walton Butterworth had already written that 'acute personal animosity between General Hodge and Dr Rhee, considered in conjunction with the fact that the latter is expected to emerge as the dominant figure, if not the titular head of the new government in south Korea' rendered Hodge's departure inevitable.[19]

The hostility of the military government to some members of UNTCOK was unchanged. Jacobs alleged that the Canadian and Australian delegates were trying to sabotage the election because they were interested in a north Korean decision to convene a conference in Pyongyang for all Korean politicians concerned with unification.[20] Jacobs and Hodge believed there was a communist group in UNTCOK, encouraged by Jackson and Patterson, working to promote the failure of the UN efforts and to ensure that south Korea fell into the Soviet sphere.[21] The elections in south Korea were held amid charges of corruption, intimidation, impersonation and the familiar concomitants of the supposedly democratic processes. The outcome was a victory for the rightists, notably Rhee's NSRRKI and the KDP. A qualified judgement was submitted by UNTCOK: the results were accepted as valid in those areas visited by members of the commission but UNTCOK did not recognise the assembly as a *national* assembly, which could lead to the formation of a national government.[22] Rhee was elected as chairman of the assembly and formed a government claiming to represent the whole of Korea. A constitution for the Republic of Korea (ROK) was approved on 12 July; this stated that the ROK represented all of Korea. On 15 July Rhee was elected President of the new state. Withdrawal of American troops was prepared by 19 May in fulfilment of Truman's decision that, 'Every effort should be made to create conditions for the withdrawal of occupation forces by 31 December 1948.'[23] Most members of the UN willing to contemplate recognition of South Korea (ROK) felt that UNTCOK's report must be considered by the General Assembly before a decision was reached on recognition. In Washington the preliminaries for recognition were being completed. Walton Butterworth noted that a constitution had been adopted, a president and a vice-president elected, and the formal launching of the state would occur shortly. The thinking in the State Department was that a statement should be issued shortly, confirming that the ROK was regarded as the government of Korea in accordance with past resolutions of the UN General Assembly. A special representative would be sent to Seoul to negotiate the transfer of functions from the military government to the ROK.[24] It was decided that an able career diplomat of wide experience, John J. Muccio, should be the representative and subsequently ambassador.[25] President Truman approved the extension of uninterrupted economic assistance to the ROK: this would continue under the aegis of the Department of the Army until the Administrator of Economic Cooperation was ready to assume responsibility.[26] Rhee wanted economic and military assistance and did not wish American troops to be withdrawn, given internal instability and the threat of a North Korean invasion.[27]

The UN General Assembly resumed its consideration of Korea in October 1948. The report of UNTCOK was submitted and decisions taken thereon. In a position paper for the American delegation it was stated that the United States should support early withdrawal of occupying forces; that steps should be urged to remove barriers between the two parts of Korea and that Korean unification be advanced through North Korean participation in the ROK; and that UNTCOK should be reconstructed as a permanent body.[28] Developments in recent months were reported to the General Assembly by UNTCOK. The government of the ROK was considered capable of performing the customary functions of a government and to offer the prospect of eventual unification, particularly through fostering economic links. Negotiations between the ROK and North Korea prior to withdrawal of American and Soviet forces were firmly advocated by UNTCOK. The Soviet Union had announced on 19 September that the evacuation of Russian forces would be completed by the end of December 1948. The General Assembly ignored the points of qualification in UNTCOK's report and passed a resolution recognising the ROK and accepting the outcome of the elections held in May. The departure of occupying forces was recommended and a new commission, the UN Commission on Korea (UNCOK), was set up as a permanent body charged with helping to attain unification. The resolution was ambiguous in not making it clear whether the ROK was being recognised as 'South Korea' or as the government of the whole of Korea. Members of the UN were invited in the resolution to recognise the ROK. Predictably the Soviet Union vetoed the South Korean application to join the UN but the ROK joined other significant organisations in 1949, including the World Health Organisation and the Economic Commission for Asia and the Far East.[29] A North Korean application to join the UN was rejected; UNCOK was in just as invidious a position as UNTCOK except that South Korea had now been given a degree of recognition denied to North Korea. The efforts of UNCOK to intervene in internal matters were rejected by Rhee. The deterioration of relations between the two Korean states diminished any faint hopes of securing a compromise and Rhee ruled out using trade to improve contacts, UNCOK being left to reflect on the unstable internal situation and the combustible nature of the border along the 38th parallel. The danger of serious conflict occurring on the border was anticipated in a motion proposed by the United States and carried in the General Assembly in 1949 authorising UNCOK to observe developments on the border and to report back on clashes that could give rise to war.[30] Observation posts were established by UNCOK and important reports were to be forwarded in June 1950, as will be seen in chapter 7.

Now to consider the establishment of the Democratic People's Republic of Korea (DPRK) and the character of the state as it developed between 1948 and 1950. Communism was solidly established in north Korea by the beginning of 1948, although there was considerable rivalry between different factions. The Soviet Union saw no need to remain in military terms and appears to have thought it was merely a matter of time before communism was extended to the southern half of the peninsula. Preparations were advanced for the establishment of a government claiming, as did the regime in the south, to represent all of Korea. A conference of the North Korean People's Council met in July 1948 and approved the proposed constitution. Kang Yang Wook, chief secretary of the council, spoke to the assembled delegates and according to the intercept of a broadcast on Radio Pyongyang said:

> This is one of the most historical events to the Korean people, who have been fighting against the American imperialists and their reactionary and treacherous collaborators who plot to colonize Korea. It has brought the Korean people to a new hope. The Constitution is put into enforcement, and then the supreme People's Council shall be established with the representatives who will be elected by general election which shall be carried out by the provisions of the Constitution. As you all know, the American imperialists carried out the ruinous separate election and organised the so-called National Assembly with the support of the traitor minority and with savage oppression upon the majority of the South Korean people. However, all the Korean people never recognized the so-called National Assembly and will never recognize it. So at this grave moment we have come to establish a supreme people's council which can represent all the Korean People and include representatives from all the classes of the Korean people.[31]

Kim Il Sung presented a report in which he deplored the division of Korea, which was itself attributable to the machinations of the Americans. North Korea had made immense progress with the assistance of the Soviet Union. Stalin had observed, when the treaty between the Soviet Union and Finland was signed, that Russia believed in true equality between states regardless of respective might. This had been proved in the relationship between Moscow and Pyongyang since 1945. By contrast, the United States had assisted traitors and reactionaries and had violated the Moscow agreement of December 1945. The people of North Korea were happy and contented; the people of South Korea in reality supported the north but were prevented by the Americans and Rhee's cronies from expressing their real opinions. The workers and peasants of South Korea were not represented in the governing structure. The constitution connoted the just aspirations of the Korean people and the yearning for the unification of the nation.[32] The British Foreign Office analysed the constitution of North Korea and compared it with the constitutions of other communist states. The constitution contained a great deal that was familiar but also differences. There were indications that some articles had been taken from the Soviet Union's constitution but there was little evidence of other constitutions having been consulted except, curiously, for the Meiji constitution in Japan. However, the latter's impact was extremely superficial and could be explained on the grounds of the familiarity of Koreans 'with the laws of their quondam masters'.[33] The essence of the

Soviet constitution was incorporated, some features having been compressed and others expanded. The constitution was intended to fulfil a propaganda role in attracting support in the south in the sense of emphasising the dedication of North Korea to radical reform and nationalism.

The leading members of the government of the DPRK were Kim Il Sung and Pak Han-yong; Pak was simultaneously Foreign Minister and leader of the South Korean Labour Party (SKLP). Pak's presence strengthened the argument for regarding the government as representing the whole of Korea and underlined the hopes that Korean unification could be achieved through a major rebellion in the south. The turbulent history of much of South Korea since 1945 suggested the likelihood of this eventuality and was further strengthened by the bloody fighting in Cheju island in October 1948, which will be discussed below. Much obscurity surrounds the views within the North Korean leadership and what exactly were the perceptions of the probable evolution of politics in the south. Pak Hon-yong needed to bolster his own role in the North Korean government and the maintenance of a revolutionary spirit in the south would assist that objective.[34] The revolutionary impetus was declining, however, in 1949–50 amid the harsh repression by the South Korean government. North Korea was forced more upon itself as a result of American success in manipulating UN recognition of the ROK. Kim and Pak visited Moscow in March 1949 for discussions with Stalin and it was evidently on this occasion – if Nikita Khrushchev's recollections are reliable – that Stalin gave somewhat grudging approval to a future North Korean attack, on the assumption that there would be a significant rebellion in the south.[35]

Between 1948 and 1950 the Soviet Union helped in building the armed strength of North Korea to a powerful level. Regular intelligence assessments of North Korean strength were prepared by different American agencies with varying results. John J. Muccio informed Washington in November 1948 that military intelligence pointed to North Korea defeating South Korea in the event of war occurring.[36] There were frequent rumours of North Korean invasion plans down to June 1950. A British estimate a year later, based largely on intelligence from American sources, concluded that North Korea would triumph in an encounter from which other countries were excluded. The Foreign Office requested an assessment from the War Office in December 1949 to clarify or confirm the analysis the Foreign Office had made of the respective strength of the two sides. The War Office wrote:

In the past it had always been our view that irrespective of strengths the North Korean forces would have little difficulty in dealing effectively with the forces of South Korea should full scale hostilities break out. This somewhat naturally (since they raised, equipped and trained South Korean forces) was not the American view. Recently, however, they have been coming round to our way of thinking regarding the capabilities of the respective forces.

... On the question of aggression by the North, there can be no doubt whatever that their ultimate object is to overrun the South; and I think in the long term there is no doubt that they will do so, in which case, as you so aptly remark, the Americans will have made a rather handsome contribution of equipment to the military strength of Asiatic Communism. As to their method of achieving their object, short of World War III beginning, I think they will adopt the well tried tactics of preparing the country from within rather than resort to open aggression, although 'frontier incidents' will doubtless continue.[37]

It seemed to be the case that three divisions and one tank regiment had returned to Korea from Manchuria but this could not be verified. Approximately 80,000 to 100,000 Korean troops (the Korean Volunteer Army) had from time to time been reported as serving in Manchuria with the communist armies but it was difficult to ascertain actual strengths. It was believed that Russia maintained a 'military mission' numbering around 3,000 in North Korea. American policy was described in terms very similar to those employed by the Foreign Office to American policy in China in 1947–49:

Regarding American policy, if in fact one exists, towards South Korea, I can only say we know little, and of their future intentions even less. Their military advisors' group consists, we believe, of 300 and the emphasis is on 'advisory'.

Whilst being in no doubt about future North Korean (or Soviet plans) [sic] regarding South Korea we think an invasion is unlikely in the immediate view; however, if it did take place, I think it improbable that the Americans would become involved. The possession of South Korea is not essential for Allied strategic plans, and though it would obviously be desirable to deny it to the enemy, it would not be of sufficient importance to make it the cause of World War III. Meanwhile, we must accept an uneasy status quo and hope for the best.[38]

The most threatening feature of the development of the North Korean armed forces lay in air power. The Soviet Union gave appreciable assistance in cultivating a significant air strength in contrast to the United States, which concentrated solely on the army in the south, ruling out aid in the air and naval spheres. An American air intelligence report in February 1950 summarised the trend in so far as this could be ascertained. The report stated that early in 1949 information indicated that an air regiment had been created in North Korea. It was believed to be based at Pyongyang and to comprise approximately 800 personnel and 36 Soviet trainers plus obsolete Japanese planes. Koreans were being sent to the Soviet Union for aircrew training and were sent back to North Korea when their efficiency had reached a satisfactory level. Intelligence suggested that personnel had recently returned and there had been a significant increase in the number of aircraft seen and in the locations at which they had been sighted. The original thirty-six aircraft had been increased or replaced by about thirty-six Soviet fighter aircraft. The latter were thought to be Yak-9s, considered 'one of the USSR's better conventional fighters, which compares well with USAF's F-51'.[39] The precise number of personnel was not known but was estimated as high as 1,500. The air unit was commanded by Senior Colonel Wang Yon, who had served in Manchuria and graduated from a Soviet military academy as an air force lieutenant in the Soviet army; he had been in North Korea since 1945. The chief of staff was believed to be Colonel Lee Hwal, who had been educated in Japan; he was thought to be responsible for the organisation of the North Korean air force. Evidence pointing to the expansion of the North Korean air force included construction of airfields in five different locations. North Korea thus possessed a line of airfields from coast to coast with four close to the 38th parallel. The location of the airfields was not logical if they were intended for defensive purposes. 'They are, however, so located as to place North Korean aircraft in decidedly advantageous positions for offensive air action against South Korea.'[40] The morale of the air force was at first excellent, this being achieved through provision of better rations and other privileges. Recently it was believed that morale had declined and that only firm Soviet and North Korean police rule was preventing defections. The report summarised the position thus:

> The North Korean Air Force is daily becoming more potent. Both psychologically and as an actual threat it weighs heavily on the minds of the South Koreans. If not now, it soon will be capable of achieving complete air superiority over south of the 38th Parallel, and of materially assisting the North Korean ground forces should they attempt to move into South Korea.[41]

While too much emphasis should not be placed upon it, intelligence pointed to the offensive capacity of North Korea being strengthened.

The American embassy in Seoul analysed current trends within the North Korean Labour Party (NKLP) at the beginning of 1950; it was based on various embassy records and on interrogations of refugees from North Korea. The NKLP was the heart of the complex of 'political parties' and 'social organizations' in North Korea, all of which were communist-controlled; the same applied to the 'façades' of the DNF and the Democratic Front for the Attainment of Unification of the Fatherland (DFUF). Membership of the NKLP was estimated at nearly 700,000 in a pyramidal structure at the base of which 'is an enormous mass of virtually illiterate farmers, numbering perhaps half a million, as well as about 180,000 uneducated factory workers'.[42] The party was controlled by a small group of Soviet-trained communists; a few leading figures had been in Yenan. Near the summit of the pyramid was a category of semi-educated members numbering a few thousand occupying subordinate positions: most of these were previously non-political residents or nationals of the Soviet Union or had links with the Chinese communists. The dominant elements were certainly the Soviet ones with the Yenan communists second and the 'native communists' having little influence. The NKLP exhibited the familiar signs of 'inflexible bureaucracy', which inhibited advancement. No evidence could be detected of significant schisms or 'nationalistic tendencies'. This observation was misleading on both counts. A continuous purge was pursued in order to rid the NKLP of those lacking genuine commitment. The NKLP had been formed in August 1946 with the unification of the Korean Communist Party and the Yenan Independence Alliance; numerous small left-wing parties were absorbed at that time or subsequently. The NKLP'S sister party in the south, the SKLP, had suffered serious reverses in 1949 at the hands of the Rhee government and was no longer the force it had once been. Rumours proliferated of disagreements between the leaders of the NKLP and SKLP and these were justified. The NKLP controlled the Democratic People's Front, which existed to present a 'democratic' façade for communist dictation and to ensure that North Koreans felt part of the political life of the state. In addition, there was the DFUF. This had been established in August 1949 in part to promote the arguments for unification under the direction of Pyongyang. The DFUF also fulfilled a strategic function in organising military training for Koreans of both sexes between the ages of sixteen and thirty. The report concluded that the Soviet Union and not the NKLP connoted the reality of power – 'The NKLP is merely an instrument of Soviet control over the northern half of the peninsula.'[43] The vigour and enthusiasm of the CCP were conspicuously absent in the NKLP. This report is interesting for the stress placed on the subservience of the NKLP to the Kremlin:

> The power delegated by the USSR to the NKLP resides in a small elite leadership of Soviet-sponsored professional revolutionaries who rule the party's relatively enormous, illiterate, mass membership with customary Communist discipline. That the party has little popular support, even within its own ranks, is shown by the fact that it is purging its own educated 'native' members who might voice discontent over the party's subservience to Soviet Russia. .... [44]

The belief that the NKLP possessed little if any independence and was a vehicle for the implementation of Soviet foreign policy was held by most American officials, including George Kennan, and was illustrated in the reactions to the events of 25 June 1950.

The Soviet press celebrated the first anniversary (March 1950) of the signing of the agreement for economic and cultural cooperation between the Soviet Union and North Korea with much emphasis. Maslonikov wrote in *Pravda* that the DPRK had made huge strides with the aid of the USSR. Economic progress was particularly noteworthy:

Thanks to the enthusiasm of the workers and the widespread emulation movement in the sphere of production, the two year plan for the development of national economy is being successfully fulfilled. ...

The 1949 plan, that of the first year of the two year plan, was fulfilled by industry as a whole by 103 per cent. Old engineering plants have been repaired and new ones built. In the two years from 1946 to 1948 industrial output as a whole increased 2.6 times, but the output from engineering works increased 6.6 times. In 1949 engineering took a big step forward.[45]

The agrarian reform had done much to improve the efficiency of agriculture and to ameliorate living standards among the peasantry. Unemployment, 'the terrible curse of capitalism', had been eliminated and the wages of workers were rising.

In *Izvestia* Tavrov wrote in similar vein that the agreements of March 1949 had strengthened the cause of peace in the Far East and throughout the world. The DPRK had won international recognition through the diplomatic relations established with the Soviet Union, the Chinese People's Republic and other countries representing 'people's democracy' in Europe and Asia, including the German Democratic Republic. Tavrov compared the achievements of North Korea with the failures in South Korea, remarking that the American imperialists had made strenuous efforts to handicap the independent, democratic spirit of the Korean people:

Their policy is aimed at making the Southern part of the country a colony without rights and a military strategic springboard for the United States. It was precisely for this purpose that the United States Government obstructed the carrying out of the Moscow Agreement on Korea, which envisaged the speediest creation of an independent Korean democratic State.

Under cover of the so-called United Nations Commission for Korea, American ruling circles set up a puppet 'Government' under the traitor Syngman Rhee, who traded away the independence and national wealth. The collapse of national industry, increased unemployment, a continuous worsening of the economic position of the working people and bloodthirsty terror – these are the results of American rule in Southern Korea.[46]

Rhee and his followers had tried to liquidate the guerrilla movement in the south but had failed. The democratic approach inherent in the guerrilla movement would triumph ultimately. The principles of Stalinist foreign policy would ensure continued support for the just aspirations of the Korean people:

The Korean people have a loyal, disinterested and great friend in the Soviet Union. Soviet–Korean friendship and economic cooperation is developing and growing stronger for the good of the peoples of Korea and the Soviet Union, thus promoting the strengthening of universal peace and international cooperation.[47]

Kim Il Sung reciprocated in an article warmly praising Soviet help before and after the agreement of 17 March 1949. Soviet aid had put North Korea on a vigorous and successful course for the future:

> Thanks to the constant assistance of the Soviet Union and the selfless labour of the Korean people in the restoration of their country on a democratic basis, the Northern part of our Republic has developed into a powerful military, political, economic and cultural base for the democratic development of the whole country, and has considerably raised the level of material and cultural life of the people of our young Republic.[48]

The Soviet Union had furnished machines, materials and raw materials essential for the growth of industry and had sent specialists to advise on economic developments. The economic attainments of North Korea were compared favourably with the poor results in the south; the latter had been adversely affected by the 'barbarous and plundering policy of the Americans'.[49] The political realities of the division of Korea made the Korean people appreciate all the more the value of the assistance provided by the Soviet Union:

> The consolidation of the eternal and unshakeable friendship formed between the Soviet and Korean peoples, thanks to the liberation and assistance by the Soviet Union will further strengthen the international democratic camp and will make a valuable contribution to the struggle against the aggressive imperialists, the instigators of a new war.[50]

Finally to turn to South Korea, and to examine the political, economic and strategic situation between 1948 and 1950. Syngman Rhee had established a strong but not invincible position in 1948. He was the most tenacious politician in South Korea and an adroit manipulator but lacking in popularity. John J. Muccio, the first ambassador to the ROK, knew Rhee well and appreciated the President's strengths and weaknesses. In retirement, Muccio recalled that Rhee was very intelligent, determined and assertive; he had reached the top at a late age and was too set in his ways, his attitude having been determined by his lengthy period in exile, amid the seemingly forlorn struggle to save Korea from Japanese colonialism. When Rhee was in a logical frame of mind, he showed an excellent historical perspective but when he became emotional, he became particularly awkward to deal with. Rhee was highly autocratic yet claimed to represent the desire for genuine democracy in Korea.[51] Rhee was concerned with consolidating his own power base, building up the strength of his regime, securing American economic and military assistance, and with achieving the unification of Korea under his leadership: this would be the crowning attainment of his long struggle. The omens for the new state were not encouraging in the first months of its existence. Muccio reported in November 1948 that economic developments were disturbing, with inflation reaching worrying proportions. Politically the situation was contentious and

Rhee had not shown the correct touch in tackling domestic problems. It was possible that this ineptitude revealed incipient senility. Corruption was a serious problem and the success of the Chinese communists had made people feel jittery.

There was much anxiety as to how South Korea would cope when American troops were withdrawn. Internal disaffection was significant in certain areas, accentuated by communist infiltration. Fear of a North Korean invasion was real and military intelligence indicated the probability of North Korean success if they attacked.[52] During 1948 unrest in South Korea reached its most serious level since the autumn harvest uprisings of 1946. A major rebellion started on Cheju island on 3 April 1948 with guerrillas advancing into coastal towns from their bases on the higher volcanic summit of the island.[53] The timing was explicable because of the vigorous SKLP campaign against separate elections. The conflict was peculiarly bloody with both sides responsible for committing atrocities. Extra police and groups of rightists went to Cheju-do to assist in restoring order. American naval and air units acted to deter the rebels. The fighting diminished after the elections but developed again in October 1948 and January 1949. It has been estimated that the Cheju rebellion involved 30,000 deaths, approximately 10 per cent of the population.[54] The guerrillas fought fiercely and effectively. The nature of the rebellion is explained by the social character of the island with a cohesive clan structure and social solidarity; the leaders included radicals who had returned from Japan and schoolteachers. The SKLP had a number of loyal supporters including some among the local police. John Merrill has concluded that the rebellion was probably not the result of conspiracy but rather of the geographical remoteness of the island, the tenuous nature of government authority, and ancient grievances against Seoul.[55] On 19 October 1948 the Yosu rebellion occurred when police about to be sent to Cheju-do rebelled. Communist infiltration of the police was clearly shown in the mutiny.[56] It is likely that about 3,000 people, divided roughly equally between supporters and opponents of the rebellion, perished.[57]

Thereafter guerrilla activity gradually subsided and the most dangerous period faced by South Korea from the viewpoint of internal unrest had been surmounted. Rhee combated dissension with a mixture of harsh suppression, new security provisions and drastic purges of dubious elements in the police force. The American embassy in Seoul reviewed the history of guerrilla activity over the past few years in April 1950. The embassy used intelligence provided by the Korean police, army and the American military mission (KMAG G-2); Korean assessments had been analysed by American military advisers. Guerrilla forces were considered to have reached their highest point numerically in September 1949 when approximately 3,000 to 3,200 were operating. Korean police and army operations had succeeded in reducing guerrilla strength by March 1950 to approximately 400. However, more guerrillas had been sent from North Korea in March 1950 and the number had tripled. The ROK army had proved effective in assailing the infiltrators and guerrilla strength on 12 April 1950 was put at about 577. The worst affected province was Kangwon. The South Korean army anticipated that an attack might be launched by North Korea to support guerrilla units in the Taebaek-san area. The vital section for the south to defend was the left flank, which protected the routes to Seoul and Inchon. The right flank was less well defended and the nature of the terrain complicated defences. At present guerrilla activity was reported in Kyongji province, north and south Chungchong provinces and on the island of Cheju. Russian advisers had been involved in border incidents but there was no evidence that they had advanced south of the 38th parallel. Russian weapons were rarely found south of the border and the guerrillas used mainly Japanese and American weapons. The Japanese weapons were derived from old stocks and the American weapons had originally been supplied to the Kuomintang forces in China, had been captured by the Chinese communists, and then passed to North Korea.

Guerrilla activity was supposedly concentrated, according to Pyongyang radio, on 'vicious landlords', 'puppet Rhee's country-ruining gang', the 'puppet army' and the 'puppet Police'.[58] In reality guerrilla action was largely indiscriminate with sporadic attacks on the occasional landlord, local official, or police post. Ordinary farmers bore the brunt of guerrilla actions. Guerrilla strength was restricted to certain mountainous regions and they had proved singularly incapable of retaining control of 'liberated areas'. Guerrillas from North Korea possessed excellent morale and were thoroughly indoctrinated in communist aims; there were few desertions and a strong bond of loyalty existed among guerrillas. They were young, usually between seventeen and twenty-five years of age. In the opinion of qualified American observers the South Korean assessment of guerrilla strength was convincing. The evidence pointed to a sharp decline in guerrilla prowess. Police and army behaviour and tactics had been improved to some extent, especially in appreciating the need for reform policies rather than simple oppression. Police and army now worked more closely together without the quarrels which had hindered operations in the past. A guerrilla reserve of approximately 3,000 was deemed to exist in North Korea. Vigilance on the border had been stepped up and large-scale infiltration should be extremely difficult. At the same time limited continuation of guerrilla activity would continue indefinitely. It was concluded that North Korean strategy was 'synonymous with Soviet strategy' and that if North Korea did not push a guerrilla campaign further, it was because this did not assist the Soviet Union.[59] While exaggerating some of the successes of the South Korean forces, the report was correct in bringing out the decline of guerrilla activity and the difficulties of transforming guerrilla operations into a major threat to the existence of the government in Seoul.

The policy of the United States regarding the defence of South Korea was to continue in 1949 with the withdrawal of American troops so that the process was completed by 30 June 1949. Economic and military aid would be furnished to render the ROK government capable of defending itself but without being very explicit as to what this meant. The NSC reviewed Korean policy in March 1949 in very similar terms to NSC 8, approved in April 1948. Once again the dilemma of maintaining the independence of South Korea without involving the United States in an open-ended commitment was examined. Once more the conclusion was that a middle policy was appropriate. All American forces would be withdrawn by 30 June 1949. An American military advisory group should be established formally, taking over from the provisional group already in existence. Congress should be asked to continue economic and military aid with the objective of achieving a well-trained, efficient army of 65,000 men, including air detachments adequate for maintaining political order inside South Korea, a coastguard of 4,000 men, and a police force of 35,000 possessing small arms and ammunition. 'In publicly announcing the withdrawal of its remaining occupation forces from Korea, the US should make it unmistakably clear that this step in no way constitutes a lessening of US support of the Government of the Republic of Korea, but constitutes rather another step towards the regularisation by the US of its relations with that Government and a fulfilment on the part of the US of the relevant provision of the GA Resolution [UN General Assembly] of December 12, 1948.'[60] This sentence admirably encapsulates the ambiguities in American policy. The ROK armed forces were to be developed so as to be capable of handling internal dissent but the issue as to its capacity for reacting effectively to North Korea was side-stepped. The ambiguity was the product of two factors: unwillingness to pay for larger armed forces and doubts as to the policy of South Korea itself. With reference to the former, Congress was unlikely to pour out vast sums of money for Korea. As regards the latter, Rhee had stated on many occasions that Korea must be reunited; given his advanced age, the President might well be tempted to accomplish this sooner rather than later. It would be dangerous to supply too much to South Korea since Rhee could not be trusted to behave responsibly if he possessed powerful forces.

The Secretary of State, Dean Acheson, warned the American mission in Seoul on 13 April 1949 that information had been received from a source believed to be reliable to the effect that serious trouble might arise in Korea within two months and that the initiative in these developments would be taken by South Korea.[61] It was necessary to exercise a restraining hand in Seoul while proceeding with the programme recommended by the NSC and accepted by President Truman. In late April 1949 the decision was taken to establish an augmented Korean Military Advisory Group (KMAG) to function as part of the American mission in Korea with responsibility for the training mission so far undertaken by the provisional military advisory group. It would be headed by Brigadier-General W. L. Roberts, currently commanding general of United States army forces in Korea.[62] Syngman Rhee was dissatisfied with American policy, which was insufficiently supportive, and he told Muccio that South Korea should be included within an essential American defence line.[63] Rhee issued a press statement raising publicly whether South Korea could rely on American assistance in the event of North Korean aggression.[64] This touched a raw nerve and Muccio was instructed immediately to see Rhee and protest at this 'grave breach [of] ordinary diplomatic courtesy'.[65] Such criticism of American policy would be counter-productive; the claims on the United States for economic and military assistance were so great that only a limited amount could be given to Korea. Under pressure from Muccio, Rhee qualified his previous remarks in a further public statement. He stressed that South Korea desired the formation of a Pacific pact analogous to the Atlantic pact; agreement between the United States and the ROK alone, or with some other nations, for mutual defence against aggressor nations; and a public declaration by the United States of a pledge to defend a reunited, democratic, independent Korea, in accordance with the policy enunciated in the Truman Doctrine. South Korea was prepared to fight alone if necessary.[66] The reference to a Pacific pact was to developing contacts between Rhee, Chiang Kai-shek and President Quirino of the Philippines to encourage the formation of an anti-communist front to be guaranteed by the United States. Chiang wished to bolster his tottering regime in Taiwan and hoped to secure bases in South Korea from which his forces could launch sporadic attacks on Communist China. Chiang also sounded out Rhee on the possibility of basing his regime in South Korea in the event of Taiwan falling. Chiang visited Seoul and was to be followed by other Kuomintang emissaries until June 1950. This is an interesting if murky subject, which will be examined further in chapters 5 and 7.

American apprehension at the danger of the ROK provoking North Korea from across the 38th parallel was reinforced by serious incidents in early May 1949. General Roberts stated that on 6 May a unit of the ROK army had advanced north of the 38th parallel to a depth of 2.5 miles (4 km) and had attacked several settlements. Muccio discussed the incidents at Kaesong and Chunchon with Rhee on 10 May: he reminded the President that UNCOK was observing developments and it would hardly benefit the cause of South Korea if the impression was conveyed to the UN that South Korea was indulging in aggression. Rhee reiterated the strategic importance of Kaesong and the necessity of standing firm against communist aggression. He gave an undertaking that his government would not adopt aggressive measures in future.[67] Muccio's considered opinion in June 1949 was that the departure of Russian and

American troops left the two sides in Korea evenly balanced and that neither side was likely to risk 'an all-out invasion' in the foreseeable future.[68] The 38th parallel offered frequent opportunities for incidents, and reports indicated strengthening of the North Korean forces. The morale of the South Korean army had improved recently. Muccio blamed North Korea for provoking two serious incidents at Kaesong and Ongjin within the past six weeks. Minor incidents would doubtless continue to arise in future.[69] The Army Department reviewed commitments in Korea and wrote to the State Department that Korea possessed 'little strategic value' in the view of the joint chiefs of staff – 'To apply the Truman Doctrine to Korea would require prodigious effort and vast expenditure far out of proportion to the benefits to be expected.'[70]

Rhee therefore failed to secure the definite promises of American support that he deemed to be essential. Indeed the tone of reports emanating from Washington between August 1949 and May 1950 gave cause for increasing alarm in Seoul over ultimate American intentions. The publication of the China White Paper in August 1949 worried Rhee, since it connoted a virtual collapse of American support for Chiang Kai-shek and the possibility of the United States preparing to recognise Communist China. The statement by President Truman on 5 January 1950, to be followed a week later by Dean Acheson's address to the National Press Club, deeply concerned Rhee, for they seemed to show that South Korea was expendable or, at any rate, that American intentions towards South Korea were ambiguous. Equally disturbing was the fact that the House of Representatives voted narrowly on 19 January 1950, by 193 votes to 191, to reject the administration's Korean Aid Bill. The defeat was attributable to resentment at the Truman administration's bankrupt policy in China, to complacency regarding the Korean bill, and to the grave ill health of Senator Vandenberg. It did not reflect particular animus over Korea but more a feeling of frustration at the setbacks encountered by American policy in the Far East in the previous two years. There was, however, growing concern over the effects of inflation in the ROK. Acheson visited Vandenberg in hospital on 21 January and the senator emphasised his support for Acheson's policy. Vandenberg was shocked at the House vote and the stupidity of many of his fellow Republicans. 'He thought that as good a case could be made for our efforts in Korea – and probably a better one – as almost anything we had done in the foreign field.'[71] In his memoirs Acheson lays much stress on the impact of the House vote and sought to play down criticisms of his own speech of 12 January; the latter criticisms had focused on Acheson having given encouragement to a North Korean attack by not making clear what the American reaction would be in these circumstances.[72] The criticisms were to be renewed after 25 June 1950. The House vote was soon reversed and Economic Cooperation Administration (ECA) aid for Korea approved. The

House carried a bill on 9 February authorising sixty million US dollars for the second part of the fiscal year 1950.

The South Korean ambassador in Washington, John M. Chang, visited the State Department on 20 January and conveyed anxiety at Acheson's speech and at the House vote:

> He [Chang] said that the fact Korea found itself on the other side of that line as defined in Acheson's address, combined with the House action yesterday, appeared to raise the serious question as to whether the United States might now be considered as having abandoned Korea. Mr Butterworth said he could not share this view. He pointed to the fact that with respect to Korea the United States had associated itself with others of the United Nations in support of Korea's cause and, in that sense, therefore, Korea's position transcended a definition of interest by a line drawn in any direction.[73]

The ambassador returned to the charge at the beginning of April 1950, just before he departed for visits to Australia and New Zealand before returning to Seoul. Chang expressed the hope that the American defence line in the Far East could be extended to include South Korea. Dean Rusk declined to discuss it other than to make the observation that

> the so-called 'defense line' to which the Ambassador had referred was in actuality merely an enumeration of those sectors in the western Pacific in which the United States held firm military commitments: i.e. our responsibilities as an occupying Power in Japan, our special interest in the Philippines as a former part of United States territory etc. The Ambassador replied that he realized that no statement could be made on this subject and he himself had avoided making any such statement which he felt might prove embarrassing. He added that he did wish, however, to impress upon the Department the importance which the Korean Government and people attached to their apparent exclusion from the defense plans of the United States in the Far East. Mr Rusk replied that the inference that the United States had decided to abandon the Republic of Korea to its enemies was scarcely warranted in the light of the substantial material aid and political support which we had furnished and were furnishing to that Republic.[74]

Soon afterwards an unfortunate press interview was given by Senator Tom Connally (Democrat, Texas), chairman of the Senate Foreign Relations Committee, which appeared in the 5 May issue of *US News and World Report*. Connally conveyed a defeatist air, commenting that he feared that the communists would overrun Korea and the same was probably true of Taiwan. Connally did not regard Korea as vitally important to American strategy.[75] Syngman Rhee's reaction was vitriolic when he met the American chargé d'affaires in Seoul on 9 May:

> Speaking in a deeply bitter and sarcastic manner, President Rhee said it was very easy for a man several thousand miles away from Korea airily to dismiss Korea and its 30 million people as of no strategic or other

importance to the United States. The President went on to say he regarded Senator Connally's remarks as an open invitation to the Communists to come down and take over South Korea. He wondered how any man in his right senses, not to mention Senator Connally ... could make such an irrational statement.[76]

The chargé, Everett Drumright, countered by reminding Rhee that the ECA was spending more than 100 million dollars in Korea at present and had perhaps its largest staff in Korea. In addition, the United States had its largest military mission in Korea except for Turkey. Rhee complained bitterly at American failure to provide an adequate level of air support.[77] In a message to the State Department on 25 May John J. Muccio rightly drew attention to the unwise nature of various statements relevant to Korea made in the previous five months:

> I refer to public statements attributed to the President, the Secretary or other high Government officials in which various countries are named as especial objects of United States interest and concern, but from which the name of Korea very frequently is omitted.
> The omissions are always noted here in Korea and they add to the sensitivity and fear of the Korean Government and Korean citizens that the United States Government is not fixed in its determination to assist Korea and will abandon Korea at the earliest opportunity. ...
> I should like to urge that those persons particularly charged with drafting speeches and statements on United States policy have this problem brought to their attention, so that in any listing of Asiatic countries in whose freedom the United States maintains a continuing interest, Korea may always be included.[78]

It was unquestionably foolish to convey the impression that Korea was expendable. North Korea and the Soviet Union could only have drawn encouragement in the belief that America would most likely not act with vigour if North Korea moved against the south to reunify the peninsula.

Apart from perturbation in Washington concerning the uncertain consequences of border clashes, the political and economic situation in South Korea gave rise to additional anxiety. The South Korean economy was heavily dependent on American support, and inflation, developing since 1945, reached grave proportions. In January 1949 Walton Butterworth warned the South Korean minister that the ROK must not repeat the mistakes of the Kuomintang in China.[79] Philip C. Jessup, Truman's ambassador at large, visited Seoul in January 1950 and held wide-ranging discussions covering political, financial and strategic matters. Jessup felt the ROK government realised the necessity of solving pressing economic problems. The difficulty lay not in identifying the issues but in tackling them resolutely. The adoption of land reform had been held up by the opposition of recalcitrant landlords. In other spheres attempts to increase productivity had been blocked.[80] Jessup considered the morale of South Korean troops to be good but he was struck by the appreciation of the strength of the North

Korean forces: the resources of the North Koreans were not underestimated by South Korean officers. Muccio spoke trenchantly to Rhee on 18 January 1950 and warned of the perils of inflation. Rhee explained the failures to control inflation as the fault of his incompetent ministers but Muccio maintained that Rhee himself was to blame. Muccio handed Rhee an American note containing advice on handling inflation and referred to the unhappy precedent of China:

> I cited that Korea seemed to be in the same position as China in 1947–1948; that the Chinese officials also continuously stated that they could put a stop to inflation at any time. They never faced the situation realistically; inflation got out of hand and contributed even more than the military inertia to bringing about the Nationalist downfall.[81]

Muccio added that Rhee's tendency to be surrounded by 'yes men' compounded the problem. On 15 March a joint meeting of representatives of the ECA and State Department was held in Washington to discuss the Korean economy. Dr Bunce, the senior ECA adviser, said that the essence of the difficulty involved personalities, particularly Rhee, Madame Rhee (who was an Austrian) and Harold Lady, Rhee's 'economic adviser'. Rhee had totally failed to understand the inflationary threat and Rhee, encouraged by Lady, bypassed the constitutional arrangements with respect to the financing of the government. Rhee's autocratic tendencies and the growth of the police state accentuated the ECA's wish to see inflation dealt with realistically. Most branches of the ROK government were now cooperating with ECA; the exceptions were the defence and police authorities, which spent on an extravagant scale. It was agreed that more vigorous representations would have to be made.[82]

In domestic politics in South Korea Rhee's growing authoritarianism and the accelerating acrimony between Rhee and his political opponents did not augur well for stability. Rhee had long displayed intolerance of dissent and his obsession with his mission to unite Korea under his leadership led him to equate criticism with treachery. Jessup reported in January 1950 that the dominance of Rhee was unquestioned and few people stood up to him. The national security law was responsible for the fears of a police state. Anyone could be arrested and accused of communist sympathies; such a person would be tried by a special court consisting of four judges from which no appeal was allowed. The South Korean justification to Jessup was that no one would be convicted, unless he or she was taking orders from a foreign power. Supposedly no danger existed of an individual being prosecuted for happening to disagree with the government but Jessup was understandably sceptical. It was obvious that Rhee had intimidated the national assembly with threats of arrest.[83] The growth of criticism of Rhee led to speculation that he might seek to postpone the elections scheduled for May 1950. Muccio recommended on 1 April 1950 that Rhee be warned that autocratic actions could adversely affect relations with Washington.[84] Dean Acheson sent an *aide-mémoire* to the ROK ambassador on 3 April protesting at the state of the economy and firmly warning against any idea of postponing the general election.[85] Despite the American criticism of Rhee, the British ambassador in Washington, Sir Oliver Franks, believed that the Truman administration was identifying itself more closely with South Korea. Feeling in Congress was less critical than it had been and Senator William F. Knowland (Republican, California), a lively critic of the administration, supported it over Korean aid while castigating the administration for the serious economic plight in which the Koreans found themselves.[86] The elections were duly held in May 1950 with more than 2,000 candidates standing for 200 positions. Numerous independents stood and did well in the elections. The outcome was widely regarded as a considerable rebuff for Rhee and a weakening of his position, underlined by the number of successful independents. However, John Merrill has qualified this assessment by pointing out that Rhee himself encouraged many independents to stand because of the weakness of his own political organisation; while a reverse for Rhee, his position after the election was rather stronger than it appeared to be.[87]

Let us conclude with a brief consideration of the state of the South Korean armed forces in 1950. Under the command of General Roberts, KMAG worked enthusiastically to improve the calibre of the ROK army. The ROK army had been occupied throughout the winter in containing guerrillas; they were under the direction of North Korea and occasionally obtained arms supplies from the north, as with a recent arms shipment landed on the east coast, the bulk of which was confiscated before it could be used inland. The anti-guerrilla activities occupied five regiments. The invasion threats, which had seemed so immediate in 1948–49, had subsided and there had been fewer incidents on the parallel. The guerrillas no longer represented a significant threat. One-fifth of the national police force (10,000 out of 50,000) had been deployed as combat police engaged in hunting guerrillas. Roberts thought the national police strength of 50,000 was perhaps too large by between 15,000 and 20,000. The police being used in fighting guerrillas in effect increased the strength of the army by 10,000; 240 of their officers were currently undergoing training at the Infantry School. Roberts commented that all the top officers of KMAG were due to depart for other posts within the next six months, which was disturbing. He recommended that his successor should be a major-general with fighting experience and not a diplomat. Roberts then reviewed the functioning of KMAG. It had not reached full strength until approximately 15 December 1949; the school system (subdivision into Infantry Staff School, Korean Military Academy, Artillery Ordnance, Engineer, Quartermaster, Finance, Medical Schools) comprised a solid foundation for the army and must be continued. Full advisers had exerted a valuable effect. A few of the divisions were in the battalion phase of training and marksmanship had shown a level of attainment second only to the United States. It was inevitable that Washington should be considering future reductions in KMAG and Roberts commented on this. The first cut should occur with the removal of advisers from battalions and a general cut in advisers to headquarters and service troops: Roberts recommended that no cuts be implemented before January 1951, as the intervening period was crucial for training purposes. He summarised the capabilities and limitations of the South Korean army as follows:

> ... If South Korea is called upon to defend itself against aggression from the North its ground army is capable of doing an excellent job. If American advisers are present (even on Regimental and Division level) it will do an even better job, for we have found Americans are leaned on heavily the rougher it gets. In other words, the advisers will almost command except in name.
> However, all G-2 sources tell that the North Koreans have up to 100 Russian planes and a training program for pilots. You know and I know what 100 planes can do to troops, to towns and to transport on roads.
> So, if South Korea were attacked today by the inferior ground forces of North Korea plus their Air Corps, I feel that South Korea would take a bloody nose. Again then, knowing these people somewhat, I feel they would follow the apparent winner and South Korea would be gobbled up to be added to the rest of Red Asia.
> This is a fat nation now with all its ECA goods, with warehouses bulging with plenty of rice from a good crop even if their finances are shakey [*sic*] with great inflationary tendencies. It is getting into the position of an excellent prize of war; strategically it points right into the heart of Japan and into the hands of an enemy it weakens the Japanese bastion of Western defence.[88]

Roberts added that what this really pointed to was the importance of having some aircraft in South Korea; at present only twelve or fourteen planes were there. The P-51s and P-47s in Japan were being replaced by jets; these might be obsolescent viewed from the highest standards but they were acceptable enough in Korea. It would be sensible if about fifty of these planes could be sent to Korea and the pilots could be found in Korea. It should be feasible to find advisers from the air force without exceeding the total of 500, allocated to KMAG. Roberts maintained that the negative attitude taken towards air power in NSC 8/2 would have to be rendered positive through its 'air detachments' being 'stretched a little'.[89] Roberts concluded that KMAG itself had operated successfully without internal disputes and that morale was good.

General Bolté replied that Roberts's successor would be Major-General Frank A. Keating, who would probably not arrive until July. He described Roberts's observations on a reduction in KMAG as timely:

Currently the JCS are studying on a global basis, the possibility of reducing missions, advisory groups and other special duty assignments. I strongly recommend that you prepare a phased plan to reduce KMAG activities effective 1 January 1951 and after approval by Ambassador Muccio, submit it to the Department of Army.[90]

Bolté asked for Roberts's advice on cutting administrative costs in Korea. Aspects of the military aid programme were under discussion in the State Department:

Most of us realize that there may be valid reasons behind such requests but the expansion of Korea's armed forces, though born of necessity, does not fall within current policy decisions of the NSC. I refer, of course, to NSC 8/2 which precludes US support of a Korean Navy, and omits mention of an Air Force. You are also familiar with the strength limitations imposed by this document in a Korean Army, Coast Guard, and Police Force supported by the US. Therefore, it is my opinion that nothing can be done to engender additional assistance of the type requested unless the State Department secures authority therefore. . . . [91]

Roberts usually spoke favourably of the development of the army, while recognising its deficiencies in equipment. He circulated a report on KMAG advisers on 5 May 1950. He recalled that the original American commitment was to supply the ROK army with an initial issue of equipment and six months' supply of spare parts for a total strength of 50,000. Since then the personnel of the army had been increased to 100,000 and there was a marked deficiency in major items of equipment. The six months' stock of parts was exhausted and it was believed that 10 to 15 per cent of the weapons and between 30 and 35 per cent of vehicles were unserviceable. According to the Department of the Army in Washington, spare parts would not arrive until some time in 1952. South Korea was incapable of providing parts from its own production or from foreign exchange. The inflationary spiral constituted a grave threat which, if not halted, could jeopardise the entire economy. Counter-inflationary measures were compelling restrictions in the military budget. Roberts ended by once more conjuring the spectre of Kuomintang China:

The significance of this situation is that unless prompt effective and vigorous measures are taken to conserve available resources the Army will be dangerously reduced in fire power, mobility and logistical support. The economy will deteriorate further and be unable to support either the military establishment or the civil and political movement toward a free and democratic country. In short, Korea is threatened with the same disaster that befell China.[92]

The crucial weaknesses of the South Korean army on the eve of the Korean War were that it lacked the range and quality of the equipment possessed by the North Korean forces and that the leadership of the

North Korean army was inspired by a fanaticism unequalled by those fighting for Syngman Rhee. In addition, South Korea had no air force or navy; air power was one of the key ingredients in North Korean prowess in the first phase of the Korean conflict.

Therefore in May 1950 the balance sheet of strengths and weaknesses between the two Korean states could be summarised as follows. North Korea was tightly organised and directed by a tough, ruthless élite. The armed forces were efficient with good equipment. There were significant factional divisions, particularly between the followers of Kim Il Sung and Pak Hon-yong. There was probably a tendency in the north to exaggerate the potential for a guerrilla-led insurrection in South Korea. As for the ROK, it was divided politically but dominated by the intransigent Syngman Rhee. Grave economic and political problems existed and the army was clearly inferior to its opponents. However, South Korea had overcome the armed challenge from within. Tension along the 38th parallel had been serious since 1948 but was worse on some occasions than on others. There was always the possibility of an obscure clash escalating into full-scale conflict. The situation in the Korean peninsula was in essence one of civil war. As in other civil wars the big question mark was the approaches to be adopted by the great powers. The responses of the United States, the Soviet Union and China would soon become clear.

# REFERENCES

1.   For a clear account of the early years of the UN, including discussion of general aspects of UN activities and of the UN in Korea, see Evan Luard, *A History of the United Nations*, vol. I, *The Years of Western Domination 1945–1955* (London 1982). See also Leon Gordenker, *The United Nations and the Peaceful Unification of Korea: The Politics of Field Operations* (The Hague 1959).
2.   Luard, op. cit., I, p. 232.
3.   Ibid., p. 234.
4.   Cited ibid., p. 235.
5.   *FRUS 1948* (6), p. 1107, Jacobs to Marshall, 12 Feb. 1948.
6.   Ibid.
7.   Ibid., pp. 1110–13, Hodge to Marshall, 14 Feb. 1948.
8.   Seoul to FO, 13 Jan. 1948, F682/511/81/G, FO 371/69937.
9.   New York (UK delegation) to FO, 11 Feb. 1948, F2280/511/81, ibid.
10.  Minute by MacDermot, F2631/511/81, FO 371/69938.
11.  FO to New York, 13 Feb. 1948, ibid.
12.  Minute by MacDermot, F2631/511/81, FO 371/69938.
13.  Luard, op. cit., I, p. 235.
14.  Ibid.
15.  *FRUS 1948* (6), p. 1167, Souers to Truman, 2 April 1948.

16. Ibid., p. 1169.
17. Hodge to JCS, 15 Jan. 1948, RG 9, box 89, Formosa File, MacArthur Memorial, Norfolk, Va.
18. Personal letter from Hodge to MacArthur, 17 May 1948, RG 9, box 148, ibid.
19. *FRUS 1948* (6), p. 1193, memorandum by Butterworth for Marshall and Lovett, 11 May 1948.
20. Ibid., p. 1180, Jacobs to Marshall, 22 April 1948.
21. Ibid., p. 1198, Jacobs to Marshall, 13 May 1948.
22. Luard, op. cit., I, pp. 235–6.
23. *FRUS 1948* (6), p. 1225, Royall to Marshall, 23 June 1948.
24. Ibid., p. 1248, memorandum by Butterworth to Lovett, 20 July 1948.
25. Ibid., pp. 1264–5, memorandum from Lovett to Truman, 28 July 1948.
26. Ibid., pp. 1288–9, memorandum from Truman to Marshall, 25 August 1948.
27. Ibid., pp. 1308–10, memorandum by Lovett on conversation with Rhee's special representative, Chough Pyong Ok, 23 Sept. 1948.
28. Ibid., pp. 1315–17, United States delegation position paper, 22 Oct. 1948.
29. Luard, op. cit., I, p. 237.
30. Ibid., p. 238.
31. Radio intercept, Radio Pyongyang, 1900 (I), 10 July 1948, Headquarters XXIV Corps, Office of Assistant Chief of Staff, G2, enclosed in letter from Holt to MacDermot, 15 July 1948, F10201/29/81, FO 371/69936.
32. Ibid.
33. Memorandum by R. S. Milward, FO Research Department, 'The constitution of North Korea', 10 Oct. 1948, F15019/29/81, FO 371/699936.
34. See John Merrill, 'Internal warfare in Korea, 1948–1950: the local setting of the Korean War', in Bruce Cumings (ed.), *Child of Conflict: the Korean–American Relationship, 1943–1953* (London 1983), pp. 158–61.
35. Ibid., p. 151, and N. S. Khrushchev, *Khrushchev Remembers* (London 1971), pp. 367–9.
36. *FRUS 1948* (6), pp. 1325–7, Muccio to Marshall, 12 Nov. 1948.
37. Letter from Major J. R. Ferguson Innes, War Office, to E. J. F. Scott, 30 Dec. 1949, FK1016/2, FO 371/84076.
38. Ibid.
39. Air Intelligence Information Report, 'Review of North Korean air power and its potentialities', 28 Feb. 1950 (based on information received by 11 Feb. 1950), Headquarters, Far East Air Forces, APO 925, State Department records, 795.00/1-750, RG59, box 4682, National Archives, Washington.
40. Ibid.
41. Ibid.
42. Drumright to Acheson, 'Current conditions and trends within the North Korea Labour Party', 7 Jan. 1950, ibid.
43. Ibid.
44. Ibid.
45. *Soviet Monitor*, 17 March 1950.
46. Ibid.
47. Ibid.
48. *Soviet Monitor*, 22 March 1950.

49. Ibid.
50. Ibid.
51. Muccio Oral History, interview between John J. Muccio and Jerry N. Hess, recorded 18 Feb. 1971, copy in Truman Library, Independence, Missouri. Through the generous assistance of Mr Richard Finn, I met Ambassador Muccio in Washington on 15 March 1982 when he kindly expanded on various aspects of his service in Seoul. This was most helpful for clarifying my understanding of American perspectives and of Rhee as a personality.
52. Muccio to Marshall, 13 Nov. 1948, forwarded by Coulter, RG9, box 175, MacArthur Memorial.
53. See Merrill in Cumings (ed.), p. 141.
54. Ibid.
55. Ibid., p. 142.
56. Ibid., pp. 143–4.
57. Ibid., p. 144.
58. Drumright to Acheson, 15 April 1950, 'Guerrilla strength and activity', State Department records, 795.00/4-1550, RG59, box 4682, National Archives, Washington.
59. Ibid.
60. *FRUS 1949* (7, part 2), p. 978, NSC report, NSC 8/2, 22 March 1949.
61. Ibid., pp. 987–8, Acheson to American Mission, 13 April 1949.
62. Ibid., p. 997, Acheson to Muccio, 28 April 1949.
63. Ibid., p. 1005, memorandum by Muccio, 2 May 1949.
64. Ibid., pp. 1011–12, Muccio to Acheson, 7 May 1949.
65. Ibid., p. 1014, Acheson to Muccio, 9 May 1949.
66. Ibid., pp. 1023–4, Muccio to Acheson, 16 May 1949.
67. Ibid., pp. 1016–18, memorandum by Muccio, 10 May 1949.
68. Ibid., p. 1042, Muccio to Acheson, 11 June 1949.
69. Ibid., p. 1043.
70. Ibid., pp. 1046–57, memorandum from Department of the Army to Department of State, 27 June 1949.
71. Memorandum by Acheson on conversation with Vandenberg, 21 Jan. 1950, folder of conversations, Jan. 1950, Acheson Papers, box 65, Truman Library.
72. Dean Acheson, *Present at the Creation: My Years in the State Department* (London 1970), pp. 354–8.
73. *FRUS 1950* (7), p. 12, memorandum by John Z. Williams, 20 Jan. 1950.
74. Ibid., p. 42, memorandum by Bond, 3 April 1950.
75. Ibid., pp. 64–6, memorandum from Rusk to Webb, 2 May 1950, discussing Connally's interview and the ramifications thereof.
76. Ibid., memorandum by Drumright, pp. 77–8, May 1950.
77. Ibid.
78. Ibid., pp. 88–9, Muccio to Rusk, 25 May 1950.
79. *FRUS 1949* (7, part 2), pp. 940–1, memorandum by Butterworth, 5 Jan. 1949.
80. *FRUS 1950* (7), p. 6, memorandum by Jessup, 14 Jan. 1950.
81. Ibid., pp. 8–9, Muccio to Acheson, 18 Jan. 1950.
82. Ibid., pp. 30–3, memorandum by Bond, 15 March 1950.
83. Ibid., pp. 6–7, memorandum by Jessup, 14 Jan. 1950.
84. Ibid., pp. 39–40, Muccio to Acheson, 1 April 1950.

85. Franks to Bevin, 14 April 1950, FK11345/5, FO 371/84147.
86. Ibid.
87. Merrill in Cumings (ed.), p. 156.
88. Letter from Roberts to Bolté, 8 March 1950, OPS 091, Defense records, RG319 (Army Staff), G-3, box 121, National Archives, Washington. Roberts had asked to be transferred, prior to retirement, because of his wife's ill health.
89. Ibid.
90. Letter from Bolté to Roberts, 23 March 1950, ibid.
91. Ibid.
92. *FRUS 1950* (7), p. 93, Muccio to Acheson, 29 May 1950, enclosing memorandum by Roberts, 5 May, 1950.

# Chapter 4

# GENERAL MACARTHUR AND THE RECOVERY OF JAPAN

Japan played a crucial role in the chain of events leading to the Korean War. Complex issues involving the termination of the allied occupation of Japan and the repercussions for all those powers interested in East Asia and the western Pacific were closely linked. The original purpose of the allies in Japan, following the Japanese surrender in August 1945, had been to reform Japanese society so as to eliminate the aggressive, militaristic character of Japanese government, which had largely explained the growth of the Japanese empire between 1894 and 1943. It soon became clear that the occupation, while formally an allied one as represented in the Far Eastern Commission (FEC) and the Allied Council for Japan (ACJ), was effectively controlled by the United States. Great Britain and the Soviet Union entertained hopes for influencing allied policy in Japan in 1945 but these were quickly dashed. Little interest in British views on Japan were shown beyond the superficial courtesies of diplomatic exchanges in Washington. The fact that the Soviet Union only entered into the Pacific War as it was about to end restricted likelihood of a prominent Soviet voice in Japan, apart from the deterioration in Soviet–American relations in Europe. The American aim was to produce a genuinely democratic constitution in place of the reactionary Meiji document; to eliminate or reduce the power of the zaibatsu; to dissolve the armed forces; to implement land reform; to foster trade unions; and, in all, to put Japan securely on a new footing. The occupation in practice was a mixture of idealism and pragmatism underpinned by a potent sense of what was in the best interests of American foreign policy.[1]

Douglas MacArthur is one of the most central and controversial personalities in the conduct of the Korean War. It is appropriate, therefore, to consider the preparation for his activities in Korea afforded by his experience in directing the affairs of Japan between 1945 and 1950. MacArthur was one of the most distinguished soldiers in the history of the United States. He had served in France in the First World War, commanded West Point, and served as chief of staff of the army before his able leadership of the allied forces in the south-west Pacific from 1942 to 1945. MacArthur was a man of brilliant, if flawed, talents. Capable of examining matters with a panoramic sweep and with a talent for adopting innovative and unexpected courses of action at vital moments, MacArthur was too readily the prisoner of his own prejudices. He gathered his own particular circle of close advisers around him and was prone to discount views that did not reflect those prevailing in his own circle. MacArthur was spurred on by a strong sense of destiny and ambition. His role at the head of the military administration was a creative one and satisfied him up to a point. He had held a greater ambition for some years, however, and this dominated him until the summer of 1952 – he wished to be President of the United States. On three occasions – 1944, 1948 and 1952 – he was a possible choice for the Republican presidential nomination.

MacArthur's political intentions must be kept in mind in assessing the various policies and initiatives for which he was responsible in Japan and Korea.[2] He wished the administration of Japan under his direction to be seen as positive, challenging and above all successful in laying the foundations for political and economic achievement in Japan. MacArthur wished to establish an enduring democratic system representing the ascendancy of the 'centre right', that is, those Japanese politicians who were firmly opposed to communism and to old-style militarism. His dedication to the task of reforming Japan meant that he committed himself to policies of fundamental reform and governmental intervention through the office of Supreme Commander for the Allied Powers, Japan (SCAP), which he would have condemned in other contexts. In the United States MacArthur was identified with the right wing of the Republican Party with condemnation of Franklin D. Roosevelt's New Deal for its 'socialistic' tendencies. Yet in Japan MacArthur established a record as a liberal reformer if one who became more conservative in the later stages of the occupation. The head of the British liaison mission in Japan, Alvary Gascoigne, met MacArthur frequently and sent back to London perceptive accounts of their discussions or, to be more accurate, of MacArthur's monologues. At a time when there was speculation as to whether MacArthur might leave Japan as part of the political developments in 1948, Gascoigne wrote in January 1948:

> ... I should say from what I can sense of MacArthur's feelings that he would continue to fill his role here as long as his health permitted him to do so. He is, as you know, 67, but I have never been amongst those who thought that he was growing old and tired ... he is, I think, just as fit as the day when I first saw him in July 1946. I should say that he was good for at least another five years of hard work and although there are various rumours about his suffering from some obscure disease which makes his hand extremely shaky, I have had it on the quiet from his medical adviser that he is sound as a bell. When the lift is out of order in his Headquarters

(a not unusual event) he leaps up the six flights of stairs and arrives at the top as cool as a cucumber, followed by a very out-of-breath Orderly Officer. If his chances for the Presidency collapsed there is presumably no other job that he could have, failing perhaps the *thankless* task of China. ... [3]

MacArthur impressed most of those who met him through his strengths of character, commitment and tenacity. Equally his theatrical gifts were appreciated, for he conveyed the air of acting a role in carefully staged manner at each of his formal encounters or luncheon engagements. MacArthur was respected but not widely liked.

Economic developments in Japan became a source of much controversy between 1948 and 1950. As in Germany, the intention in 1945 had been to deprive Japan of the economic resources to wage war in the foreseeable future. The Japanese colonial empire was swiftly dismantled even though some regrets were later to be expressed at the Japanese departure from Korea and Taiwan. The zaibatsu – the powerful financial combines headed by Mitsui, Mitsubishi, Yasuda, Sumitomo and Okura – were regarded as the cornerstone of Japanese activities and it was accordingly a priority to break down their authority. Not surprisingly the substantial economic burdens of administering Japan fell heavily on American shoulders; it was not long before economy-minded members of Congress began to express doubts about economic policy in Japan. MacArthur was not personally much interested in economic matters and he was faced in 1947–48 with vocal pressure for a new approach to economic questions. The British journal, *The Economist*, reported in April 1948:

> Plans now taking form call for leaving the Japanese practically all of the industrial capacity with which they waged the war and for financial assistance to get into full production again. Restoration of a 'self-supporting' Japanese economy, it is revealed, has become a 'primary objective of the occupation'.[4]

American industrialists, critical of the performance of the occupation, had urged a reversal of policy so as to increase Japan's capacity to stand on her own feet and not to receive excessive subsidies from the United States. In April 1947 a policy paper placed before the FEC had envisaged an industrial level designed to give the people of Japan a standard of living approximately equal to that experienced in 1930–34. The Draper mission advocated a far higher level of industrial growth even to attain the living standards of the early 1930s. ' "Off the record", military and diplomatic policy makers now say that Japan must become the fulcrum of American policy in the Far East. It had been hoped, they say, that China might emerge as the new "workshop of Asia" but China is prostrate and the rest of Asia is weak. ... "[5]

Alarm was provoked within the British Commonwealth and South-East Asia at the news of the new American policy. Within Britain the textile and shipbuilding industries were vociferous in urging limitations on Japanese revival.[6] *The Economist* observed:

> The present American tendency is to ask what a country can now do for itself and for the United States, not what it might do in other circumstances, nor yet what it deserves.
>
> It is not to be expected, however, that the killing of the fatted calf for the prodigal son will evoke any more enthusiasm in his virtuous brother than it did in the scriptural parable. Australians and Chinese, who have borne the burden and heat of the day in the war imposed by Japanese aggression, naturally take a dim view of Washington's new policy and ask how Japan is going to behave once it gets back its industrial strength.[7]

It was essential for the United States to explain to those countries which had supported the allied war effort against Japan how the dangers posed by a Japanese economic revival could be surmounted. There was much sense in the American wish to see the Japanese economy functioning efficiently again, 'But in Canberra, Nanking, and Manila their conversion to innocence requires to be demonstrated more convincingly than it is by the optimistic hand-outs from General MacArthur's headquarters.'[8]

Gradually incentives to growth in the economy were provided. In November 1948 a trade agreement between Japan and various members of the British Commonwealth was concluded, indicating more than a threefold increase in trade between Japan and the sterling group, which included Australia, New Zealand, India, South Africa plus Britain and her colonies. The agreement would last for a period of twelve months as from 1 July 1949, with a dual trade flow amounting to about £55 million. Goods exported by Japan would include cotton textiles, industrial machinery, raw silk, caustic soda and other chemicals, rayon, paper and bunker coal. Exports from the sterling area to Japan would include raw materials, such as raw wool, iron ore, salt, raw cotton, cereals, rubber, tin, jute and manganese.[9] The fears of the British textile industry preoccupied British officials for much of the time between 1948 and 1950. Raymond Streat, chairman of the British Cotton Board, noted in his diary that apprehension in Lancashire was warranted, ' ... for the Japanese low cost producer can sweep us off our feet, no matter how efficient we might become'.[10] Streat was devoting much effort to reorganising and streamlining British textiles; he ruefully noted that part of the difficulty resulted from the attitudes of vested interests among trade unions and the less adventurous managements, which were dominated by 'narrow motives of selfish interest'.[11] Streat worked to try to achieve common purpose and interest with American textile interests but was handicapped by a certain reluctance to go too far and by MacArthur's reluctance to receive a joint Anglo-American mission in 1950. Streat visited Japan in May 1950 and met MacArthur. His description of their encounter conforms to the usual descriptions with the general's immense sense of presence and concomitant dramatic side-effects. Streat congratulated MacArthur on his 'momentous' achievements and then warned him against encouraging Japanese competition to the point where strong antagonism was aroused in western and eastern countries. Streat urged that Japan should not supply more than her fair share of world cotton trade:

> When I passed at this point MacArthur said perhaps I would like to hear his summary as a soldier and as no businessman or textile expert. He proceeded to speak with extreme lucidity and the liveliest expression on his face. He is an uncommonly good talker and easy indeed to listen to. He knew all the figures of spingleage pre-war and post-war and most of the figures of Japanese trade. He said that before the war Japan had built up a large international textile trade, part of which in his view, was legitimate and part illegitimate. Insofar as they provided cheap goods of low quality for the coolies of eastern countries, who could not afford anything better they performed a service to the world and created for themselves a trade which conformed to their opportunities and resources. That was the legitimate half. Insofar as they intruded on the very different trade in superior goods which Britain and Germany and USA could make better than they could and for which these and other countries had established legitimate mark[et]s and insofar as this intrusion was achieved by methods of subsidy and selling at less than cost it was an illegitimate trade and very disruptive in world trading circles.[12]

MacArthur maintained that the moves he had taken to break up the large banks would prevent a repetition of the devious methods formerly used to provide a subsidy for Japanese textile exports. He added that part of the difficulty before the Pacific War had resulted from low labour costs; steps had been taken to raise the cost of labour to an appropriate level. Streat doubted some of MacArthur's remarks, including his sharp distinction between 'legitimate' and 'illegitimate' trade.

Streat asked MacArthur for his views on trade with China to which the general replied that an increase in trade between Japan and mainland China would not occur immediately but that he was convinced that this could occur within the next four or five years. Neither the Soviet Union nor China herself was capable of meeting the demand for textiles: Japanese textiles would eventually be accepted in exchange for Chinese commodities, including minerals, since Japan was the obvious market.[13] The Japanese economy was developing significantly before the start of the Korean War. The war itself gave an immense stimulus to trade, leading to an increase of 60 per cent in Japanese exports in 1950 to be followed by an increase of similar proportion in 1951 on the 1950 figures.[14]

Apart from the economic motive for making Japan more self-sufficient, a major consideration was the part that Japan would play in American strategy in East Asia. Here again perspectives changed with the passage of time and the new international relationships that occurred. In 1945 most opinion in the allied countries held that Japan must be wholly disarmed and that Japan should not possess armed forces in future. MacArthur insisted that the new Japanese constitution, accepted by the Japanese government upon his insistence in 1946, contained a clause renouncing war. The Emperor was transformed from a divine figure into a constitutional figurehead. Various generals and admirals who had been prominent in the war effort were put on trial for their lives in the International Military Tribunal for the Far East (IMTFE), which met in Tokyo between 1946 and 1948. Even in 1945 some Americans anticipated Japan assisting the United States in a war against the Soviet Union, and General Willoughby, head of G-2 (intelligence) branch within SCAP, recruited former army and navy officers authorising the official use of their old ranks in the imperial forces.[15] MacArthur was dedicated to the extirpation of militarism and did not favour the development of defence forces. In an image employed on a number of occasions MacArthur observed that he wished Japan to become the 'Switzerland' of the Far East, pledged permanently to the renunciation of aggressive war and with a formal status of neutralisation written into a peace treaty.[16] MacArthur was conscious of the latent danger of militant nationalism in Japan and had no wish to undermine the work of the occupation through permanently embracing a positive concept of Japanese defence forces.

The repercussions of the Cold War in Europe and the adoption of the Truman Doctrine and Marshall Aid brought about a change in thinking in Washington. Opinion in the Pentagon moved towards the belief that Japan was assuming more importance in global terms and that Japan must remain within the American sphere. For this reason the Defense Department opposed the early conclusion of a peace treaty because of the basic uncertainties over Japan's position at the end of the occupation: the generals were not attracted by an idea of Japan as an Asiatic Switzerland. The State Department on the whole supported the conclusion of an early treaty and was sympathetic to the British view that the indefinite prolongation of the occupation would be counter-productive politically and would encounter growing resentment from the Japanese people. George F. Kennan, head of the Policy Planning Staff within the State Department and architect of the policy of containment, visited Japan in February–March 1948. Kennan described his mission as an 'educative' one, intended to broaden his own understanding of the situation in Japan so that the State Department could recommend a realistic policy for Japan in the future. Kennan met MacArthur for lunch on 1 March; MacArthur stated that there had previously been only one successful military occupation in history and this had been Julius Caesar's achievement in the subjugated barbarian provinces.[17] For the first time in history the Japanese people were enjoying real freedom rather than the autocracy and totalitarianism which they had suffered prior to August 1945. He regretted that his proposal for a peace conference a year ago had not been acted upon, as he was confident the Soviet Union would have participated at that time with beneficial effects for the whole world. MacArthur believed the Soviet Union and China would gain from a peace settlement, since the alternative was that the occupation would continue and Japan would more obviously become an American satellite.[18] Kennan requested MacArthur's assessment of the defence of Japan. MacArthur stated that it was imperative to prevent the dispatch of an amphibious force. It was vital to concentrate defences in the western Pacific in the region, including the Aleutians, Midway, the former Japanese-mandated islands, the Philippines and particularly Okinawa.[19] From Okinawa it would be feasible to control all the ports of northern Asia, which could be used as bases for an amphibious expedition. Air striking power was essential for this purpose. As regards the Japanese islands, MacArthur felt it would not be practicable for the United States to keep bases after the signing of a peace treaty. Britain and the Soviet Union would want bases in Japan if the United States possessed them and the only wise policy was to ensure that no power had bases on Japanese soil.[20]

In a subsequent discussion on 23 March, MacArthur advocated an early peace conference despite the problems that would arise from Soviet obstruction. If the other participants approved a solution it would assist in persuading the Russians to join in eventually. It would be impossible to withdraw American forces if this gave the Soviet Union the opportunity to move into Japan. The possibility of Japanese defence forces taking over after the peace treaty was opposed by MacArthur: it would be a violation of existing commitments, would be contrary to SCAP policies hitherto and in any event could not transform Japan into a significant military power. The strain on the Japanese economy of a heavy defence burden could not be supported: as it was, even with American aid, a large deficit was being accumulated. In addition, the Japanese people would not accept extensive or prominent armed forces. He reiterated the necessity of remaining in Okinawa and of developing a permanent garrison there.[21] Kennan believed that it was necessary to permit the Japanese greater freedom and that the interventionist role of SCAP should be reduced. Internal security must be handled by the Japanese themselves.[22]

Rumours began to appear in the press concerning differences between the American State and War departments over policy regarding Japan. Gascoigne saw MacArthur on 21 May and drew his attention to an article that day in the *Nippon Times* discussing the dissent within the American government. MacArthur replied that there was no basic divergence but there was much jealousy and bitterness. As regards American defence policy, MacArthur denied that the United States was preoccupied with building up Japan against the Soviet Union. There was no desire in Washington or Tokyo to see Japan transformed into a country again capable of undertaking aggressive action. Gascoigne deduced disagreement over long-term aims between the War and State departments.[23] At the same time Gascoigne's military adviser, Brigadier A. K. Ferguson, submitted a report revealing that there was divergence between different sections of GHQ as to the treatment of Japan. Ferguson added:

> There would, however, appear to be one question on which there is unanimity of opinion and that is that Japan must be protected as far as possible from Communistic influences and from infiltration from the USSR. The motive behind this unanimity is definitely American fear of Russian penetration and the desire to use Japan as a bulwark.[24]

In the military sphere certain steps had been taken, which included strengthening air bases far beyond the normal requirements of the occupation, as for example in the extension of runways, allegedly for coping with B-36 bombers. Japanese army and navy ammunition storage facilities in certain places, particularly at Sasebo and Yokosuka, had been extended and improved. It was known that underground Japanese oil storage facilities had not been destroyed and had even been put into a state for use in some areas. Ferguson stressed that the American actions need not be interpreted as aggressive but rather as part of defence against a possible Soviet offensive. If American intentions were aggressive, then the training of Japanese in modern war methods could be expected, including the training of technicians and radar operators. Ferguson tried to provide a balanced conclusion by viewing the situation from the Russian perspective:

> It must be admitted, however, that although there is no doubt in our own minds that preparations of the US Army in Japan are purely precautionary and defensive, seen from the Russian viewpoint, many of the activities of the Americans here may appear extremely aggressive.[25]

The Soviet press was already castigating American policy in Japan for condoning a recovery by Japanese capitalists with the ultimate purpose of consolidating the American hold on Japan. An article in the Soviet defence publication, *Red Fleet*, in January 1948 commented:

> The American imperialists are trying in every way to realise the plans of establishing their world domination. Japan occupies a prominent place in these plans. The Americans have converted Japan into their colony, into a patrimony of American monopolist capital. This allows them to build without hindrance places d'armes on the Japanese islands against the Soviet Union and those countries of Asia which have risen to fight for liberty and independence against the forces of imperialism and reaction.[26]

George Kennan returned from his visit to Japan in a critical spirit as regards significant aspects of the occupation. He believed the reform measures had been too radical and were undermining the fabric of Japanese society. While the new constitution was broadly satisfactory, there were defects, as with the abolition of the Ministry of Interior and the decentralisation of the police forces. Communists could infiltrate local government and local police forces. The purge within Japanese defence personnel had gone too far and the same applied to the purge of politicians. The Soviet Union could affect the situation through skilful action with serious consequences for the whole strategic situation. Kennan echoed MacArthur's fears that the Russians were well placed to assume control of the whole of Korea. Soviet forces were present in the Kuril islands and south Sakhalin in addition to possessing a major base at Vladivostok. If a peace treaty were signed within the near future the danger was that Soviet pressure could be applied against a demilitarised Japan. For this reason it was felt in Washington that the occupation had to be extended and a peace treaty deferred.[27] The NSC examined American policy towards Japan in a report forwarded to President Truman in October 1948. The recommendations included refraining from concluding a peace treaty because of divergent views among interested countries and because of the Soviet Union's pursuance of militant expansion. When a treaty was eventually arrived at, it should be succinct, generalised and relatively magnanimous; the psychological impact of the presence of occupation forces on the Japanese people had to be countered through flexible policies including reduction of total numbers of both tactical and non-tactical forces. The report clearly looked towards the likelihood of American forces remaining in Japan after the signing of a peace treaty; this would be determined according to the international situation when the negotiations for a treaty had been completed.[28]

The success of the Chinese communists late in 1948 and early in 1949, together with the effects of the European crisis, accentuated concern over the vulnerability of Japan. In February 1949 MacArthur told Max W. Bishop, head of the division of North-East Asian Affairs, that the fluid state of affairs in the Far East rendered it impossible to achieve a peace treaty. Bishop told MacArthur that the State Department fully appreciated the necessity of developing Okinawa as a strong base, as contemplated in NSC 13/2. MacArthur criticised the American military for wishing to 'scuttle the Pacific'.[29] The Pentagon was obsessed with the Atlantic and had devoted inadequate attention to the problems of the Pacific. MacArthur emphasised the great importance of preventing the Chinese communists from gaining Taiwan; this was vital to American policy in the region. He maintained that there was no doubt that if Taiwan fell, then it would be made available by the Chinese communists for Soviet use as a base whenever desired. Taiwan was delicately situated for preserving American lines of communication between Okinawa and the Philippines. At the same time MacArthur opposed the rearming of Japan, which would be 'a great mistake'.[30] Japan could be of much importance in the event of war and it might be feasible for the Japanese to fight for the United States after a war had begun. From the viewpoint of American security, it was imperative to hold the 'Asiatic fringe of islands with Japan as a neutralised area'.[31] Bishop believed that change was essential and reported on his return to Washington that there was undue complacency in Tokyo; the vested interests in the occupation bureaucracy believed that American dominance in Japan must be continued for a considerable period and Bishop held that tough action would be required in order to transform attitudes and to terminate the occupation. American business men were dissatisfied because of the difficulty of communicating with MacArthur and the senior members of SCAP. Ironically the British case was effectively advanced by 'Joe' Gascoigne and his staff.[32]

The joint chiefs of staff reviewed the role of Japan in defence policy and recommended to James Forrestal, the Secretary of Defense, on 1 March 1949 that in consequence of the serious world crisis and the probability of this crisis deepening, appropriate measures should be taken at an early date so that the 'military potential' of Japan could be utilised should events warrant it.[33] Simultaneously MacArthur expressed his views publicly in an interview with the British correspondent, G. Ward Price, which appeared in the *Daily Mail* on 2 March. MacArthur stated his affection for the British people, recalling that his grandfather had come from Scotland. After the initial courtesies, he stated that the Pacific represented a primary line of defence for the United States. It had never been intended and was not his desire that Japan should become an ally of the United States; rather Japan should be recognised as a neutral. If Japan was subjected to aggression, American support would certainly be forthcoming. However, MacArthur doubted whether the Soviet Union would attack Japan – 'Even if the Soviet Government had aggressive intentions towards her it would be incapable of carrying them out, unless it could secure mastery of the air and either had a Far Eastern fleet of its own or possessed the means of neutralising any action by our own fleet.'[34] He added that Russia could not secure control of the air.

The outcome of State Department deliberations in the first four months of 1949 was that the character of the occupation must be changed so as to afford the Japanese more legitimate freedom of action.[35] Dean Acheson informed various American ambassadors in late April 1949 that the Japanese government had to be given more authority so as to re-establish civilian government properly. It was hoped that the countries represented in the FEC would cooperate in this policy. Japan was approaching the crossroads and it was imperative that Japan be guided into the most desirable course of action – fully into the western fold as a sovereign nation. Acheson explained, 'Jap[an]s[e] will either move toward sound friendly relationships with non-communist powers or into association with a communist power system in Asia.'[36] The NSC produced a further important report (NSC 13/3) on 6 May 1949, which revised NSC 13/2, issued on 7 October 1948. It was recommended that the United States should not urge a definitive peace settlement with Japan at this time owing to the Soviet Union's policy of militant communist expansion. If the allied powers could agree on procedure, then the United States should be prepared to advance with negotiations. The psychological effect of the occupation on the Japanese people should be modified through reduction of forces. American tactical forces should remain in Japan and the ultimate American decision concerning the presence of forces in Japan should be deferred until the peace negotiations were in progress. It was further recommended that Okinawa be retained and that whatever was needed by way of other facilities should be obtained in the Ryukyus. The Japanese police should be strengthened and the Japanese government unobtrusively permitted greater political and economic freedom, subject to the qualifications that Japan's war potential should be restricted through stockpiling strategic war materials in Japan. Manufacture of military weapons and civilian aircraft should not be allowed, restrictions on industrial production should be minimised.[37]

Soviet resentment and alarm at the trend of American policy were made explicit by Andrei Vyshinsky, the Russian Foreign Minister, at a meeting of the Council of Foreign Ministers held in Paris in June 1949. Ernest Bevin was in the chair when Vyshinsky inquired what was happening concerning a peace settlement with Japan and proposed that the assembled foreign ministers should proceed with it. Vyshinsky made what Bevin described as 'an interminable speech' in which he quoted extensively from the agreements reached at Potsdam and stated that under the Potsdam terms the Council of Foreign Ministers and not the FEC was the relevant body for negotiating a peace treaty.[38] Vyshinsky's speech was clearly made for the dual purpose of endeavouring to depict the Soviet Union in a more conciliatory light in global terms and to try to gain a voice in the negotiations leading to a treaty. Shortly afterwards the Chinese communist press issued a statement supporting the views expressed by the Soviet Union.[39] This was followed by a statement from the New China News Agency on 6 July conveying the desire of the Chinese communists to take part in peace negotiations over Japan.[40] Britain firmly and – except for a brief period in March 1951 – consistently advocated the conclusion of an early peace treaty. This view was held for political and economic reasons. British diplomats in Tokyo believed that increasing signs of restlessness could be perceived and that it would not be wise to delay a peace treaty for much longer. More selfish economic motives were also involved, given the British wish to see limitations imposed on Japanese economic development, which could form part of a treaty. However, the issue also reflected the fundamental unease of the British Foreign Office at the absence of a clear-cut American policy in the whole of the Far East, affecting China and Korea in addition to Japan.

Esler Dening, one of the principal British officials specialising in far eastern matters, met W. Walton Butterworth in Washington in early September 1949 and reiterated the arguments in favour of a peace treaty.

Dening criticised the inconsistency and failure to clarify objectives on the part of the United States; he conceded that there could be difficulties over Chinese representation in talks between the powers, given the collapse of the Kuomintang and the imminent proclamation formally of the communist government in Peking.[41] On 17 September Bevin and Acheson met in the State Department; Acheson stated that the American government had decided it was necessary to proceed with a peace treaty within the near future.[42] MacArthur remained sceptical and told Gascoigne he doubted whether Washington meant business on the treaty: in his opinion it was a 'smokescreen' intended to mollify those allied countries who had made representations.[43] MacArthur was the better guide where actual progress was concerned, since Acheson was unable to advance as he had notified Bevin, owing to basic disagreement with Louis Johnson, the Secretary of Defense. The joint chiefs were unwilling to support a treaty at this juncture for strategic reasons. Acheson informed the British ambassador in Washington on 24 December 1949 that because of inability 'to find satisfactory answers to certain basic problems confronting us', it would not be possible to adhere to the schedule originally decided with Bevin in September.[44] Acheson added that the Soviet Union was already endeavouring to spread subversion in Japan and that the potential Soviet threat to Japan was such that the risks inherent in concluding a treaty could not be entertained in present circumstances.[45]

MacArthur was far more concerned with the threat posed by Communist China than by any menace posed by the Soviet Union. In a conversation in July with Cloyce K. Huston of the American mission in Japan, MacArthur reverted to his former view that a peace treaty should be arrived at as soon as possible. Japan's security could be safeguarded through obtaining a pledge from all nations involved to respect the neutrality of an unarmed Japan. When Huston expressed doubts over the extent to which a Russian promise would be respected, 'he remarked that the Soviets might indeed be difficult to deal with, but in his experience he had found that the Soviet Government always endeavoured to keep its plighted word'.[46] MacArthur added that the Soviet failure to fulfil repatriation commitments regarding Japanese prisoners of war in Russia, was the product of physical inability to comply and not to unwillingness to act as agreed. MacArthur repeated his desire for a treaty in the context of the continuing exchanges within the American government later in the year. His personal representative, Colonel Stanton Babcock, met officials in Washington on 2 November and conveyed MacArthur's latest thoughts. A treaty was urgently required and strenuous efforts should be made to secure participation and cooperation with the Soviet Union. Unarmed neutrality, underwritten by the major powers, was the best course to protect Japan. He remained opposed to any suggestion that Japan should be rearmed: such a step would be contrary to the new constitution and it would be unwise for the allies to encourage Japan to abandon its renunciation of the use of force.[47] MacArthur understood the danger from the Soviet Union and now stated that he knew a Soviet promise to observe Japanese neutrality could not be relied on. He conceded that his preferred solution of involving the Soviet Union in a guarantee was impracticable for the time being but it remained the most satisfactory long-term solution.

MacArthur's recommended strategy consisted of keeping naval and air bases in Japan after a treaty, principally to make it absolutely clear to the Soviet Union that aggression against Japan would lead to a full-scale conflict with the United States. He did not consider it necessary to establish Japanese defence forces to reinforce the American presence. If war broke out he did not believe that the Soviet Union would mount a localised attack on Japan. MacArthur's plan would involve the United States in keeping options open to increase forces in Japan according to circumstances. Negotiations should take place on a basis of equality with Japan to decide how American bases in Japan would operate: the outcome should be reflected in a discrete United States–Japan agreement to apply simultaneously with the implementation of the treaty. Babcock felt MacArthur would probably approve a treaty clause calling for a re-examination of Japan's security situation five or ten years after signature of the treaty. MacArthur deemed it vital that 'if and when the Japanese are permitted an army that it not be run by the "old crowd" and in the old way but that, as Colonel Babcock put it, be a "democratic army" '.[48] MacArthur knew of the extent of Japanese disillusionment with militarism. Policy requirements should be met through the development of a constabulary possessing rifles, machine guns and other equipment. Economic restrictions to industry should only apply to those connected with armaments. MacArthur was confident that the creative work of the occupation would remain after Japan regained independence. Taiwan must not come under communist control; it was not essential for the United States to control the island but the Chinese communists must not capture it. It would be preferable for Taiwan to be returned to Japan rather than fall into communist hands.[49] The Ryukyus should be retained as an integral part of the island chain. Major-General Carter B. Magruder stated that he and his colleagues in the Pentagon

> did not share General MacArthur's view that reactivation of Japanese forces at this time was unnecessary and undesirable. This school of thought holds that Japanese ground forces could be of military value in the defence of Japan, and that their establishment would release US forces for service in other areas where they would be fully needed in the event of war.[50]

The gulf between the State and Defense departments was so large that no progress could be made until President Truman was ready to resolve the conflict. Truman was not prepared to do so as yet, despite the fact that in general he fully supported Acheson. Truman owed a personal debt of loyalty to Louis Johnson, who had served as treasurer of Truman's re-election committee in 1948 at a time when most commentators had consigned the President to ignominious defeat at the hands of Governor Dewey. Further Truman wished the dust to settle over the recognition issue in China before embarking on a Japanese treaty.[51] MacArthur was identified, ironically enough, with the State Department against the Pentagon. When Philip Jessup visited MacArthur in January 1950 the general stated that the Soviet Union should perceive the advantages to be derived from a Japanese treaty and he was sure that a diplomat like Jacob Malik would appreciate the position. MacArthur held that efforts to secure a treaty should proceed even if the Soviet Union and China declined to participate. He brushed aside the views of the joint chiefs of staff, ascribing their opposition to ignorance of the Far East. General Bradley was familiar with Europe, not Asia, and General Vandenberg lacked perspective. Admiral Sherman, on the other hand, was able and understood the Pacific: General Collins had served in Guadalcanal.[52] In a personal letter to Acheson, Jessup described MacArthur as being 'quite outraged' at the rejection of his own recommendations and at the recalcitrance displayed by the joint chiefs. MacArthur thought Louis Johnson was the real obstacle and that Bradley simply conveyed the attitude of the Secretary of Defense. MacArthur urged Acheson to raise the matter with Truman and persuade the President to overrule Johnson; he added that Truman should grasp the opportunity provided by the treaty for regaining the initiative in East Asia from the Soviet Union.[53]

A dimension of growing significance concerned the attitude towards a peace treaty and strategic matters adopted by the Japanese government itself. Considerable thought was given to the extremely important principles involved by different sections of the Japanese bureaucracy between 1945 and 1950.[54] The Foreign Ministry set up a study group on a peace treaty in November 1945, although it was clearly premature to pursue the problem at this time. Much activity took place in 1947 when it appeared as though sudden progress might be made. Schemes were devised by an Inter-Ministerial Committee for Coordination and leaks appeared in the press. The Japanese draft revealed particular interest in territorial matters involving the northern islands under Soviet occupation. It was hoped that Japan could re-establish herself to some extent in the islands of Habomai and Shikotan while the Kurils should come under a UN mandate. As regards other islands, Okinawa, the south-west Pacific islands, the Bonin and certain other groups could be retained by the allied powers for strategic reasons if necessary but compensation would be expected eventually.[55] The continued pressure of allied troops in Japan after the signing of a peace treaty should be separately negotiated. The Foreign Minister and Prime Minister for part of this period, Ashida Hitoshi, was active in pressing Japanese views in 1947–

48. Ashida contacted General Eichelberger, commander of the Eighth Army, and exchanged views with him. Eichelberger was vehemently hostile to communism and favoured some degree of Japanese rearmament; MacArthur was opposed to such action.[56] Eichelberger told Japanese representatives that he feared the outbreak of war with the Soviet Union and this could include a sudden attack based on southern Sakhalin and the Kuril islands after allied forces had left Japan with the conclusion of a peace treaty. Eichelberger thus expressed precisely the apprehensions of the Japanese government.[57] The so-called 'Second Ashida Memorandum' for the first time envisaged the possibility that, if the UN was not capable of protecting Japan, the United States would be permitted to send forces to Japan and utilise bases in order to defend Japan. Police forces should be strengthened to deal with internal security; this was rendered more significant by the labour unrest in Japan earlier in 1947. As Reinhard Drifte has observed, 'Here for the first time, the idea of a Japan–US security treaty emerges along lines of the actual treaty of 1951.'[58] Ashida's views were conveyed to Washington but a decision was taken against separate peace treaties with Germany and Japan.

The central personality on the Japanese side was Yoshida Shigeru.[59] Yoshida was a former diplomat of Anglophile inclinations; he had firmly disapproved of the ascendancy of the military before and during the Pacific War and had been imprisoned in the latter part of the war. Yoshida was no radical and did not wish to see drastic changes taking place within Japan. Emperor Hirohito must be supported and the forces of moderate conservatism strengthened within Japan so as to resist a future challenge either from the left or from a regalvanised extreme right wing. Yoshida was frequently underestimated by contemporaries and was regarded as an elderly garrulous figurehead. In fact he proved the most formidable politician of postwar Japan with a good claim to be the architect of the domestic and external systems which have guided Japan's evolution from the late 1940s to the 1980s. Upon taking office as Prime Minister in October 1948, Yoshida summarised the priorities of his administration as fostering democracy in Japanese society, encouraging the Japanese economy so as to secure greater self-sufficiency, and restoring Japan's status in the world. Yoshida stressed that labour unrest must be diminished so that trade unions and workers understood their responsibilities as well as their rights. The head of the British liaison mission reported that Yoshida had indicated his views on a peace treaty and associated issues:

> Yoshida also took the opportunity to say that while, of course, the decision must rest with the Allies, the Japanese felt that an early Peace Treaty was most desirable. He stated, however, that if conditions in Japan at the time of the Peace Treaty remained the same as at present, he thought that it would be necessary for a number of Allied troops to

remain in Japan even after the Peace Treaty, since the Japanese police were too few and their armament inadequate to maintain public order should the Communists attempt an offensive in Asia as they had already done in Europe. Yoshida considered that there was a danger that radical and ultra-nationalistic activities would increase in Japan and said that his Government was already considering the possibility of establishing a Committee of Un-Japanese Activities to combat them.[60]

Gascoigne regarded Yoshida as amiable but devious. 'Yoshida, who is likeable enough, is an intriguer and a trouble maker. He would love to split us and the Americans and to complicate our inter-Commonwealth relations.'[61] Gascoigne warned Yoshida in February 1949 to show more skill in handling labour unrest; this underlined the more assertive attitude adopted in the Foreign Office under Ernest Bevin's inspiration wherever labour problems arose. Yoshida declared himself to be a liberal opposed equally to the excesses of the left and right.[62] A British official observed that, 'The truth is that Mr Yoshida, although able in his own way, does not give the impression of being particularly well-qualified to cope with the intricate political and economic situation in which Japan now finds herself.'[63]

Yoshida handled the range of problems challenging him with subtlety and a considerable measure of success. He proved the master of evasion and calculated indiscretion. Whatever some observers regarded as a blundering approach was a skilful way of navigating the dilemmas confronting him. MacArthur did not regard him as particularly able and remarked on the disappointment he felt at the failure of Japanese politics to produce outstanding personalities. There was some friction in their relationship beneath the surface, since MacArthur wished to determine the nature of a peace treaty and for purposes of formal ratification of a treaty the circumstances in which a peace conference met; it was his intention that a conference should be held in Tokyo under his own chairmanship.[64] Ironically when the peace conference was held in September 1951 it met in San Francisco, not Tokyo; Yoshida attended to sign on behalf of Japan and MacArthur was not present. Yoshida wished to see Japan restored to true independence but he did not wish to see Japanese armed forces re-created. There were several reasons for this: the delicate state of recovery within the economy meant that it would be foolish to contemplate a significant defence burden falling on Japanese shoulders; the question of Japan's future foreign policy was extremely contentious within the country and there was vocal hostility to any suggestion of reviving an active or adventurous approach to foreign matters; furthermore Yoshida had personally suffered at the hands of the military and had no wish to see the old guard of the Japanese armed forces making a come-back.[65] Yoshida had to reconcile these conflicting pressures as best he could. Speculation has raged as to whether he did privately support rearmament but the likelihood is that he did not do so before the start of the Korean War. Yoshida's attitude to communism was pragmatic: while he disliked communism as an ideology, it was necessary to deal with the world that existed. This was illustrated in his famous statement in the Diet early in 1949:

> I don't care whether China is red, white, or green, we are willing to do business with her. China is our neighbour. There is danger that trade between our countries might be permanently cut, but I believe that we shall eventually transcend ideological differences and progress together.[66]

Yoshida held that Chinese communism would prove very different from the Russian variety and that the historical and cultural values of China would assert themselves over the principles of Marxism-Leninism as applied by Moscow.[67] The Soviet Union was more of a menace to Japan but Yoshida did not believe an early Soviet attack was likely. However, the potential danger had to be recognised and continued cooperation with the United States would persuade Washington to be more magnanimous and simultaneously protect Japan.

In the spring of 1950 decisions were reached in Washington that at last pointed the way forward towards a peace treaty. The disagreement between the State and Defense departments could not continue for much longer and President Truman, in the light of representations from the allies and bearing in mind the restless attitude developing in Japan, determined to proceed. On 24 April a joint meeting of officials from the two departments was convened. The atmosphere was acrid, as shown by Louis Johnson's opening remarks that he hoped the deliberations would not be leaked by the State Department. General Bradley, supported by Admiral Sherman, stated that a peace treaty would be premature. Sherman viewed the situation as a choice between concentrating American defence policy on the island chain including Japan, Okinawa and the Philippines or whether Japan and Okinawa should be abandoned with a retreat to focusing on Guam and the Philippines, as in the Pacific War.[68] It appeared that the Chinese communists would gain Taiwan within the next six months, which would exacerbate defence anxieties. General Vandenberg said he had derived the impression from his exchanges with MacArthur that the general regarded a peace conference as having propaganda value in the sense of improving relations with Japan and of isolating the Soviet Union; in Vandenberg's opinion, MacArthur was not concerned with strategic repercussions.[69] He felt that MacArthur was not interested now in a peace conference actually meeting but rather of putting forward the proposal in order for the Soviet Union to reject it. Johnson mordantly remarked that the only propaganda for such a conference emanated from the State Department; he endorsed the recommendations of the joint chiefs that no conference be held. Dean Acheson responded that the unhappy stalemate which had existed for a lengthy period could not be extended. It was essential to determine future American policy over Japan and to be clear as to the American commitment to Japan. Acheson alluded to the reference in the recent Sino-Soviet treaty, signed in February 1950, to the desirability of holding a peace conference; if the Soviet Union brought forward a proposal, it would be highly embarrassing.[70]

Just before this meeting MacArthur told Gascoigne he had been in contact with Senator Robert A. Taft and, in a five-page letter, had urged on Taft the importance of concluding a peace treaty speedily. Owing to the grave illness of Senator Arthur H. Vandenberg, Taft had become more influential within the Senate Foreign Relations Committee. When asked about the attitude of the Pentagon, MacArthur dismissed the 'illogical and half-baked' views expressed by the 'military' specialists there.[71] He commented that the Pentagon was split between the advocates and opponents of a treaty. Earlier in the conversation MacArthur discounted suggestions that Walt Butterworth would assume responsibility for dealing with a treaty. Butterworth was 'on the skids', having been made a scapegoat by Acheson for the bankruptcy of American policy in China; Butterworth would shortly be posted abroad, which was correct as he soon afterwards departed to be American minister in Stockholm.[72] The key figure in handling the Japanese treaty was John Foster Dulles. Dulles was the chief specialist on foreign affairs in the Republican Party and was closely associated with Governor Thomas E. Dewey of New York, twice unsuccessful candidate for the presidency. Dulles belonged to the internationlist wing of the party and fully supported the bipartisan policy regarding Europe, devised by Vandenberg. Over China Dulles was critical of the administration, as was Vandenberg. Dulles appreciated the growing significance of Japan and was anxious to see a satisfactory settlement accomplished. He enjoyed a good relationship with Acheson and it suited both men for Dulles to be closely involved in policy formulation: Acheson because it would diminish at least some of the acrimony in Congress and Dulles because he wished to consolidate his record so that he could become Secretary of State in the next Republican administration. Truman was initially less enthusiastic over the appointment owing to criticisms expressed by Dulles in the previous campaign in New York state. However, Truman was persuaded by Acheson to appoint Dulles in April 1950 as consultant on foreign affairs.[73] The following month it was announced that Dulles would specialise on matters concerning the peace treaty and Truman approved arrangements for Dulles to visit Japan and Korea in June in order to confer with MacArthur and the Japanese government.[74]

In May 1950 Yoshida dispatched a highly confidential mission to Washington headed by the Finance Minister, Ikeda. The mission was so secret that Yoshida, who was Foreign Minister in addition to Prime Minister, did not inform his own officials of the aims of the mission.[75]

Yoshida's decision resulted from the deductions he had drawn from Acheson's major speech on 12 January 1950 in which he had indicated the principles of American policy in East Asia.[76] Ikeda handed a personal message from Yoshida to Dodge at a meeting in the Defense Department in early May. Yoshida desired a peace treaty as soon as possible; he recognised that a treaty would probably involve American forces remaining to verify compliance with the treaty and indicated the willingness of the Japanese government to meet American wishes. It was stated that authorities on the Japanese constitution did not see difficulty in fitting security provisions into a treaty or placing it in a discrete American–Japanese treaty.[77] Yoshida's proposal was intended to achieve the best outcome in the circumstances from both the American and Japanese viewpoints. It is likely that Yoshida also wanted to obviate the possibility of the Soviet Union making a proposal linked with the fate of Sakhalin and the southern Kurils.[78] Yoshida's initiative did not have a dramatic effect but did assist in smoothing out some of the problems in reaching a settlement.

In May Acheson visited London for discussions with Bevin. Most of their time was devoted to European issues and China but a Japanese peace treaty was pursued. Bevin emphasised the accumulating problems resulting from the fact that little progress had been made: he had encountered difficulties at the British Commonwealth conference held at Colombo in January 1950 and there were criticisms of the United States for not having given a lead. In order to defuse the pressure Bevin had proposed the establishment of a Commonwealth working party; however, it was impossible to discuss matters further without a contribution from the United States. Acheson replied that the obstacle was one of security. The American defence chiefs were alarmed at the threat from the Soviet Union and China and did not relish the thought of their participating in a treaty. Equally if the Soviet Union did not participate, this could provide room for Russian meddling. He explained that Louis Johnson and General Bradley were visiting Japan near the end of May and should return to Washington by 12 June. The situation should then be clarified. There were two possibilities in the opinion of the State Department. The first was a treaty incorporating the minimum of enforcement provisions to be accompanied by a separate section whereby as many FEC countries as possible would sign a treaty with each other and with Japan, the purpose being to prevent aggression and to afford protection to Japan. In return Japan would extend military facilities in her territories. Alternatively there could be an intermediate phase during which the occupation controls would be dismantled and sovereignty restored to Japan; Japan would then be free to develop relations with other powers. However, SCAP and the occupation would continue to exist to defend Japan. Acheson said that the joint chiefs of staff preferred the latter course of action.[79]

Gascoigne informed the British Foreign Office on 12 June that the

Japanese were becoming bolder in their criticisms of the occupation and at the absence of a long-term policy. If the American policy of drift continued, the consequences would be grave. Gascoigne observed of the Russian and Chinese perspectives:

> Meanwhile, Russia, and to a lesser degree Red China, must be looking on with considerable satisfaction at the indecision which is being displayed by the United States as regards her future treatment of Japan. Putting one's self in Stalin's shoes, the present period of indecision must appear to be an opportune moment for him to step into the arena to suggest to Japan that she should make peace with the Kremlin and with Peking. Stalin and Mao would produce attractive terms (which of course would not be honoured) and this would be embarrassing to us. The Allies would be still at war with Japan, while Russia and China would be at peace – a situation which would be fraught with obvious dangers and embarrassments from our point of view.[80]

MacArthur did not indicate how the problems over the treaty could be resolved; he did not disagree with Gascoigne's assessment of the simmering undercurrents of discontent in Japan. MacArthur had acted decisively with two recent tough moves against the Japanese Communist Party, which included purging the party's central committee and press organ.

MacArthur's enthusiasm for a treaty had waned by June 1950. The appointment of Dulles could not have been welcome to him, for Dulles carried great weight in the Republican Party and would rival his own authority as the principal expert on Japan. Gascoigne had commented in April that, 'He also spoke slightingly of John Foster Dulles, who he said knew nothing whatever about the Far East.'[81] In the past MacArthur had frequently reiterated his wish for an early peace treaty but this had not happened recently. Gascoigne suspected that MacArthur wanted a peace conference to take place because it would convey the impression of activity to the Japanese but that MacArthur did not necessarily desire a treaty to emerge from it.[82] Much would depend on Dulles's mission and how he handled the thorny matters confronting him. Dulles's role will be considered further in the light of developments in the month of June 1950 culminating in the outbreak of war.[83]

It is instructive to conclude with an assessment of the significance of Japan in the origins of the Korean War. The Soviet Union was conscious of the historic record of confrontation and suspicion between Russia and Japan extending back to the late nineteenth century. Apprehension over Japanese revival was not as great as the Soviet fears over a German revival but the trend of American policy towards Japan could only be regarded as alarming from the Soviet perspective. The Soviet Union had been kept out of the administration of Japan other than the futile complaints of the Soviet representative in the ACJ. While SCAP had sponsored major changes in Japanese society, these were less extensive than originally expected and the result of SCAP policies was to strengthen the forces of moderate conservatism and capitalism in Japan. There was little if any prospect of the left gaining support and still less power in Japan after MacArthur's resolute handling of labour unrest and of the Communist party. Despite the disagreements in American policy-making circles, Japan was effectively being incorporated into an American sphere of interest; the likelihood was that United States forces would remain in Japan when a treaty was signed and that the general peace settlement would reflect American wishes. It was unclear whether Japanese armed forces would be developed significantly but given the covert encouragement given by General Willoughby and others to Japanese defences – of which the Soviet Union could not have been unaware through intelligence activities – disquiet was bound to increase. The gradual re-emergence of a strong Japan with an accelerating economy would pose a threat to North Korea and, less directly, to the Soviet Union's far eastern territories. The contentious problem of the northern islands would become critical. It could therefore be argued that it was in the interests of the Soviet Union to see the Korean peninsula in the hands of a friendly regime and American–Japanese interests pushed out of the Asian continent. Developments in Japan between 1948 and 1950 heightened tension from the Soviet viewpoint.

For the Chinese communists the memories of the atrocities of the Sino-Japanese War were very real and the fears of a resurgent Japan appreciable. However, it must be remembered that the Chinese communists resembled the Kuomintang in using captured Japanese personnel for their own purposes after 1945 and indeed during the Chinese intervention in Korea from October 1950.[84] In 1949–50 China was a weak, vulnerable country devastated by war and civil war with a whole range of daunting political, economic and strategic challenges facing the new government. It would be erroneous to overstate this apprehension, for there was another aspect to the argument. China would require trade and economic assistance; Japanese politicians and capitalists were willing to provide this, as made clear by Yoshida himself. In addition, relations between Moscow and Peking were marked by considerable strain, as the length of the negotiations in Moscow from December 1949 to February 1950 demonstrated. If relations with the Soviet Union deteriorated, Japan could be helpful. Nevertheless suspicion of American policy in Japan and the implications for China were dominant. The problem of Taiwan caused more friction. Certainly the United States should be kept out of the Asian continent and it would be beneficial for the Korean peninsula to be ruled by a communist government. China would not wish Russian interest in Korea to be increased but it was more likely that a regime headed by Kim Il Sung would move along lines independent of Moscow. It would be fair to conclude that the trend in Japan caused concern to Peking but not to the extent that it did in Moscow.

The two regimes in Korea shared bitter recollections of harsh Japanese suppression between 1910 and 1945. Both were intensely nationalistic and neither had any desire to see Japan play an active part in Korea. To North Korea Japan posed a powerful latent threat: the United States and Japan combined could install themselves in South Korea, boost its economy and armed forces, and encourage subversion against North Korea. This would strengthen the case of Kim Il Sung moving sooner rather than later to defeat Syngman Rhee and transform the whole of Korea into a communist state. For South Korea there was no love of Japan and there was the current controversy arising from Japanese treatment of the sizeable Korean community living in Japan. South Korea required support and the combination of the United States and Japan was important: the Americans were committed to Japan to an extent not applicable to South Korea and the South Korean aim was to draw the Americans in further. A powerful Japan could work either for or against South Korea; so long as the United States exercised a controlling influence over Japan, it would work for rather than against South Korea.

Great Britain was broadly favourable to the work of MacArthur. There was dissatisfaction because of inadequate consultation between Washington and London and discontent at the American inability to move more decisively towards a peace settlement. British officials believed the indefinite prolongation of the occupation to be dangerous, particularly because of the restlessness provoked thereby in Japan. Scepticism existed as to the duration of the political changes promoted by MacArthur. It was feared that once Japan was restored to independence, right-wing conservative nationalism would assert itself with at least some of the characteristics of prewar Japan emerging again. Japanese economic competition was feared, although the anxiety was based more on memories of competition in the 1930s than the new competition that developed so vigorously in the 1960s. In defence terms Britain was perturbed by moves to rearm Japan and was influenced by the alarm felt in Australia and New Zealand. Britain was affected by the Cold War and by the need for Japan to be unequivocally within the western sphere of interest. The British leaned towards a middle line whereby Japan would be tied to the West but not in such a way as to stimulate aggressive tendencies.

In 1950 the likely future evolution of Japan was open to diverse interpretation. The undoubted components were that American policy in Japan had become more sympathetic to the aspirations of moderate conservatism and that a peace treaty would probably be concluded within a year or so, resting on generous treatment and with Japan locked into the system of western strategy directed against the threat of Soviet expansion.

# REFERENCES

1.  For a general account of the occupation see K. Kawai, *Japan's American Interlude* (Chicago 1960). For a lucid assessment of Anglo-American perspectives, see Roger Buckley, *Occupation Diplomacy: Britain, the United States, and Japan, 1945–52* (Cambridge 1982). See also Gordon Daniels, 'Britain's view of post-war Japan, 1945–9', in Ian Nish (ed.), *Anglo-Japanese Alienation, 1919–1952* (Cambridge 1982), pp. 257–77.
2.  There is no comprehensive study of MacArthur in Japan between 1945 and 1950. For a colourful account, see William Manchester, *American Caesar: Douglas MacArthur, 1880–1964* (London 1979), pp. 459–544.
3.  Letter from Gascoigne to Dening, 9 Jan. 1948, F1368/662/23/G, FO 371/69885. For a discussion of British views see Peter Lowe, 'British attitudes to General MacArthur and Japan, 1948–50', in Gordon Daniels (ed.), *Europe Interprets Japan* (Tenterden 1984), pp. 117–26.
4.  *The Economist*, **154** (24 April 1948), 670.
5.  Ibid., p. 671.
6.  For the subsequent representations of the British textile industry, see Buckley, op. cit., pp. 168–9.
7.  *The Economist*, **154** (1 May 1948), 706.
8.  Ibid.
9.  Ibid., 13 Nov. 1948, 'Notes of the week'.
10. Diaries of Sir Raymond Streat, vol. 15, 14 May 1948, cited by kind permission of Sir George Kenyon.
11. Ibid.
12. Ibid., vol. 16, 8 May 1950.
13. Ibid.
14. Reinhard Drifte, *The Security Factor in Japan's Foreign Policy, 1945–1952* (Ripe, East Sussex 1983), p. 98.
15. Ibid., p. 34.
16. It should be noted that the comparison with Switzerland requires clarification in that the Swiss have shown determination to defend themselves if attacked and this is exemplified in the tradition of military service for all male citizens. Exactly what MacArthur meant in the Swiss analogy is not clear but it is usually taken as denoting neutrality.
17. *FRUS 1948* (6), p. 697, report by Kennan, 25 March 1948, enclosing memoranda of conversations with MacArthur, 1 March 1948.
18. Ibid., pp. 697–8.
19. Ibid., pp. 700–1, 5 March 1948.
20. Ibid., p. 701.
21. Ibid., pp. 707–10, 23 March 1948.
22. Drifte, op. cit., p. 81.
23. Gascoigne to Bevin, 21 May 1948, F7999/662/23, FO 371/69887.
24. Report by Ferguson, 22 May 1948, ibid.
25. Ibid.
26. *Red Fleet*, 7 Jan. 1948, article by K. Eidens, enclosed in Chancery, British embassy, Moscow, to Japan and Pacific department, FO, 8 Jan. 1948, F769/769/23, FO 371/69889.

27. *FRUS 1948* (6), pp. 803–6, memorandum of conversation prepared in Canadian Department of External Affairs, 3 June 1948.
28. Ibid., pp. 857–62, note by Souers to Truman, 7 Oct. 1948, enclosing NSC report.
29. *FRUS 1949* (7, part 2), p. 656, memorandum of conversation by Bishop, 16 Feb. 1949.
30. Ibid., p. 657.
31. Ibid.
32. Ibid., p. 662, memorandum by Bishop, 18 Feb. 1949.
33. Ibid., p. 672, memorandum by joint chiefs of staff to Forrestal, 1 March 1949.
34. *Daily Mail*, 2 March 1949.
35. *FRUS 1949* (7, part 2), pp. 694–6, memorandum by Bishop, 1 April 1949: pp. 708–9, memorandum by Butterworth, 15 April 1949.
36. Ibid., p. 714, Acheson to certain diplomatic officers, 22 April 1949.
37. Ibid., pp. 730–5, report by NSC, NSC 13/3, 6 May 1949.
38. UK delegation to Council of Foreign Ministers (Bevin) to FO, 20 June 1949, F8971/1021/23, FO 371/76211.
39. BBC Monitoring, communicated to FO, 24 June 1949, F9484/1021/23, ibid.
40. Reuters to BBC Monitoring, summarising statement by New China News Agency, 6 July 1949, F10200/1021/23, ibid.
41. Record of conversation between Dening and Butterworth, 9 Sept. 1949, F14202/1021/23G, FO 371/76212.
42. Record of meeting in the State Department, 17 Sept. 1949, F14555/1021/23G, ibid.
43. Letter from Gascoigne to Dening, 19 Sept. 1949, F14735/1021/23G, FO 371/76213.
44. *FRUS 1949* (7, part 2), p. 927, informal memorandum from Acheson to Franks, 24 Dec. 1949, Sir Oliver Franks reported to London that while Acheson would not be explicit on the nature of the trouble, he (Franks) believed Louis Johnson was responsible and that there had been a serious clash between Acheson and Johnson; see Washington to FO, 9 Dec. 1949, F18486/1021/23G, FO 371/76214.
45. Ibid., p. 928.
46. *FRUS 1949* (7, part 2), p. 806, memorandum by Huston, 16 July 1949.
47. Ibid., p. 891, memorandum of conversation by Fearey, 2 Nov. 1949.
48. Ibid., p. 893.
49. Ibid., p. 894.
50. Ibid.
51. For Truman's relationship with Johnson, see H. S. Truman, *Memoirs: Years of Trial and Hope, 1946–1952*, paperback edn (New York 1965), pp. 70–1, 387–92. See also Robert Donovan, *Tumultuous Years: The Presidency of Harry S. Truman, 1949–1953* (London 1982), pp. 53, 64–5, 159–60, 177, 263–7.
52. *FRUS 1950* (6), pp. 1109–14, memorandum by Jessup, 9 Jan. 1950.
53. Ibid., p. 1115, letter from Jessup to Acheson, 10 Jan. 1950.
54. A useful table summarising Japanese discussions is to be found in Drifte, op. cit., p. 79.
55. Ibid., p. 73.

56. Ibid., p. 74.
57. Ibid., p. 75.
58. Ibid., p. 76.
59. For a stimulating revisionist assessment of Yoshida's career, see J. W. Dower, *Empire and Aftermath: Yoshida Shigeru and the Japanese Experience 1878–1954* (London 1979).
60. Tokyo to FO, 22 Oct. 1948, F14829/44/23, FO 371/659825.
61. Personal letter from Gascoigne to Dening, 22 Oct. 1948, F15706/44/23, FO 371/69827.
62. Dispatch, Gascoigne to Bevin, 21 Oct. 1949, F16818/1015/23, FO 371/76179.
63. Minute by F. S. Tomlinson, 17 Feb. 1949, ibid.
64. Dispatch, Gascoigne to Bevin, 21 Oct. 1949, F16818/1021/236, FO 371/76213. In 1948 MacArthur described Yoshida as lazy and incompetent, see Dower, op. cit., p. 311.
65. See Drifte, op. cit., pp. 88–96 for a useful discussion of Yoshida's attitude. Note also Dower, op. cit., pp. 373–83.
66. Cited in Drifte, op. cit., p. 128.
67. Ibid., pp. 127–8.
68. *FRUS 1950* (6), p. 1177, memorandum by Howard, special assistant to Acheson, 24 April 1950.
69. Ibid., pp. 1177–8.
70. Ibid., p. 1179.
71. Letter from Gascoigne to Dening, 17 April 1950, FJ1021/67G, FO 371/83830.
72. Ibid.
73. Acheson discussed the appointment of Dulles with Truman on 4 April 1950. According to the account in Acheson's papers, 'The President stressed that he would like the appointment to be one which would not harm Mr Dulles's dignity, but that because of his ideas as expressed in last fall's campaign on domestic matters, he did not feel he could make him part of the Administration domestically. The Secretary agreed with the view.' Memorandum of conversation with Truman, 4 April 1950, folder, April 1950, Acheson Papers, Truman Library.
74. *FRUS 1950* (6), p. 1207, footnote, summarising memorandum by James Webb, acting Secretary of State, to Truman, 22 May 1950.
75. Drifte, op. cit., p. 92.
76. See Dean Acheson, *Present at the Creation* (London 1970), pp. 354–8.
77. Drifte, op. cit., pp. 92–3.
78. Ibid., p. 93.
79. 'The London Conference, May 1950, United Kingdom Record,' 10 May 1950, FJ1021/73G, FO 371/83830.
80. Dispatch from Gascoigne to Younger, 12 June 1950, FJ1021/93, FO 371/83831.
81. Letter from Gascoigne to Dening, 17 April 1950, FJ1021/67G, FO 371/83830.
82. Letter from Gascoigne to Dening, 16 June 1950, FJ1021/96, FO 371/83831.
83. See Chapter 7 below.
84. For an illuminating discussion of the attitudes of the two sides in China to

Japanese troops working for them, see D. G. Gillin and C. Etter, 'Staying on: Japanese soldiers and civilians in China, 1945–1949', *Journal of Asian Studies*, XLII (May 1983), 497–518.

# Chapter 5

# THE DEMISE OF THE KUOMINTANG AND THE TRIUMPH OF CHINESE COMMUNISM

Developments in China in the second half of the 1940s were of crucial importance for the sequence of events in 1950, culminating in the Chinese intervention in Korea in October–November 1950. The traditional American attitude towards China had been one of sympathy for the sufferings and aspirations of the Chinese people but without any profound understanding of the forces at work in China.[1] The Kuomintang, under the leadership of Generalissimo Chiang Kai-shek was regarded favourably by politicians and the general public. Chiang had emerged as the dominating personality but not dictator within the Kuomintang in 1927 and had symbolised resistance to Japanese aggression during the Sino-Japanese War of 1937–45. Within the United States government disillusionment with China developed from the middle period of the Pacific War, stimulated by the negative contribution made by China to the defeat of Japan. It had been hoped originally in Washington that China could play a vigorous part in undermining Japan with coastal territory recaptured from the Japanese being used to facilitate bombing of the home islands of Japan. As General Joseph W. Stilwell discovered, the enthusiasm for fighting the Japanese in the temporary wartime capital of Chungking was extremely limited.[2] The top Kuomintang officials and generals were primarily interested in exploiting large-scale American aid for their own benefit; corruption was rife and extended to a high level, although Chiang himself was apparently not corrupt. However, Chiang was preoccupied with his long-term feud with the Chinese communists, notwithstanding the supposed 'United Front' against the Japanese, formed in 1937. Chiang's policy during the Pacific War was to obtain as much aid as possible from the Americans and to husband his resources for the eventual decisive struggle with the communists when Japan had been defeated. President Roosevelt wearied of Chiang and might have adopted a tougher line towards him in 1944 but for domestic political complications, linked with Republican sympathy for China and the imminence of the presidential election.

The Kuomintang gradually declined, having forfeited the revolutionary zeal of the 1920s. Numerically the Kuomintang forces were markedly superior to the communists but in morale, commitment and leadership the communists were far ahead of the Kuomintang, as the civil war was to reveal. The communists, under the astute, forceful leadership of Mao Tse-tung, had recovered from the setbacks experienced in the first two decades of the party's existence.[3] Mao transformed the CCP into a formidable, tenacious foe, imbued with fervent nationalism and a deep faith in the Chinese masses. The small number of American officials, who met the communist leaders and visited Yenan, the CCP's capital in remote Shensi province, were impressed by the spirit of dedication and mission, together with the absence of the corruption that was the hallmark of the Kuomintang.

After the Japanese surrender in August 1945, the United States hoped for a new approach from the Kuomintang, including the CCP participating in the Chinese government. While suspicion of the communists existed, it was felt that the CCP was different from the Russian variety of communism and that Chinese communism would be less dangerous, provided that the Kuomintang possessed the upper hand in their cooperation. General George Marshall devoted much time, between December 1945 and January 1947, to a futile attempt to bring the two sides together. The failure of his mission led Marshall and most officials in the State Department to lose interest in China and to feel that little could be accomplished beyond giving economic assistance to China within certain limits. American policy rested on 'letting the dust settle' and seeing what emerged from the civil war between 1947 and 1949.[4] The Truman administration was principally interested in Europe where the constructive aspects of American policy were advanced by Truman, Marshall and Dean Acheson. Great Britain wished to resume her prewar role in the former treaty ports, particularly in Shanghai, and to recapture some of the old pre-eminence in the China trade. There was little faith in the prospects of the Kuomintang but equally little anticipation that Chiang Kai-shek's power would decline at such a catastrophic pace in 1949. British officials were conscious of the diminished British standing in China and that the United States would determine – or not as the case might be – the western response to the evolution of China. The nature of American policy in China was viewed with accelerating cynicism by the Foreign Office and the diplomats in Nanking.

The Soviet Union followed a cautious approach between 1945 and 1949 and one less sympathetic to Chinese communism than might have been expected. The evidence indicates that the Kremlin had considerable doubt about the character of the CCP and the prospects for the CCP taking power throughout China. Russia had signed a treaty of friendship with the Kuomintang government in 1945 and Chiang Kai-shek sometimes supported the Soviet Union over wider questions, such as the conclusion of a Japanese peace treaty in 1947. Stalin had followed a mistaken and ultimately disastrous policy in China in the 1920s and was well aware of the independent spirit within the CCP encouraged by Mao. It would not be in the Soviet Union's interest to have a strong China, albeit a communist one; historical, geographical and cultural reasons would render it difficult or impossible for the Soviets to dictate to Mao. Stalin appears to have anticipated a slow decline of the Kuomintang balanced by a gradual growth of the CCP; this would point towards a division of China, perhaps with the regions north of the Yangtze dominated by the CCP and those south by the Kuomintang. This explains the preservation of diplomatic relations with the Kuomintang until a surprisingly late stage with the Soviet ambassador retreating with the Kuomintang bureaucracy from Nanking to Canton in February 1949 by which time it was obvious that the CCP would succeed on the mainland within the near future. The Soviet Union had assisted the communists to gain control of Manchuria but this could be explained on the grounds that Russia possessed the ports in the Liaotung peninsula as a result of the Yalta agreement of 1945: subsequent events indicate that the Russians hoped to persuade the local CCP officials to collaborate with them.[5]

In 1946–47 the Kuomintang had seemed to be reasonably well placed in the sense that military defeat did not appear to be imminent. The economic problems facing the Nanking government were rapidly worsening as the wartime inflation continued to gather momentum. In 1947–48 the situation changed drastically. Chiang Kai-shek erred in attempting to regain Manchuria for reasons of prestige. The morale of his forces was poor, officers were frequently corrupt, and ordinary soldiers were treated with sickening brutality.[6] Reports from the American minister-counsellor in Nanking indicated that the position was discouraging, despite Chiang's sanguine statements. Members of the government realised how grave it was and this pessimism was communicating itself to the people – 'The Nanking regime continues to lose popular support. Both ordinary people and civil servants are inclined more and more to attribute the ills of the times to bad government and in the North the Communists, through offers of higher pay and better working conditions, are actually luring Government workers from their jobs.'[7] Policy statements of the CCP included vehement criticism of the United States. Mao Tse-tung issued a personal statement on 25 December, 1947 condemning American imperialism as a 'major enemy' of the Chinese people.[8] John Leighton Stuart, the American ambassador in Nanking, observed that while attacks on the United States had grown recently, this was the first time that a prominent leader had expressed such views publicly.[9] O. Edmund Clubb, the experienced consul-general in Peking, held that three possibilities faced the United States – continuing support for the Kuomintang, as constituted, a sympathetic attitude to the reform movements with the aim of changing the character of the Kuomintang and, as a parallel move, consulting the Soviet Union. Reform groups had become vociferous in 1947–48 but Clubb doubted whether liberalism could make progress as long as Chiang Kai-shek remained in power. Clubb remarked on the significance of developments in Korea:

> Reference to events in Korea would seem to indicate that possibly the Soviet political leaders are prepared to embark upon a more radical line of action in respect to China in the event that a compromise settlement in China, giving substantial authority to the Chinese Communists within clearly established limits, proves infeasible. .... [10]

The Truman administration had moved away, however, from its earlier advocacy of a coalition government in China. Appreciable aid was given to Nanking but falling short of what the State Department deemed intervention in the Chinese civil war. General Marshall met the House of Representatives Foreign Affairs Committee in February 1948 to speak in support of continued aid. Alistair Cooke reported in the *Manchester Guardian* that Marshall had not raised China with any enthusiasm but was responding to pressure from certain prominent Republicans for greater assistance to Chiang Kai-shek. Cooke commented that isolationist Republicans were promoting the campaign – 'It is not that they love China more but that they love Europe less.'[11] Governor Thomas E. Dewey of New York, campaigning actively for the Republican presidential nomination, had demonstrated vocal interest in China. Senator Arthur H. Vandenberg of Michigan, the architect of the bipartisan foreign policy embracing Europe, was critical of the administration over China.[12] When Marshall met the House committee he radiated gloom on the prospects for the Kuomintang. In response to a question at a press conference on 19 March, Marshall stated that the United States still favoured communist participation in the government of China; the problem was that the communists were in a state of rebellion and the international scene had darkened since the communist coup in Czechoslovakia the previous month.[13] Truman dissented and made it clear that he did not favour communist involvement in government anywhere.[14] Much of the pressure for increased aid to China came from a small group of Congressmen headed by a former missionary Walter Judd (Republican, Minnesota). There was no evidence that American public opinion felt strongly over China and the so-called 'China Lobby' did not possess the influence it was to exert after the start of the Korean War.

In July 1948 Leighton Stuart reported deep alarm among military and political leaders over the future of the Kuomintang. General Li Tsung-jen, a prominent figure in the Kwangsi clique and a long-standing rival of Chiang Kai-shek, thought the government's position was hopeless and that existing civil unrest could soon affect the army.[15] Criticism of the United States was being expressed for sustaining Chiang Kai-shek in office. A desire for peace at almost any price was developing rapidly, according to Stuart.[16] Despite a brief interval of stability in August the Kuomintang encountered further military setbacks, including the fall of Tsinan. Unhappiness and frustration grew in Washington but it was unclear how the situation could be resolved. Marshall sent a statement of his views to Stuart in late October 1948. He emphasised that the chief consideration in policy formulation had been that the United States must not assume responsibility for maintaining the Kuomintang in military or economic terms. Armed intervention in China would be contrary to traditional United States policy. The China Aid programme was intended to provide breathing space to permit the Nanking government to reform itself and establish the basis for recovery. An attempt to eradicate communism in China would connote a vast commitment amounting to taking over the administration of China. In the light of recent events it was most unlikely that any American action could put the government on a solid foundation. The Truman administration would continue to support the Kuomintang as long as it remained a significant force. What would happen in the event of a collapse of the Nanking regime or of a section of the Kuomintang deciding to merge with the communists, as rumoured, would have to be determined at that point in time.[17]

Speculation grew at the end of 1948 and beginning of 1949 as to whether Chiang Kai-shek might stand down tactically or because the Generalissimo had wearied of the setbacks that had occurred. In an interview with the *New York Tribune* in October 1948 Chiang spoke of the world menace of communism and of the need to support Chinese resistance to communism. Chiang linked his message with communist activities in Korea and Japan:

> Moreover I should like to point out that the Communist bandits with whom the government is engaged in fighting is linked up with Japanese and Korean communists who in turn receive support of the Communist International.
>
> What is more obvious is that without an integral Northeast, there will be no independent Korea, nor will there be a peaceful East Asia.[18]

A feature of the decline of the Kuomintang was Chiang's interest in forging links with Syngman Rhee and his reference to Korea was one of the first signs of the trend. Chiang and the clique surrounding him had reached the conclusion that the only hope for the salvation of the Kuomintang lay in a third world war; this, too, was a consistent theme to the outbreak of the war in Korea and after. In January 1949 Chiang ostensibly retired and the Vice-President, Li Tsung-jen, became acting President. Chiang had not resigned and exercised effective power from behind the scenes. Li fruitlessly endeavoured to reshape the Kuomintang and entered into peace exchanges with the communists; the latter proved abortive, as the CCP had no intention of compromising, since the prospect of full power was looming. The continued slide downwards for the Kuomintang was alarming principally because of fears that the defeated regime might sanction attacks on foreigners and their property and in all follow a policy of negative destruction. Some attacks did take place, notably in Canton, and the Kuomintang generals ruthlessly extorted whatever they could out of Shanghai before leaving the city. On the whole, however, the retreat of the Kuomintang to Taiwan, while disorderly and humiliating, was not as difficult as had been anticipated.[19]

Attention in Washington and London focused more intensively in 1948–49 on the character of Chinese communism and whether or how to come to terms with it. Mao Tse-tung produced an article entitled 'Revolutionary forces of the world rally to combat imperialist aggression' to commemorate the 31st anniversary of the October revolution. The theme was the close identification in common struggle of the Russian and Chinese peoples. The Russian Revolution had 'erected a bridge between the socialist West and the enslaved East' in the battle to defeat world imperialism.[20] Tribute was paid to the 'brilliant' leadership of Lenin and Stalin. Mao went out of his way to denounce the possibility of a 'middle way' or 'third path' by those who disliked Marxism and the achievements of the Soviet Union.[21] This could be taken as a repudiation of the small liberal centre groups in China, although Mao was prepared to cooperate with them on the basis of their being rendered powerless by the CCP, as later events demonstrated. The CCP was based on the model of the Soviet party and was moving along similar lines. Mao castigated the role of the United States in world affairs:

> Instead of fascist Germany, Italy and Japan, it is now American imperialism and its servants in the various countries who are feverishly preparing a new world war and who are menacing the whole world. This is a reflection of the extreme decay that has set in throughout the capitalist world, its fear of impending doom. Imperialism, however, the enemy of the working peoples of all countries, is still strong. That is why the revolutionary forces in every country must be united and consolidated, why they must daily strengthen the united anti-imperialist front headed by the Soviet Union, why they must pursue a correct internationalist policy, for otherwise they can never be victorious.
>
> The great people's democratic revolution in China which is being carried out under the leadership of the Chinese Communist Party is an integral part of the international anti-imperialist camp. The working people of China have won great victories in their selfless struggle against the vicious aggression of American imperialism and against the reactionary Kuomintang Government which has betrayed the fatherland and the interests of the people.[22]

Mao proudly recalled the series of defeats inflicted on the Kuomintang and the huge areas liberated by the CCP's forces. The tasks of the revolution were to complete the liquidation of the Kuomintang and to expel American imperialism totally. The article ended by affirming loyalty to the principles of Sun Yat-sen, identified the CCP once more with communist parties elsewhere in the world, and asserted the courage of the Chinese masses. Mao's sentiments gave additional evidence to those who argued that the CCP was working closely with Moscow. It had to be borne in mind that a statement celebrating the Bolshevik revolution was bound to include sentiments of this character and that Mao was irate at continued American help for Chiang Kai-shek.

At around the same time General Marshall explained his views at a meeting of the United Nations General Assembly held in Paris. Marshall said that in its desperation the Nanking government was requesting an increase in military supplies, the appointment of a leading American general as a military adviser, and that members of the existing American military mission should be distributed among Chinese divisions. Marshall stressed that there was no intention of meeting the demands. The quantities of supplies wanted by the Kuomintang were excessive and amounted to a 'major operation'.[23] It would not be feasible to provide a senior military adviser; the military situation was too complicated and intelligence showed that the communists would pursue their advance southwards. Marshall did not mention that Chiang Kai-shek would have welcomed the appointment of General MacArthur and that MacArthur was apparently willing to entertain such a proposal, provided that it was additional to his existing responsibilities in Japan and not a substitute for them.[24] Marshall added that American policy would support Chiang 'for as long as he was supportable'.[25] It was clear that the Truman administration were 'at their wits' end for any palliative even for the present situation'.[26] The incompetence of the Kuomintang army was such that it appeared impossible of solution. Furthermore the administration had given priority to Europe and greater involvement in China would mean a reduction in American efforts to assist WEU or the Atlantic pact. The Soviet Union would desire just such a development and the United States would not be drawn into the trap. Marshall went on to consider the Chinese communists. While they were undoubtedly Marxist-Leninist, they were different from other communists. Marshall therefore believed there was some prospect of preventing the relationship between the Chinese communists and the Soviet Union becoming too close.[27] Marshall's remarks were in harmony with a report earlier in 1948 from the NSC and a report in September 1948 from the Policy Planning Staff, headed by George Kennan.[28]

Britain quickly appreciated the complexities associated with recognition of a Chinese communist government and was anxious to begin consultation with the United States. While it was appreciated that it would prove contentious, it could not have been forecast that the subject would be so peculiarly difficult, that it would be the most dangerous example of Anglo-American divergence to have arisen so far, and that it would take more than twenty years for the United States to take the first significant steps towards recognition. The establishment of the new government was proclaimed formally by Mao in Peking on 1 October, 1949.[29] The British attitude to recognition was essentially straightforward and devoid of ideological bias. A government should be recognised officially when it was clearly in effective possession of most or all of the territory of the state and when it appeared reasonably certain that the new regime would fulfil treaty commitments. In contrast the approach of the United States was more complex. Recognition was not simply a fulfilment of the criteria employed by Britain but amounted to approval of the character of the new government. This would necessarily incorporate unqualified acceptance of international obligations and fair treatment of United States nationals in China. In the course of the communist advance friction had been occasioned in places by clashes between American officials and communist authorities. The clashes, for which the Americans were partly responsible, overshadowed the arguments over recognition. The most serious obstacle was engendered by the impact of the Cold War. George Kennan had originally intended his concept of containment to be used in specific contexts and not in a universalistic way. An element of carelessness in the drafting of his proposals together with the simplistic approach shown by members of the Truman administration and others led to the phobia over communism that came to dominate American perspectives from the late 1940s to the 1970s, if not beyond.[30] A growing number of Americans began to lament the loss of China, happening before their eyes. In contrast to Europe where an imaginative and constructive policy was adopted, the administration was floundering in China without a policy or at any rate one that had registered a degree of success. China had already been seized on by the Republican Party as a stick with which to beat the administration. The unexpected defeat of Dewey in the 1948 election exacerbated tensions for a party that had been out of office for a lengthy period and which contained much internal conflict within its own ranks. It would be necessary to tread warily to ensure a consensus before proceeding.

In January 1949 Dean Acheson became Secretary of State. On policy matters there was no disagreement between Acheson and his predecessor, Marshall: the United States must play a dynamic role in the world, the priority was Europe, and little could be done about China. The difference was that Marshall was widely respected for his honesty, integrity and forthrightness, cultivated during a lifetime's service to the United States army. Acheson was also a man of integrity and vigour but was a controversial figure. Acheson's manner and bearing personified the eastern establishment liberal and grated on various people in Congress. Acheson's response could be arrogant at times and he never suffered fools gladly. Senator Vandenberg, a shrewd judge of congressional reactions, respected Acheson but did not regard Truman's choice as a wise one; Vandenberg commented in his diary that had Truman consulted him on the appointment he would have recommended against it.[31] Acheson experienced a tempestuous term of office in the State Department but arguably was the most capable Secretary of State in the twentieth century. President Truman trusted him implicitly and usually supported him unequivocally; their relationship was probably the most congenial between a President and a Secretary of State in recent times.[32]

In January 1949 British representatives raised recognition at a meeting in Washington with Philip Sprouse, head of the China division. Sprouse stated that meticulous consideration had to be given to the topic and stressed that it would be controversial. The hope was expressed that Britain would not extend *de jure* recognition without consultation. In response it was indicated that the Foreign Office viewed recognition as a bargaining counter to protect British economic interests.[33] Sporadic attention was devoted to recognition in the following months but it was not feasible to advance further until the communists had absorbed additional territory. On 18 March the Foreign Office regarded the frontiers of communist territory as fluid and believed that a situation analogous to that in the Spanish Civil War (1936–39) might arise. The range of issues required careful consideration and Britain would not rush into recognition.[34]

Meanwhile the NSC reviewed American policy and recommended that freedom of action be preserved by following an approach calculated to accentuate tendencies towards a rift in Sino-Soviet relations. Such a policy would allow, with adequate safeguards, restoration of ordinary economic relations between China on the one hand and Japan and the western powers on the other. Trade between Japan and China should be encouraged on a quid pro quo basis. Full controls over trade with China should be implemented by the United States government.[35] This paper pointed cautiously to an attempt to work with the Chinese communists. The American consul-general in Peking commented on the communists' desire to increase trade with Japan: they wished to export salt, coal, soya beans, particularly coal. Clubb, the consul-general, proposed that he reply sympathetically but also underlined that trade could not be developed until the communists gave United States consular establishments the usual facilities. On the more overt political side Clubb expected the communist campaign against American imperialism to continue for some time but the CCP's line might be reconsidered. He fully supported an attempt to insert a wedge in relations between the Chinese and Moscow.[36] The consul-general in Tientsin, Smyth, believed that a softer approach towards foreigners was slowly occurring but this could be explained through a wish to allay apprehension before the communists entered Shanghai; it could also be part of a strategy to secure western recognition of the new government.[37] MacArthur concurred in the State Department's views on fostering trade with north China; he did not intend to take an initiative himself over trade but would leave commercial transactions to the consul-general to pursue.[38] The State Department did not want matters to proceed too rapidly and were conscious of the importance of not extending formal recognition to communist representatives going to Japan to discuss trade. Accordingly MacArthur was informed that it was doubtful whether he should receive representatives; a reply was sent to Washington on 6 July, 1949 that SCAP did not think it appropriate at the present time to allow into Japan a trade mission accompanied by representatives of the communist regime.[39]

The head of the ECA mission to China, Roger D. Lapham, fully supported efforts to put relations with the communists on a more secure footing. Lapham was a Republican and former mayor of San Francisco; he had been in China since June 1948 for the purpose of supervising economic assistance to China. Lapham believed that the Kuomintang regime was doomed and it would be futile to try and save it. Political objectives could be attained by economic means; commerce could lead to improved relations with the communists. He proposed that no restrictions be placed on American exports to China other than supplies of military goods, including strategic materials. He recalled that the aim of United States policy should be to prevent domination of China by a hostile government: the development of a 'satellite' relationship between the Soviet Union and China must be obviated. Lapham candidly remarked that the United States had supported the losing side with economic aid, arms and ammunition. Any thought of assisting the Kuomintang further in military terms or of giving help to any anti-communist groups that might appear should be resisted; instead American policy should be directed at assisting the peasant masses of China through the work of American advisers motivated solely by the wish to raise the standard of living.[40] The overall head of ECA was a prominent business man and a Republican, Paul G. Hoffman, to whom Lapham's memorandum was addressed; Hoffman had made a statement in January, while visiting Shanghai, implying that American aid should be given to a communist government.[41] Lapham's term of office in China ended on 24 Mar, 1949. In an interesting final report he discussed his work and the difficulties he had faced. Currency inflation was one of the worst features which he illustrated by remarking that when the ECA mission first reached China, one US dollar could purchase 1.4 million Chinese dollars; some months later one US dollar could buy almost 12 million Chinese dollars. The Kuomintang's counter-offensive against inflation had proved a fiasco whereby ordinary Chinese were forced to surrender gold, silver or other valuables in return for a worthless new currency. He believed the mission had discharged its task effectively in the circumstances. His report ended with wise words: 'One thing this year has taught me – you cannot afford to hold to fixed ideas. You must keep fluid, face things as they are and not as you would like to have them'.[42]

The consul-general in Shanghai, Cabot, took a similar view. It would be best to follow a united approach among the powers over recognition if possible but the British were anxious to advance more swiftly. A policy of using trade controls was unlikely to work because it would require unanimity among the powers and Britain would evidently not support utilising trade controls in exchange for recognition. The final phase of Kuomintang rule in Shanghai was appalling; it amounted to 'a gigantic and sickening racket to strip the town clean before they hand it over'.[43] He added that the Kuomintang was departing the mainland assured 'of unusual and permanent execration'.[44] Cabot had previously served in Yugoslavia and brought a fresh mind to bear on Chinese matters, reinforced by the knowledge of how Marshal Tito had broken with Moscow. At the end of May 1949 he produced a reflective survey of Chinese communism to provide a new perspective for Washington. Cabot talked of the vacillation in assessments of the CCP from, at an earlier stage, discounting the fact that the CCP was fully communist, at least in the European sense, to a tendency to categorise it as no different from the Kremlin. What was significant was not the respect in which Chinese communism resembled the Soviet variety but the divergences. Among the latter were that the Sino-Soviet treaty of 1945 was a snub to the CCP; the Soviet embassy was the only one to move from Nanking to Canton with the retreating Kuomintang; the fact that Vyshinsky had seen the Kuomintang ambassador in Moscow before the latter's departure to become Foreign Minister; that negotiations in Sinkiang had been with the Kuomintang, not the CCP; the relative failure of the Soviet Union to help the CCP, which could be compared with the Greek experience; the deportation of Anna Louise Strong; the apparent refusal to glorify the Chinese achievements at the 1 May parade in Moscow; and the closure of the Soviet consulates in Peking and Shanghai. From the Chinese side indicators included a growing respect for foreign private property and the infrequency with which Stalin's portrait was displayed. It was still too early to reach a conclusion on Soviet–Chinese relations but all relevant aspects had to be considered.[45]

The evidence could be interpreted in either direction in the summer of 1949. The consul-general in Peking, Clubb, reported an indirect approach, allegedly from Chou En-lai, revealing willingness to improve relations with Washington.[46] The State Department was cautiously favourable but regarded prompt settlement of current disputes to be fundamental.[47] On the other hand, Mao's speech of 15 June laid stress on the complete defeat of imperialism and its 'running dogs'.[48] Leighton Stuart considered the full text of Mao's *On People's Democratic Dictatorship* to be a frank statement of where the CCP stood and revealed the potent effect of Stalinism emphasising identification with Moscow more strongly.[49] Cabot's concluding thoughts, before he departed to a new post, were that the Kremlin did not exert significant power over the CCP. It was manifest that a communist government would soon rule China and this had to be realised. The most urgent challenges facing the new regime would be economic and these might compel basic changes in policy.[50] Stuart, who tended to oscillate, believed that the CCP was unquestionably Marxist-Leninist and would prove tenacious. The United States should follow the traditional policy of supporting the legitimate aspirations of the Chinese people and an improvement in relations could be secured by flexible economic and political initiatives. It was a somewhat muddled appeal for a middle path, explicable psychologically from a distinguished educational administrator, who had spent the greater part of his life in China and who was attempting to reconcile American procedures and principles with the realities of CCP policy.[51]

Between July and December 1949 lengthy exchanges took place between London and Washington over recognition. The British government was vitally concerned about economic interests in China and at preserving agreement within the British Commonwealth. The latter was particularly important in the case of India, for Jawaharlal Nehru considered himself the spokesman of the 'new Commonwealth' and was determined to recognise the new government of China sooner rather than later; Nehru was encouraged by the effervescent Indian ambassador in Peking, K. M. Panikkar, who was to play a controversial role in the speculation over the Chinese attitude to the Korean War in the autumn of 1950. Ernest Bevin met Dean Acheson in Paris in June 1949 and Bevin characteristically hoped that Anglo-American consultations over far eastern problems could be forwarded through 'matey' discussions.[52] Acheson responded positively in July, rather to Bevin's surprise, and sent a memorandum on far eastern matters. The issues examined included attitudes towards the Kuomintang and communist regimes, trade, the position of foreign nationals in China, how far problems should be coordinated with other interested governments. It might be best for the first steps to be taken by Asiatic states under Indian leadership.[53] Bevin welcomed Acheson's initiative and proposed to discuss it with him when he accompanied the Chancellor of the Exchequer to Washington in the autumn; he was currently preoccupied with the Middle East and Kashmir.[54] The Foreign Office prepared a memorandum for submission to the Far Eastern (Official) Committee, which was involved in the formulation of policy. The Kuomintang regime was described as moribund and there was little point in considering it further except in the context of timing of recognition. The leaders of the CCP were regarded as orthodox Marxist-Leninists and the new communist state would pose a definite threat to western interests in China and South-East Asia. The most sensible western strategy would be to impress on the new government the value of western economic aid and the incompatibility of Soviet and Chinese interests, for example in Manchuria. Britain wished to avoid confrontation with the CCP but would not adopt appeasement in order to avert it. Private western companies engaged in business could make a distinct contribution to developing a new relationship. There would be awkward problems to surmount but British firms had 'weathered many storms in the past'.[55] It would not be wise to facilitate increases in the military might of China but ordinary trade of a civilian nature should be pursued. The evacuation of British residents was not favoured; merchants and missionaries could assist positively in the era of transition.

On recognition itself, it was necessary to remember that the charter of the UN was so devised that unless there was a Chinese representative to the Security Council the latter could take decisions solely on procedural issues. It followed that *de jure* recognition should not be withdrawn from the existing government until it could be transferred to the new government. The question was not an immediate one in that the communists had to bring their southern campaigns to a successful conclusion. However, this would probably be accomplished rapidly and the new regime proclaimed formally. Looking ahead to the likely nature of relations between the West and the communist government, these could develop either in the Soviet satellite pattern or on the Yugoslav model. While it would be foolish to hasten into recognition, it must be accepted that 'to withhold recognition from a government in effective control of a large part of China is legally objectionable and leads to grave practical difficulties regarding the protection of Western interests in China'.[56] Excessive delay in granting recognition would be counter-productive.

Conflicting reports continued to be produced in Washington but the trend was in the direction of a tougher attitude to the CCP. President Truman had little interest in the Far East and was normally content to leave his colleagues to handle them. He detested communism and thought of it in simplistic terms as a monolithic force. Truman was annoyed at the clashes that had occurred over the rights of American consuls and other cases involving the detention of United States nationals. In late August Truman set in train a reappraisal, since he believed that the views contained in NSC 41, adopted in February, which had included emphasis on economic incentives and gaining the trust of the communists, were no longer feasible. Truman also gave instructions that the scope for assisting Li Tsung-jen and Pai Chung-hsi, who were still opposing the communists, should be examined.[57] Congressional criticism of the failure of American policy in China was growing. Dewey visited Acheson and said that while he had no wish to rake over the past, 'he thought our policy had been full of mistakes and that we had practically lost Asia'.[58] Hardliners opposed to an understanding with the communists contemplated the prospects for aiding the disparate elements fighting the communists in China. A memorandum prepared for Truman in November was couched in classic Cold War 'domino' terms. Russia's possession of the atomic bomb and the progress of communism in China necessitated a drastic reinterpretation of policy. Complete success of communism in China would mean, 'it is only a question of time when all Asia is beyond the possibility of cooperation with the West and is in the anti-American orbit'.[59]

The Kuomintang's retreat had supposedly been quickened through inability to send material assistance in time. The various Kuomintang forces resisting the communists were estimated at just over one million embracing Taiwan, Hainan, and parts of Kweichow, Hunan, Szechuan, Sikang and Yunnan. Given leadership, organisation and support, guerrilla forces could oppose the communists for a prolonged period. The Kuomintang required new dynamic leadership and this could be provided by General Sun Li-jen, who was capable, American-trained and efficient. Sun had just become commander-in-chief of Chinese Army Training Headquarters, Taiwan. Maintenance of troops would connote appreciable payments and a sum of forty-five million US dollars should be allocated over a two-year period. Time was pressing and the consequences of the Chinese communists sitting in the UN Security Council had to be grasped.[60] Walt Butterworth submitted a commentary on the arguments to Webb, the acting Secretary of State, but this was apparently not passed to Truman. The defect with the arguments in his opinion was that they exaggerated the potential for further resistance; the Kuomintang forces were fast declining, if not disintegrating, and CIA intelligence did not correspond with the estimates in the memorandum. He was not convinced by the arguments and felt they should not be pursued further. It is difficult to penetrate the obscurity over the American relationship with the anti-communist forces in mainland China but it is probable that some assistance was extended to guerrilla groups on the mainland over the next few years.

Britain advanced gradually but inexorably to recognition. After full exchanges with the ambassador in Peking, Sir Ralph Stevenson, it was decided to withdraw the ambassador for consultations once it was clear that the proclamation of the communist government in Peking was imminent. This was intended to circumvent recognition immediately upon the formation of the government and to give freedom to announce recognition at the most suitable time.[61] Bevin had explained his intentions to the American ambassador when they met on 26 August:

> We believed ... that the Chinese Communists were first and foremost Chinese and that they were not capable of becoming Russians overnight. I then said that it seemed to me that the American White Paper had effectively dismissed Chiang Kai-shek as being unworthy of any further American support but the United States Government did not seem to have any alternative to put in his place. The Ambassador admitted that there was some force in this.[62]

On 1 October 1949 Mao Tse-tung declared the formal establishment of the Chinese People's Republic at a ceremony in Peking; it was an astonishing achievement for a party which had encountered such serious reverses in the later 1920s and 1930s. Stevenson, who was about to depart from China, recommended to London that steps be taken to establish an informal relationship; the formula that he suggested referred twice to the formation of the 'Central People's Government'.[63] Stevenson maintained that this did not constitute *de facto* recognition, which he deemed inappropriate as yet. Stevenson's proposal was accepted and the statement duly conveyed to Peking.[64] Shortly afterwards the French government pointed out that the statement could be construed as extending *de facto* recognition because of the use of the term 'Government'. Legal opinion subsequently concurred in this observation.[65] The Foreign Office comforted itself with the thought that the Chinese communists had previously made it clear that they were interested only in *de jure* recognition.[66] The United States showed no inclination to follow in Britain's footsteps; Butterworth sardonically remarked to the British ambassador in Washington that he hoped Britain's 'bolt into the blue' would end with a landing on solid ground.[67] Two of the leading American newspapers differed in their attitudes; the *New York Times*, which frequently represented State Department opinions, was cautious but the *Washington Post* advocated recognition.[68]

The lengthy process ended for Britain in December 1949 with the approval by the Cabinet of recognition. Acheson was informed that Britain had delayed for some months but the important issues could be postponed no longer. The presence of large Chinese communities in Hong Kong, Malaya and Singapore rendered recognition essential. To delay recognition would be to assist the aims of the Soviet Union; it would be dangerous for China to be isolated and subject to intensified Soviet pressure. The British government did not approve of Communist China but recognition was irrelevant, since Britain recognised Russia and the satellite states. It was expected that recognition would be accorded on 2 January 1950.[69] Stevenson having now returned to London, the chargé d'affaires, John Hutchison, dealt with the procedural aspects. He was based in Nanking but expected to transfer to Peking after recognition. The British communication to the communist authorities stated that this was a response to Chairman Mao's statement of 1 October; the action was being taken because the government was in 'effective control of by far the greater part of the territory of China' and that *de jure* recognition was now declared.[70] The Kuomintang regime, based in Taiwan, was notified of withdrawal of recognition but Britain retained representation at the consular level in Taiwan.[71] Anglo-American relations were strained considerably and this strain was exacerbated at various times during the Korean War. Britain did not gain as much out of recognition as had been hoped, for China was determined to end the final relics of western imperialism except for Hong Kong. Dean Acheson hoped that a gradual reduction in American relations with the Kuomintang could be effected and in private he believed there was much to be said for the British decision.[72] The political realities of Washington precluded any idea of American recognition for some time to come.

Lastly let us consider Taiwan (Formosa). This was extremely significant in political and strategic terms. Taiwan was the scene of Chiang Kai-shek's final stand; if Taiwan fell the last shreds of Chiang's credibility would vanish. There was talk of Chiang's definitive retirement, perhaps to Switzerland, but the Generalissimo had no intention of departing. He believed he had a historic task to fulfil as the successor to Sun Yat-sen and felt that the Kuomintang could be saved at the eleventh hour, provided that he could operate with other trenchant anti-communists such as Syngman Rhee and President Quirino of the Philippines and induce the United States to accept the obligation to defend Taiwan and South Korea. A third world war could be the salvation of the Kuomintang. Chiang appeared in effective control of Taiwan, although there was speculation on a possible coup, perhaps to advance General Sun Li-jen. The influx of numerous refugees was resented by the native Taiwanese who had suffered enough already from the Kuomintang, notably in the harsh suppression of the 1947 rising. There had been some American interest in the Taiwanese autonomy movement, especially in 1948–49 when the complete disintegration of the Kuomintang was feared. The fact that large numbers of troops were evacuated from the mainland with the air force and loyal sections of the navy postponed the collapse and eliminated the likelihood of advancing the Taiwanese cause. The strategic position of Taiwan was the vital question for American policy-makers; they had long ago given up hope of Chiang's revival, as the China White Paper demonstrated. Chinese communist possession of Taiwan could pose a threat to the concept of the American frontier in the western Pacific, formulated in the later 1940s. The key aspect was precisely how important was Taiwan? Was it so valuable as to justify American intervention to prevent the communists capturing it? This was the focus of intense debate in Washington in the autumn of 1949 and in the course of 1950 until the question was decisively answered by the events of June and November 1950.

The relationship between Taiwan and Japan is a significant area to examine. Economic relations were close and the political connections between General MacArthur and the Kuomintang are a fascinating if obscure subject. Trade between Taiwan and Japan had revived by 1948 to the point where the formation of a trade association to promote commerce was envisaged in Taiwan.[73] In addition, trading contacts with South Korea were being developed. The descent of large numbers of refugees in 1948–49 worsened the economic problems in Taiwan with the onset of serious inflation. In 1948–49 production of manufactured sugar, Taiwan's most valuable export, had risen from 260,000 tons in 1948 to 620,000 tons in 1949. The biggest single contract for sugar exports was with SCAP, although the bulk of the sugar was exported to countries within the sterling area and purchases were made by the British Ministry of Food. It was estimated in July 1949 that there were over 400,000 soldiers in Taiwan, all of whom had escaped from the mainland, plus approximately half a million civilian refugees.[74] Taiwanese autonomy movements operated in part from Japan. American press reports from Tokyo in September 1948 discussed the activities of the Taiwan independence movement, stimulated by the arrival in Tokyo from Taiwan of Peter K. Huang, one of the most vigorous exponents of the cause. The headquarters of the Formosan League for Re-emancipation was located in Hong Kong and the movement was said to have a significant number of agents in Japan and the Philippines. The group's policy was that the UN should assume responsibility for Taiwan pending the holding of a plebiscite. It had advocated autonomy rather than independence for Taiwan but had moved more towards the latter; coordination with the other movements opposing the Kuomintang regime, the Anti-Government Democratic League and the Communist Party, had not so far been established. The most prominent leaders of the Formosan League were W. K. and W. I. Liao, large property owners resident in Hong Kong. In general terms Taiwanese autonomy was viewed sympathetically within Japan and the Kuomintang alleged that Japanese were financing it together with 'other foreign interests'.[75] The British consul in Taiwan, E. T. Biggs, reported Kuomintang apprehension that the frequent tales of incompetent, oppressive rule in Taiwan might lead the United States to support the autonomy movement. There was considerable interest in the concept of Taiwanese autonomy in Washington and it is likely that MacArthur facilitated the activities of the autonomists in Japan at a time when the fate of the Kuomintang was uncertain.

MacArthur believed firmly that Taiwan must be denied to the communists. He urged the provision of more assistance to the Kuomintang and SCAP gave discreet help where feasible. One form comprised unofficially permitting former Japanese military personnel to visit Taiwan to advise the Kuomintang. Alvary Gascoigne, head of the British mission in Tokyo, informed London in September 1949 that MacArthur had for some months laid stress on Taiwan as an essential constituent of the 'Island line', including Japan, Okinawa and the Philippines. General Willoughby, MacArthur's intelligence chief, told Malcolm MacDonald, Britain's high commissioner in South-East Asia then visiting Tokyo, that he (Willoughby) included Taiwan in the line of vital American defence. As Gascoigne remarked, this must have been the view of MacArthur.[76] Willoughby had recently been asked by journalists for information on Japanese smuggled to Taiwan to assist the Kuomintang. Willoughby replied that probably a few had departed in this way and it could not be prevented, given the limited numbers of police in Japan. A British representative questioned one of Willoughby's subordinates on 17 September and he admitted that General Nemoto and a small number of former senior and junior officers had gone to Taiwan since June 1947.[77] A CIA memorandum by Admiral Hillenkoetter, drafted on 21 November 1949 and to be found in a sanitised form in the Truman Papers, summarised a private luncheon meeting between General Claire L. Chennault and MacArthur in Tokyo at which 'General MacArthur expressed regret that the present United States policy prevents him from helping the Chinese; he asked Chennault to convey word-of-mouth message to the Generalissimo and Pai Chung-hsi, urging them 'to fight to the end'.[78] MacArthur had urged Chennault – who surely needed little encouragement – to urge the opponents of communism to fight as vigorously as they could. MacArthur's chief of staff 'let slip' that Japanese volunteers, chiefly aviators, were being allowed to leave Japan for Taiwan.[79] Undoubtedly MacArthur was well informed of developments in Taiwan and did what he could to inspire continued resistance by the Kuomintang. It was one of the indications, before the Korean War began, of the divergences between MacArthur and the Truman administration in the sense that MacArthur felt a political commitment to support the Kuomintang, which was certainly not the policy of the administration.

The joint chiefs of staff and the NSC spent much time evaluating the strategic significance of Taiwan in 1948–50. The basic principles of their assessments remained consistent, although points of emphasis varied at different times. In November 1948 the joint chiefs submitted a report describing Taiwan as most important strategically, for the island could be used as a staging post for troops or for strategic air and naval operations. The joint chiefs believed that Taiwan should be denied to the Chinese communists by diplomatic and economic pressures.[80] The NSC produced a comprehensive report in January 1949. The Taiwanese autonomy movement was termed weak, having been effectively crushed by the Kuomintang regional administration in 1947; the communists in Taiwan were similarly weak. The island had been badly governed since 1945, the Kuomintang having revealed its familiar genius for inept administration. It would be possible for the United States to occupy Taiwan under the terms of the Japanese surrender in 1945 with the consent of the Kuomintang or after the disintegration of the latter. As an alternative, an arrangement for American extraterritorial or base rights in Taiwan could be negotiated. Politically the United States could support a rump Kuomintang regime or promote a Taiwan autonomy administration. The aim of the United States should be to prevent the communists taking Taiwan or the Pescadores. Given the prevailing uncertainties, flexibility should be maintained with policy options left open. It was imperative that a new regime in Taiwan, whatever its political commitment, should function fairly and effectively.[81] The joint chiefs reported to Forrestal, the Secretary of Defense, in February summarising the principal aspects and emphasising that while Taiwan should be denied to the enemy if possible, they believed that there could be no United States commitment to defend Taiwan owing to onerous global responsibilities.[82] In March 1949 the joint chiefs were contemplating the possibility of having to act in Taiwan through a show of military force if the situation deteriorated to the stage where this was necessary. Acheson told the NSC that it was important to act in conjunction with other interested powers:

> If we are to intervene militarily on the island, we shall in all probability, do so in concert with like-minded powers, preferably using UN mechanisms and with the proclaimed intentions of satisfying the legitimate demands of the indigenous Formosans for self-determination either under a UN trusteeship or through independence.[83]

The State Department moved in the summer of 1949 to preferring the installation of a temporary administration, under UN or American auspices, which would prepare a settlement on the basis of self-determination for the people of Taiwan; the Kuomintang was effectively finished.[84] Shortly afterwards the joint chiefs submitted a revised statement reiterating that while Taiwan was strategically important, Taiwan and the Pescadores were not of such compelling military value as to commit United States forces to occupation short of a major war; in the circumstances military occupation was not recommended.[85] By October the joint chiefs favoured economic aid to Taiwan and the re-establishment of a military advisory group. Economically Taiwan should be made self-sufficient but the Chinese administration must reform and eliminate the grave defects of their rule on the mainland.[86] Towards the end of 1949 MacArthur and the joint chiefs placed more emphasis on the importance of Taiwan.

MacArthur explained his views in December. Taiwan was essential to 'out littoral island defense' and could be retained 'with very little effort'.[87] Taiwan was legally part of Japan until a peace treaty had been signed. The Kuomintang government had acted as a custodian on behalf of the allies in occupying Taiwan. Should Taiwan be threatened with invasion, all the allies should combine to defend it:

> Such a defense could be made without the necessity of committing US troops, merely by a declaration under the Potsdam Agreement that the US would treat any attempt to invade Formosa as an act of war, and similarly that it would be treated as an act of war for the Nationalist Government itself to use Formosa as a base to launch an attack against China.[88]

It could be decided subsequently that Taiwan should become an independent nation. An appreciable part of the sum of seventy-five million US dollars allocated for Chinese matters could be used to defend Taiwan. MacArthur's concluding thoughts were thus summarised by Tracy S. Voorhees, Under-Secretary of the Army:

It would be fatal to split the US line of littoral bases by letting the Communists put an air force on Formosa thereby threatening both Clark Field in the Philippines and our fields on Okinawa. However, placing US Forces on Formosa is not favoured.[89]

Louis Johnson sent a memorandum to President Truman explaining that the State and Defense departments were conferring on policy and that

Generally speaking, the staffs agree that efforts should be continued and perhaps increased to deny Formosa to the Communists. The nature and extent of such efforts are now being considered in some detail. ... They include political and economic aid, and also military advice and assistance short of overt military action.[90]

The joint chiefs recommended a modest, well-organised and supervised programme of military aid to Taiwan in the security interests of the United States: this should be combined with an increased political, economic and psychological programme as an intensified version of the existing programme. Their recommendations had to be seen as 'part of the overall problem of resisting the spread of Communist domination of East Asia'.[91]

Dean Acheson's thinking was running along different lines. He was attracted at the prospect of separating Peking from Moscow in the wider interests of American global policies. Acheson worked to bring the finer points of the situation to Truman's attention. Truman devoted little thought to the Far East and when he did tended to see it in terms of communism as a monolithic force. He was capable of appreciating alternative arguments, however, when these were carefully brought to his attention. On 17 November Acheson had arranged a meeting with Truman and the 'consultants' accompanying Acheson. According to Acheson's record of the conversation, Truman 'had gotten a new insight into the reasons for the Communist success in China, a better understanding of the whole situation and found himself thinking about it in a quite new way'.[92] The President intended to review far eastern policy in total when Philip Jessup returned from the Far East. Acheson told Truman that as he saw it, the choice facing the administration was between two courses of action:

One might be to oppose the Communists [sic] regime, harass it, needle it, and if an opportunity appeared to attempt to overthrow it. Another objective of policy would be to attempt to detach it from subservience to Moscow and over a period of time encourage those vigorous influences which might modify it. I pointed out that this second alternative did not mean a policy of appeasement any more than it had in the case of Tito. If the Communists took action detrimental to the United States it should be opposed with vigor. ... [93]

With the joint chiefs urging a tougher approach in December the Secretary of State arranged a meeting for 29 December, attended by Generals Bradley and Collins, Lieutenant-General Norstad, Admiral Sherman with Rusk, Butterworth and Merchant from the State Department. Bradley said the basic attitude of the joint chiefs had not changed: Taiwan had always been considered important. The Kuomintang air force had now moved to Taiwan with their families and this reduced the danger of defections. Collins spoke of the need to prevent communist dominance of Indo-China, Burma and Thailand. He agreed that the danger was one of infiltration and subversion rather than Chinese communist invasion.[94] There was no thought of sending combat troops to Taiwan and the joint chiefs preferred former officers being employed as advisers. Acheson believed facts had to be faced; there was no real base from which Chinese opposition to communism could be conducted. The communist threat in South-East Asia would be advanced through subversion, not attack. Sino-Soviet relations had already encountered strain because of the Soviet attempt to detach certain northern provinces; furthermore Mao Tse-tung was not an uncritical adherent of the Kremlin, since he had come to power through his own efforts:

> This situation, I pointed out, is our one important asset in China and it would have to be for a very important strategic purpose that we would take an action which would substitute ourselves for the Soviets as the imperialist menace to China. For this reason we oppose waging economic warfare against China.[95]

The problem with the Kuomintang in Taiwan was that they might succumb to the same features of internal decline that had affected them on the mainland. If absolutely necessary a policy of postponing a communist take-over of Taiwan for one year could be adopted but it should only be done for vital defence purposes.

Growing pressure from leading Republicans to increase aid for Taiwan was applied in November–December. Senator H. Alexander Smith (New Jersey) put forward the proposal that Taiwan was still Japanese territory and that the United States could develop a protectorate there. Senators William F. Knowland (California) and Robert A. Taft (Ohio) with the support of ex-President Herbert Hoover publicly urged that the United States navy be deployed to defend Taiwan.[96] Truman and Acheson concluded that the time had come for definitive statements to curb the incessant speculation. Truman issued a press statement on 5 January, 1950 to the effect that Taiwan was clearly Chinese territory and the United States harboured no ulterior motives concerning Taiwan. There would be no involvement in the Chinese Civil War, neither would military assistance or advice be furnished to Taiwan. So far as the administration was concerned, Taiwan had sufficient resources to defend the island. Assistance from the ECA would be continued.[97] Acheson quickly followed with a major speech delivered on 12 January, 1950 at the National Press Club. The speech was carefully prepared and given on the basis of 'a page or two of notes'.[98] It was a crisp, forthright address covering much ground but too explicit on a few aspects that would have been better cloaked with at least some opaqueness. Acheson emphasised that Chiang Kai-shek and his party had failed because of their own ineptitude and for no other reason. The Chinese communists had captured revolutionary nationalism 'and ridden to victory and power' on it.[99] The Soviet Union represented communist imperialism and was the enemy of China. Acheson next turned to military security: the essential line of defence for the United States lay in the chain of islands ranging from the Aleutians in the north through Japan to the Ryukyus and the Philippines. This line would be strongly defended. He did not refer to South Korea or Taiwan but the implication was unmistakably clear that these were not deemed vital in Washington. Acheson covered himself with a vague reference to the UN:

> So far as the military security of other areas in the Pacific is concerned, it must be clear that no person can guarantee these areas against military attack. ...
>
> Should such an attack occur ... the initial reliance must be on the people attacked to resist it and then upon the commitments of the entire civilized world under the Charter of the United Nations which so far has not proved a weak reed to lean on by any people who are determined to protect their independence against outside aggression.[100]

The statements of Truman and Acheson were too blunt, given the fact that it was arguably not in America's interest that Taiwan should fall within the near future and not desirable that South Korea should be liquidated. Hostages to fortune were given and the United States acted to assist South Korea and Taiwan within less than six months. The speeches could only have conveyed the impression that the United States was unlikely to act.

It was not tactically wise for Acheson to refer to Sino-Soviet relations in the way he did when the leaders of the two countries were engaged in lengthy, complex and probably acrid discussions from which emerged the Sino-Soviet treaty of February 1950. Mao Tse-tung had travelled to Moscow in December 1949 for his first excursion outside China. When he arrived at the railway station on 16 December he made a short speech paying tribute to Stalin's leadership of world communism but also indicating indirectly that China must be treated as a great nation and not in a position analogous to the satellite states of eastern Europe.[101] Difficult issues were bound to arise, the fundamental aspect being the incompatibility of two revolutionary movements that had come to power in very different ways with different cultures and attitudes. In more concrete terms problems surrounded the Russian presence in Manchuria and the arrangements that would obtain for the economic aid China required. It could be argued that the statements made by Truman and Acheson in January would allay Chinese suspicions and push Mao into a more obstinate response. Equally their remarks might be viewed as a crude attempt to drive China and the Soviet Union further apart. Again it might be said there was no impact on the Sino-Soviet talks. The duration of Mao's stay in Moscow provided evidence for the deduction that a harmonious identification of interests had not been arrived at. The British ambassador in Moscow, Sir David Kelly, reported on 31 January that it was most unusual for a visiting communist leader to remain for a period approaching seven weeks. Kelly's assessment was that both Stalin and Mao had been unyielding and that serious divergence had occurred.[102] Esler Dening of the British Foreign Office believed economic aspects, border problems affecting Sinkiang, Inner Mongolia and Manchuria, and Mao's inexperience of top-level diplomacy were the key features.[103] Chou En-lai arrived in Moscow a fortnight earlier, which showed that Chou's formidable diplomatic skills were required.[104] The British chargé d'affaires in China, Hutchison, was told that economic questions were the most contentious and that the talks were going badly.[105]

The Sino-Soviet agreements were signed in Moscow on 14 February. They comprised a treaty of friendship, alliance and mutual assistance, an agreement on the Chinese Changchun railway, Port Arthur and Dairen, an agreement extending credits from the Soviet Union to China, and two exchanges of notes, one of which abrogated the Sino-Soviet treaty of 1945. The texts were published in English in the *Soviet Monitor*. The treaty of alliance pledged joint cooperation against 'the rebirth of Japanese imperialism and a repetition of aggression on the part of Japan or any other State which should unite in any form with Japan in acts of aggression'.[106] Article I provided for full cooperation to meet any future threat posed by Japan: if Japan 'or States allied with it' attacked either Russia or China, the other would render military assistance. Article II called for the swift conclusion of a peace treaty with Japan, jointly with the other powers who had fought against Japan in the Second World War. Article III was a mutual pledge not to participate in a coalition against the other signatory. Article IV stipulated that consultation should take place on all major international matters. Article V was a statement of mutual respect with a promise to consolidate economic and cultural links and to render economic assistance to one another. Article VI indicated that it came into effect upon ratification. The concluding paragraph stated that the treaty would last for thirty years. In the agreement on Manchuria the Soviet Union transferred all its rights in the Chinese Changchun railway either upon conclusion of a peace treaty with Japan or not later than the end of

1952. The naval base at Port Arthur would be handed over to China by the end of 1952 at the latest. The future of Port Dalny would be determined on the conclusion of a peace treaty, but the administration of the port belonged to China. The economic agreement consisted of a Soviet undertaking to grant 300 million US dollars; credits would be on favourable terms of 1 per cent annual interest. China would redeem the credits, as well as paying interest with deliveries of raw materials, tea, gold, American dollars. Redemption of credits would be effected in ten years in equal annual parts.

The British Foreign Office's analysis of the cluster of agreements concluded that on the surface there was no indication of friction between the signatories and China would feel encouraged. If the treaty and agreements were examined more closely, however, the Soviet Union emerged as less generous. The treaty itself was in essence a propaganda instrument condemning the danger of a Japanese military revival. In a war the Soviet Union would gain more than China because in a Russo-American conflict the United States would probably use Japanese bases; in such circumstances China would most likely be committed to entering the war. Neither the United States nor Japan would, in all likelihood, become involved in hostilities with China alone and the Soviet guarantee was therefore less valuable. The Manchurian provisions did not have to be implemented before the end of 1952 and, it was prophetically observed, might not materialise even then. The financial credits, while possibly generous given Russia's own problems, were paltry when seen against the enormous problems facing China.[107]

The relevance of China to the outbreak of the Korean War is in the context of the sharp decline of Sino-American relations in the period after 1945. Many Americans were disillusioned with the incompetence of the Kuomintang; some believed the Truman administration had contributed, deliberately or through negligence, to the eclipse of Chiang Kai-shek. Chinese communism was viewed with suspicion or hostility by most Americans. It represented an alien ideology and might be no more than a branch of the Kremlin. Heightened domestic tensions in the utilisation of China by certain prominent members of the Republican Party accentuated the dimensions of the problem. Taiwan complicated matters greatly, since it was inextricably linked with the fate of Chiang Kai-shek, American strategy in the west Pacific, the role of General MacArthur, and American domestic politics. The Chinese communists felt much bitterness at the American aid to the Kuomintang, the rebuilding of Japan as a conceivable future threat under SCAP, and at American refusal to contemplate recognition of Peking or the latter's securing membership of the UN Security Council. Sino-Soviet relations were not close and contained great tensions but it was unlikely that a rift would occur for a number of years. A clash between the United States and China could easily arise at any time and might be precipitated by one of a range of issues.

# REFERENCES

1.  For a concise general survey of Sino-American relations in the twentieth century, see Michael Schaller, *The United States and China in the Twentieth Century* (New York 1979). For a valuable collection pursuing issues examined in this chapter, see Dorothy Borg and Waldo Heinrichs (eds), *Uncertain Years: Chinese-American Relations, 1947-1950* (Guildford 1980).

2   For Stilwell's graphic portrait of the difficulties encountered in grappling with the Kuomintang, see Theodore White (ed.), *The Stilwell Papers* (New York 1948). See also Barbara Tuchman, *Stilwell and the American Experience in China, 1911-45* (London 1970).

3.  See S. R. Schram, *Mao Zedong: A Preliminary Reassessment* (Hong Kong 1983) for a valuable analysis of Mao's impact upon the CCP. For the importance of the Yenan era, see Mark Selden, *The Yenan Way in Revolutionary China* (Cambridge, Mass. 1971).

4.  The nature of American policy in China is assessed cogently in N. B. Tucker, *Patterns in the Dust: Chinese-American Relations and the Recognition Controversy, 1949-1950* (New York 1983).

5.  See C. B. McLane, *Soviet Policy and the Chinese Communists, 1931-1946* (New York 1958).

6.  For a penetrating discussion of the conflict between the Kuomintang and the CCP, see Suzanne Pepper, *Civil War in China, 1945-49* (Berkeley and Los Angeles 1978).

7.  *FRUS 1948* (7), p. 12, Clark to Butterworth, 7 Jan. 1948.

8.  Ibid., p. 28, Stuart to Marshall, 9 Jan. 1948.

9.  Ibid.

10. Ibid., p. 103, Clubb to Marshall, 19 Feb. 1948.

11. *Manchester Guardian*, 23 Feb. 1948.

12. See A. H. Vandenberg, Jr (ed.), *The Private Papers of Senator Vandenberg* (London 1953), pp. 335, 351, 450-2. In an election broadcast in October 1948 Vandenberg stated that there were areas in which the bipartisan policy did not obtain and gave as examples China, Palestine and Japan, ibid., pp. 450-2.

13. Washington to FO, 27 March 1948, F4635/190/10, FO 371/69585.

14. Washington to FO, 12 March 1948, F4026/190/10, FO 371/69584.

15. *FRUS 1948* (7), pp. 348-51, Stuart to Marshall, 12 July 1948.

16. Ibid., p. 388, Stuart to Marshall, 30 July 1948.

17. Ibid., pp. 512-17, Lovett to Stuart, 26 Oct. 1948, enclosing Marshall to Stuart.

18. Dispatch, Stevenson to Bevin, 3 Nov. 1948, enclosing text of press interview, *New York Tribune*, 31 Oct. 1948, F16032/33/10, FO 371/69542.

19. See Pepper, op. cit., pp. 7-195, for the closing stages of Kuomintang rule on the mainland. See also R. M. Blum, *Drawing the Line: the Origin of the American Containment Policy in East Asia* (London, 1982).

20. 'Revolutionary forces of the world rally to combat imperialist aggression', enclosed with FO minutes in F16917/33/10, FO 371/69544.

21. Ibid.

22. Ibid.
23. UN General Assembly, Paris (UK delegation), to FO, 20 Nov. 1948, F16331/190/10, FO 371/69586.
24. For MacArthur's advocacy of funds and military assistance to the Kuomintang government, see Tucker, op.cit., pp. 182, 185, 187, and W. W. Stueck, Jr, *The Road to Confrontation* (Chapel Hill, NC 1981), pp. 39–40.
25. UN General Assembly, Paris (UK delegation) to FO, 20 Nov. 1948, F16331/190/10, FO 371/69586.
26. Ibid.
27. Ibid.
28. See draft NSC assessment on United States aims in China, 24 March 1948, NSC 6, *FRUS 1948* (8), pp. 44–5, and ibid., memorandum by Policy Planning Staff, 7 Sept. 1948.
29. For a lucid account of the British perspective, see Ritchie Ovendale, 'Britain, the United States, and the recognition of Communist China', *Historical Journal*, **26** (March 1983), pp. 139–58.
30. See G. F. Kennan, *Memoirs, 1925–1950* (London 1968), pp. 250–1, 294, 319–20, 322, 358–9.
31. Vandenberg (ed.), op. cit., p. 469.
32. For Truman's views, see H. S. Truman, *Memoirs: Years of Trial and Hope, 1946—52*, paperback edn (New York 1965), pp. 485–9. For Acheson's views, see Dean Acheson, *Present at the Creation: My Years in the State Department* (London 1970), p. 366.
33. Letter from Graves to Scarlett, 5 Jan. 1949, F415/1023/10, FO 371/75810.
34. FO to Washington, 18 March 1949, F3505/1023/10, ibid.
35. *FRUS 1949* (9), 826–34, NSC report, NSC 41, 28 Feb. 1949.
36. Ibid., pp. 974–6, Clubb to Acheson, 30 April 1949.
37. Ibid., pp. 982–3, Smyth to Acheson, 11 May 1949.
38. Ibid., pp. 985–6, Webb to Clubb, 27 May 1949.
39. Ibid., pp. 990–1, Webb to Clubb, 21 June 1949, with a footnote on pp. 990–1 summarising a report from the counsellor of mission in Japan (Huston) dated 6 July.
40. Ibid., pp. 262–30, memorandum by Lapham, sent to Hoffman (ECA administrator), 9 March 1949.
41. Ibid., p. 616, memorandum prepared in the Office of Far Eastern Affairs, 25 Jan. 1949.
42. Ibid., pp. 656–67, report from Lapham to Hoffman, 30 June 1949.
43. Ibid., p. 309, letter from Cabot to Butterworth, 11 May 1949.
44. Ibid., p. 310.
45. Ibid., pp. 356–7, Cabot to Acheson, 31 May 1949.
46. Ibid., pp. 357–60, Cabot to Acheson, 1 June 1949.
47. Ibid., pp. 384–5, Webb to Clubb, 14 June 1949.
48. Ibid., pp. 392–4, Clubb to Acheson, 20 June 1949.
49. Ibid., pp. 405–7, Stuart to Acheson, 6 July 1949.
50. Ibid., pp. 436–40, Cabot to Acheson, 16 July 1949.
51. Ibid., pp. 430–5, memorandum by Stuart, 14 July 1949.
52. Letter from Lewis Douglas (US ambassador) to Bevin, 22 July 1949, F10976/1023/10G, FO 371/75813.

53. Memorandum enclosed in letter from Douglas to Bevin, ibid.
54. Letter from Bevin to Douglas, 22 July 1949, ibid.
55. FO memorandum, 8 Aug 1949, F11653/1023/10, ibid.
56. Ibid.
57. *FRUS 1949* (9), pp. 870–1, memorandum by Merchant to Sprouse, based on conversation with Rusk, 24 Aug. 1949.
58. Memorandum by Battle on conversation between Acheson and Dewey, 21 Sept. 1949, folder September 1949, box 64, Acheson Papers, Truman Library.
59. *FRUS 1949* (9), p. 582, memorandum, undated, unsigned, enclosed in Webb to Butterworth, 14 Nov. 1949 (pp. 582–8).
60. Ibid., pp. 586–8.
61. Commonwealth Relations Office to various Commonwealth members, 1 Sept. 1949, F13271/1023/10, FO 371/75814.
62. Conversation between Bevin and Douglas, 26 Aug. 1949, F12843/1028/10, ibid.
63. Nanking to FO, 1 Oct. 1949, F14782/1023/10, FO 371/75816.
64. FO to Paris (and other capitals), 5 Oct. 1949, ibid.
65. FO to Paris (and other capitals), 10 Oct 1949, F14878/1023/10, ibid.
66. Ibid.
67. Washington to FO, 1 Nov. 1949, F16417/1023/10, FO 371/75818.
68. *New York Times*, 17 Oct. 1949, and *Washington Post*, 18 Oct. 1949 and 16 Nov. 1949. On the latter occasion the *Post* stated a government should be recognised when clearly in control of a country, as laid down many years before by Secretary Buchanan. However, the case of China was complicated by the detention of Angus Ward, the consul-general in Tientsin; it was possible that the Soviet Union had been involved in Ward's incarceration, according to the *Post*.
69. FO to Washington, 16 Dec. 1949, F19057/1023/10, FO 371/75828.
70. FO to Nanking, 23 Dec. 1949, F18896/1023/10, FO 371/75827.
71. FO to Tamsui (Taiwan), 3 Jan. 1950, ibid.
72. Tucker, op. cit., p. 191.
73. Biggs (British consul, Tamsui) to Lamb (British embassy, Nanking), 24 July 1948, F15592/565/10, FO 371/69621.
74. Report in *The Times*, 20 July 1949.
75. Biggs to Lamb, 12 Oct. 1948, F15622/565/10, FO 371/69621.
76. Tokyo to FO, 17 Sept. 1949, F14000/1015/10G, FO 371/75770.
77. Ibid.
78. CIA memorandum by Hillenkoetter, 21 Nov. 1949, sanitised copy, folder CIA memoranda, 1949, Harry S. Truman Papers, PSF, Truman Library.
79. Ibid.
80. *FRUS 1949* (9), pp. 261–2, NSC 37, note by Souers, 1 Dec. 1948, enclosing memorandum from joint chiefs of staff to Forrestal, 24 Nov. 1948.
81. Ibid., pp. 971–5, NSC 37/1, draft report by NSC, 19 Jan. 1949.
82. Ibid., pp. 284–6, NSC 37/3, memorandum by joint chiefs of staff to Forrestal, 10 Feb. 1949.
83. Ibid., pp. 294–6, memorandum by Souers, 3 March 1949, enclosing statement by Acheson at NSC.
84. Ibid., pp. 356–64, memorandum by Kennan, 6 July 1949, and pp. 369–71, memorandum from State Department to Souers, 4 Aug. 1949.

85.  Ibid., pp. 376–8, memorandum by JCS, 22 Aug. 1949.
86.  Ibid., pp. 392–7, NSC 37/8, note by Souers, 6 Oct. 1949, enclosing draft memorandum.
87.  Memorandum by Voorhees to Johnson, 14 Dec. 1949, Formosa file, RG6, box 8, MacArthur Memorial.
88.  Ibid.
89.  Ibid.
90.  Memorandum from Johnson to Truman, 15 Dec. 1949, ibid.
91.  *FRUS 1949* (9), pp. 460–1, note by Souers, 7 Dec. 1949, enclosing joint chiefs of staff memorandum, 23 Dec. 1949.
92.  Memorandum by Acheson, 17 Nov. 1949, folder, memorandum of conversations, November 1949, box 64, Acheson Papers, Truman Library.
93.  *FRUS 1949* (9), p. 464, memorandum by Acheson, 29 Dec. 1949.
94.  Ibid., p. 466.
95.  Acheson, op.cit., p. 350.
96.  Ibid., p. 351.
97.  Ibid., p. 354.
98.  Ibid., p. 356.
99.  Ibid., p. 357.
100. Ibid.
101. *FRUS 1949* (8), p. 642, Kirk to Acheson, 21 Dec. 1949.
102. Moscow to FO, 31 Jan. 1950, FC10338/29A, FO 371/83313.
103. Minute by Dening, 2 Feb. 1950, ibid.
104. A lively portrait of Chou En-lai is to be found in Dick Wilson, *Chou: The Story of Zhou Enlai, 1898–1976* (London 1984).
105. Nanking to FO, 6 Feb 1950, FC10338/33, FO 371/83314.
106. 'Treaty of friendship, alliance and mutual assistance between the USSR and the People's Republic of China', 14 Feb. 1950, reproduced in FC10338/88, FO 371/83315.
107. Analysis of treaty and agreements, Far Eastern Department, 13 March 1950, ibid.

# Chapter 6

# THE COLD WAR IN EUROPE

Developments in Europe after 1945 were vitally important for establishing the attitudes that were to determine the western response to the crisis in Korea in June 1950. The Soviet Union was viewed in the United States and Britain as dangerously expansionist, intent on exploiting every opportunity that occurred in order to extend Soviet dominance. The Americans were obsessed by 1950 with the extreme menace of communism as an ideology and believed that the Kremlin manipulated events so as to secure the advancement of Marxist-Leninist concepts. The British were alarmed, too, by the ideology but did not reveal the extremes manifested in the United States and were perhaps more preoccupied with Russia as a great power. By 1950 a third world war was regarded as very possible but this prospect was held in check by the realisation of the full horrors that would be engendered through it, particularly since the Soviet Union had exploded the first atomic weapon in 1949. The growth of the Cold War had thus produced an uneasy armed peace and an atmosphere of deep tension in which any serious incident could escalate out of control unless handled with meticulous awareness of the potential consequences. This was so different from the optimism of the alliance between the Soviet Union, the United States and Britain between 1941 and 1945 when it was believed that genuine cooperation, despite some unavoidable differences of opinion, could be continued following the defeat of Germany and Japan. The emerging rift between East and West was the product of the Soviet desire for security in central and eastern Europe, of the erratic recovery of western Europe and a determination to resist Soviet pressure, and of the consensus within the American establishment that the security of the United States necessitated the pursuance of an interventionist policy in Europe. The traditional view of the origins and course of the Cold War held in the West saw the struggle as the outcome of unprovoked aggression by the Soviet Union, which was intent upon controlling as much of Europe as possible and with extending Soviet dominance into the Middle East and Far East. Revisionist interpretations have depicted the Soviet Union as a defensive if not passive agent and have regarded American policy as assertive, motivated by hatred of communism and by a wish to seize every chance to promote the interests of American capitalism. Neither interpretation is convincing as stated; the Cold War resulted from actions, calculated and mistaken, for which East and West were held responsible and it is not convincing to see it as solely or overwhelmingly the responsibility of either side. The Cold War was a traditional contest between two great powers, accentuated by the role of ideology and transformed by the scope of the weapons of mass destruction available.[1]

The central personalities in the confrontation were Joseph Stalin and Harry Truman. Much remains obscure over the conduct of Soviet foreign policy and over the functioning of the Kremlin, given the inaccessibility of Soviet records. The broad features of Stalin's policy-making appear clear even though the finer points remain a matter of speculation. Stalin was utterly ruthless, cynical and opportunistic. The savagery and suffering of his rule in the Soviet Union from the 1920s to the 1950s is abundantly demonstrated in the massive purges of Russian society, of the Communist Party, and of the Red Army for which he was responsible; the 'Gulag' labour and death camps were poignant evidence of extreme totalitarianism as implemented by a malevolent dictator. Stalin's domestic policies of rapid industrialisation and drastic suppression of actual or potential internal opposition resulted from his appreciation of the dangers posed by Russia's isolated world position and from his own pathological fear of a challenge to his leadership.[2] Stalin was determined to avoid a repetition of the circumstances in which the Soviet Union had been propelled into the Second World War in June 1941; this was the principal reason for the swift consolidation of Russian control in central and eastern Europe immediately before and after the Second World War. Contrary to the impression often illustrated in western pronouncements, Stalin was not interested in conquering western Europe or other strategic areas in the Middle East or Far East. Naturally he would utilise the opportunities presented by fate but Stalin was inherently cautious and unadventurous. Russia was still in the early stages of recovering from the traumatic experience of the struggle against Germany and was in no state to contemplate participation in a major war.

Harry Truman was one of the few American presidents to come from the Midwest or Far West; he came from a humble background and had advanced his career through native wit and shrewdness. Truman never possessed great personal wealth and was not particularly interested in material rewards. He was driven on by a staunch sense of duty and patriotism together with a relatively uncomplicated view of the world: the United States stood for freedom and decency and the Soviet Union for repression and enslavement. Truman was forthright, vigorous, indomitable. His domestic position before the election in 1948 was not strong for he had succeeded to the presidency with scant preparation on the sudden death of Franklin Roosevelt in April 1945 and was considered by many to be an interim incumbent of the White House. The Republicans had taken control of both the House of Representatives and of the Senate in 1946 and were supremely confident of winning in 1948.[3] After eighteen months' experience of dealing with the Russians, Truman wrote in a private letter: 'There is too much loose talk about the Russian situation. We are not going to have any shooting trouble with them, but they are tough bargainers and always ask for the whole earth, expecting maybe to get an acre.'[4] Truman therefore favoured a resolute policy in the belief that this would avert conflict if consistently pursued. The President held that the United States must play an active part in world affairs and could not retreat into the deceptive isolationist opinions that had prevailed for much of the interwar era. At least from 1946 Truman supported an interventionist policy but it was imperative to ensure that this commanded bipartisan endorsement in Congress. In this context he obtained immense assistance from Senator Arthur H. Vandenberg of Michigan, from Governor Thomas E. Dewey of New York and from John Foster Dulles, a leading authority on foreign relations in the Republican Party.

The chief landmarks in the construction of American policy were the acceptance of the need to assist Greece and Turkey when Britain decided she could no longer sustain a major commitment to Greece, the announcement of the Truman Doctrine, and the commitment to Marshall Aid to help European recovery. In 1945–47 rapid demobilisation of American forces was accomplished in a period when the longer-term aims had not been defined; while relations with Moscow were gradually deteriorating, Secretary of State James F. Byrnes tried to maintain an effective dialogue and was less inclined than Truman towards an obstructionist line.[5] Given the serious divergences over Poland, Germany and eastern Europe, it was impossible to sustain a meaningful exchange. Byrnes was too assertive and ambitious for Truman's liking and was dismissed at the beginning of 1947 to be replaced by General George Marshall. Marshall possessed enormous experience of the Washington bureaucracy and was capable, loyal and devoid of personal ambition; his health was not good and he served through a strong sense of responsibility to his country. Marshall entirely endorsed Truman's view that Europe was the priority and that American commitments should be stipulated with some urgency. The Truman Doctrine, enunciated in March 1947, was a response to British inability to fulfil obligations to Greece and to the President's belief that the time had come for an uncompromising statement of American intentions. Truman had been present at Winston Churchill's famous address in June 1946 at Fulton, Missouri when the former Prime Minister had sombrely described the descent of an 'iron curtain' across much of Europe. Evidently Truman had concurred in Churchill's appraisal but had not deemed the moment opportune for a statement of his own. The Truman Doctrine was a fundamental statement of policy which became enshrined as a basic constituent until the later stages of the Vietnam War. The United States was committed, subject to congressional approval of necessary funds, to assisting any free country threatened with subversion. The statement was designed, of course, to meet a particular situation but it did so in terms that were too sweeping and insufficiently qualified by the peculiar features that would distinguish specific problems when these arose. However, it served the purpose of awakening American public opinion and of paving the way for developments in the next two years.

Marshall Aid connoted the recognition by the State Department of the demoralised state of western Europe and of the need to promote economic and political recovery. Marshall put forward his ideas in a speech at Harvard in June 1947 and Ernest Bevin, the British Foreign Secretary, took the initiative in urging the application of Marshall's prescription.[6] In a penetrating reassessment of European recovery from 1947 to 1953, Alan Milward has argued that the basic economic revival already existed before the commencement of Marshall Aid and that the significance of the American contribution was political rather than economic.[7] This would seem convincing but contemporaneously the American role in the economic revitalisation of western Europe was regarded as extremely significant. The Soviet Union regarded the development of American policy in 1947 as a direct threat to Russian interests and would not permit the states of eastern Europe to accept Marshall Aid.

The British government warmly welcomed the more forthright direction of American policy. The Labour administration of Clement Attlee was committed to innovative economic and social policies at home and to solving urgently British responsibilities in the Indian sub-continent, Burma and in Palestine. The base of the British economy was now so weakened that it was impossible for Britain to accomplish an active policy of blocking Soviet expansion. The United States was regarded with a mixture of awe and exasperation. The power of the American economy was unquestioned and the resources of the United States could make a huge contribution to resisting the Soviet Union. Past American policies had been marked by tergiversations of unpredictable character and the fear entertained by Attlee, Bevin and their colleagues was that the United States might underreact or overreact in combating a Soviet probe. What the Washington bureaucracy lacked was the experience of British officials in navigating complex issues.[8] Some consideration was devoted in London to the possibility of a third force being constructed from the British Commonwealth and western Europe to stand on a basis of autonomy alongside the United States and the Soviet Union. This was attractive to those who harboured doubts on American reliability and to those who disliked America. It was formally considered by a committee headed by the permanent Under-Secretary to the Foreign Office, Sir William Strang, in 1949. The concept of the 'Third Power' was rejected for several reasons. The British Commonwealth was in no sense a homogeneous unit and had been developing along increasingly independent lines since the First World War. While there were still important links with the Commonwealth, it could not be seen as containing the prospect of a new power. A powerful western Europe was not feasible and could only be achieved in future through the remilitarisation of Germany. American assistance was making and would continue to make a distinct major contribution to the security of western Europe. The latter should prove more capable within the next ten to twenty years of defending itself but a close relationship with the United States should still exist. The only suitable conclusion was that the trend of the previous two years should be pursued for the foreseeable future.[9]

In the intensification of the Cold War in Europe two crises were responsible more than anything else for sharpening the acrimony – the communist assumption of full power in Czechoslovakia in February and the Berlin blockade, which lasted from June 1948 to May 1949. These events repay careful study. There was nothing surprising over the course of events in Czechoslovakia between 1945 and 1948: if there is an element of surprise, it is occasioned by the precise timing rather than the outcome. When Czechoslovakia came into existence after the First World War, it was effectively controlled by the political forces of the moderate centre; communism did not pose a significant threat and the most ominous feature concerned agitation among the Sudeten Germans, exacerbated by Hitler's attainment of office. Conservatism and bourgeois liberalism were equally discredited by the Munich settlement of September 1938 followed by the complete German absorption of the state in March 1939. Czechoslovakia's independence had been surrendered without a fight: the Communist Party could benefit in representing nationalism and the desire for radical social reform. Edward Benes, the leading moderate after the death of Thomas Masaryk, led a government-in-exile in London during the war and returned to Prague in 1945, believing he could preserve the independence of his country through following a policy acceptable to Moscow and through manipulating the parties belonging to the newly formed grand coalition government. Benes's errors were to underestimate the Communist Party, to overestimate the resolution of the non-communist parties, and to misjudge the impact of external developments on the fate of Czechoslovakia.[10] Czechoslovakia functioned on the basis of limited independence from 1945 to 1948. The principal examples of independence were afforded by President Benes himself, the existence of political pluralism, the strength of the non-communist political groups in Slovakia, the fact that the army was predominantly officered by prewar personnel rather than by communist officers, and that all were aware of the delicate nature of the political equilibrium within the country. Against this was the powerful position held by the Communist Party in Bohemia and Moravia, the brooding presence of the Soviet army on Czechoslovakia's frontiers, and the problems of preserving independence when relations between the Soviet Union and the United States were rapidly worsening. In the general election of May 1946 the Communist Party secured approximately 40 per cent of the votes in Bohemia and Moravia, emerging as the largest single party with 93 seats; the next largest, the National Socialists, obtained approximately 24 per cent and possessed 55 seats (the National Socialists comprised a party of moderate bourgeois character led by supporters of Benes – they should not be confused with German National Socialism).[11] The government was a coalition comprising Communists, National Socialists, People's Party and the Social Democrats. In Slovakia the Democratic Party was the strongest with about 61 per cent of the votes and 43 seats; the Communist Party obtained about 30 per cent and 21 seats.[12] The Communist Party gained appreciably from the Russian role in liberating the country and from the prominent communist participation in the resistance movement: party membership increased dramatically from approximately 28,000 before 1938 to 50,000 in 1945 and at least 1 million in the spring of 1946.[13] The communists enjoyed a strong power base among the working class; trade unions were powerful and party members were particularly active within them.

In the main the government worked effectively to 1947; this was achieved through acceptance of reforming policies and by each of the parties subordinating ulterior aims to the maintenance of the administration. However, the Communists held a number of leading posts, most crucially the Ministry of Interior, which controlled the police; there is no doubt that the police force was organised as the Communists desired and this was highly significant in 1948. Friction developed within the government in 1947 as a consequence of the problems encountered in the economy and of rivalry connected with the impending general election in May 1948. Rumours circulated that the Communists might be forced out of the government or that Benes might install a non-communist as Prime Minister in place of Gottwald.[14] There was little the United States could do to influence developments other than influencing the form of commercial and cultural agreements.[15] Tension increased in January and early February 1948 amid alarm by the more right-wing parties in the Prague government at further communist interference with police appointments. A British official remarked that the Czechs were 'notoriously a nation of calculators and fence sitters' and supported the opinion of the British representative in Prague, Sir Pierson Dixon, that: ' ... the present political situation in Czechoslovakia is like a house of straw. If the Communists blow, the whole edifice will collapse.'[16] Dixon saw Benes on 11 February and conveyed a message of support from Bevin with a request for a frank statement of the situation as perceived by Benes. The President was optimistic and felt that the danger of a communist coup could be avoided. However, Dixon was struck by Benes's poor health and difficulty in speaking clearly. Benes was insistent that the collapse of democracy could be 'absolutely excluded' and asked Dixon to communicate this to Bevin.[17]

The crisis came to a head on 13 February when the members of the National Socialist, People's and Democratic parties tendered their resignations in protest at communist policy regarding the police.[18] It was a singularly foolish step, since they had no clear idea of what they would do afterwards and there was no anticipation of the ruthlessness with which the Communists would respond to the opportunity. The Communists had been afraid of losing support in the coming elections and now had the chance to strengthen their position irreversibly. The Communist Party used its strength in the trade unions and associated bodies to rally support on the grounds of a bourgeois reactionary threat to the achievements of the state since 1945. Speculation in the West centred on the role in the crisis played by the Soviet Union. Zorin, a deputy Soviet Foreign Minister, was in Prague in February and was involved in consultations with Czechoslovak Communist leaders.[19] However, it is unlikely that the Soviet Union masterminded the whole operation; rather the Czech party had been preparing itself for assertive action for some months and the naïvety of the other parties afforded them the opportunity.[20] Benes vacillated amid Communist-organised demonstrations; he could have dismissed the Communist ministers and called on the army to intervene. He feared that bloodshed would occur in such an eventuality and his own bad health doubtless contributed to his decision to acquiesce. His irresolution was equalled by that of the leaders of the non-communist parties, none of whom showed any wish to resist the Communists. Gottwald, Zapotocky and their colleagues decided to form a new government and to exclude anybody from other parties who could not be relied on to be subservient; this would soon be followed by an extensive purge and consolidation of the Communist regime. Faced with mass demonstrations on 24–25 February, Benes capitulated and accepted the composition of the government proposed by the Communists.[21] The American and British governments watched events helplessly. Lewis Douglas, the American ambassador, saw Bevin at the House of Commons on 25 February and inquired what if anything could be done to assist the Czechs. Bevin replied:

> ... that I did not think it would do any good. It was too late and the sending of notes was of no avail. The only thing which could stop communism from carrying out the same policy right through Europe was action and unless the Western Powers, including the United States, were prepared to discuss action I thought Italy might go next.[22]

General Marshall's view was similar to Bevin's: nothing could be done directly but the right lessons should be drawn for other parts of Europe.

Jan Masaryk remained in the government as non-party Foreign Minister, apparently in the hope that he could exert a moderating influence. In talking to the American ambassador on 27 February Masaryk claimed to have saved the lives of some 250 people. He described Benes as a broken figure and had tears in his eyes as he conceded that the Communists now dominated the government completely.[23] On 10 March Masaryk's body was found beneath the windows of the Foreign Ministry. It is unclear whether he committed suicide or was murdered; it is probable that it was suicide, as the only honourable way out for Masaryk, who had been criticised by opponents of communism for remaining in the government. In addition, suicide was one form of protest designed to embarrass the new regime when it was seeking to establish its credibility.[24] Benes wished to resign but was persuaded by Gottwald to continue for the time being. He was physically and psychologically exhausted, as all he had wished to achieve vanished as Czechoslovakia slid totally into the Soviet orbit. He strongly disapproved of the nature of the new government, of the proposed constitution, and of the elections, now to be held under vigorous intimidation and direction. Benes told the American ambassador on 29 May 1948, that he firmly condemned communist methods in seizing power and was determined to resign.[25] He did resign on 7 June and was succeeded as President by Zapotocky. The Communist Party now occupied significant positions of authority. The result of the Czechoslovak crisis in 1948 was predictable and had been since at least 1945. It was, however, strange that the non-communist parties had so played into the hands of the Communists and that Benes, too, had gravely underestimated Communist intentions.[26] The real importance of the crisis in its wider effects is that it heightened tension in the Cold War and accentuated apprehension over a Soviet attempt to extend communism elsewhere, perhaps to west Berlin.

The Berlin crisis of 1948–49 was the most dangerous menace to world peace before the start of the Korean War. It originated in the growing divergence of aims for the future administration of Germany between the four occupying powers, the United States, Britain, France and the Soviet Union. Was Germany to remain divided and, if so, under what constitutional provisions? Where would Berlin fit into whatever pattern emerged? Among the three western powers differences of opinion existed, particularly because of French insistence that Germany must not be permitted to develop in such a manner as conceivably to threaten European peace for a third time. Accordingly France had argued in favour of maintaining the division of Germany, of restricting the economic growth of west Germany, and of preventing rearmament. Britain sympathised with France to some extent but held that political and economic realities meant that advances had to be made in the direction of the restoration of autonomy so long as certain safeguards were incorporated. The United States was conscious of the vulnerability of the western-occupied zones to possible Soviet expansion and wished to proceed more rapidly towards the creation of a west German state. The Soviet Union was deeply distrustful of any moves culminating in an independent German state. However, as Avi Shlaim has remarked, there was ambiguity as to whether Russia wished to see a weak, divided Germany for the foreseeable future or whether a communist state should be fostered.[27] Berlin itself was situated well within the Soviet zone and was divided into two parts, which coexisted uneasily and with growing difficulty. The political trends within east and west Germany were markedly divergent in 1947–48 and a confrontation surrounding Berlin was highly probable. Western preparations for such an eventuality were slight and the implementation of the measures to beat the Soviet blockade were far more successful than was believed possible when the crisis began. The governor of the American zone, General Lucius D. Clay, was a tough, unpretentious southerner, vehemently hostile to communism and contending that the only method of dealing with the Russians successfully was to be adamant and refuse to be intimidated. Clay felt war could probably be averted through an unyielding response; his views had considerable impact in Washington and Clay acted on occasion with astonishing independence in taking crucial decisions.[28] The failure of the meeting of foreign ministers representing the occupying powers at the end of 1947 resulted in the United States and Britain moving towards establishing a separate state in west Germany; this was the first step in precipitating the crisis.[29] Soviet suspicion of western intentions were in part understandable, according to Kenneth Royall, Secretary of the Army, in a private letter written in April 1948:

> The Soviets have some basis for their argument in view of the tripartite actions we have been forced to take regarding Germany, as a result of the breakdown of the Council of Ministers last December. They can argue with some logic that the Three Power talks on Germany, initiated in London in February ... are proof of our intention to abandon four-power control.[30]

At the end of February 1948 the British Foreign Office considered the situation to be dangerous and it would be necessary to pursue a resolute yet prudent policy. Determination to remain in Berlin despite Soviet pressure must be conveyed but 'bombastic' utterances eschewed. Circumstances might arise in which western withdrawal from Berlin might be unavoidable but in such a contingency the western powers themselves should decide the timing of withdrawal and not allow the Russians to do so.[31] Ernest Bevin attached great importance to standing firm after developments in Czechoslovakia. The Foreign Office advised Bevin that there were two courses of action: a planned withdrawal from

Berlin as part of a new approach to governing west Germany or to remain in Berlin for the near future while recognising that withdrawal would have to be effective when the western presence became physically untenable. Bevin grimly minuted, 'We must stay.'[32] British policy-makers were concerned that General Clay might overreact and were not mollified by Clay's observations when he met Sir William Strang and General Robertson, the British commandant, on 28 April:

> He thinks that the Russians consider it so vital to get us out of Berlin that they will face the prospect of war in doing so, though they may try to contrive that we fire the first shot. He regards an early war with the Soviet Union as inevitable, i.e. within the next year or 18 months, and judges that on a comparison of present and future resources on the two sides the Soviet Government would think it advantageous not to wait too long. He believes that the Russians will progressively intensify their pressure and that a point will sooner or later be reached – and it may well be sooner – at which we shall have to face the alternatives of war or of ignominious retreat from Berlin. He does not think that the US public would tolerate the piling up of indignities upon the American forces in Berlin and will demand that the situation be resolved at some point either by action or by withdrawal. But even before this point is reached, he thinks that there may be shooting on one side or the other and that this will mean war.[33]

Strang informed Clay that Britain wished the western presence to be maintained but any incidents that arose need not lead to conflict: some could be isolated. Strang conceded that if a Soviet blockade was applied stringently, western withdrawal might be inevitable. Clay reiterated that American opinion would not accept humiliation.[34]

The issue that prompted the breakdown of exchanges between the Soviet Union and the West was that of currency reform. It had originally been hoped that agreement could be reached for a joint policy to be formulated and discussion to this end proceeded between April and June 1948. Clay advocated the attainment of a monetary union embracing Berlin and the Soviet zone on the understanding that four-power agreement between the respective commandants determined the quantity of Soviet marks to be circulated.[35] The French were reluctant to risk a breach with Moscow and only concurred reluctantly in Clay's preparations for introducing the new currency.[36] The aim was to introduce the new currency on 20 June. Clay fully appreciated that a unilateral decision to introduce the new currency would be seen by the Russians as provocative but he held that it was imperative to act firmly.[37] On 16 June relations deteriorated with a Soviet departure from a meeting of the Berlin Kommandatura because of an alleged insult from the outspoken American commandant, Colonel Frank (Howlin' Mad) Howley.[38] When Clay officially informed the Russians that the currency changes would be applied as from 20 June the Soviet Union acted to halt rail and road traffic in and out of Berlin and subjected freight to tight regulation, supposedly to prevent increased circulation of the discarded currency. The Russian military governor, Marshal Sokolovsky, accused the western powers of rupturing existing agreements. He threatened to establish a new currency in Soviet-controlled territory, including Berlin.[39] Clay responded diplomatically by offering to discuss the position to see if an agreed solution could be secured. A meeting took place on 22 June but broke down because of the Russian insistence that the Soviet Union alone should control arrangements concerning circulation of the Soviet mark.[40] Clay then decided without consulting his government to use the authority he had been given two months earlier to implement the new currency scheme. Clay therefore announced his decision on 23 June. As Avi Shlaim has commented, this decision was wholly in keeping with Clay's personality and conduct but is none the less remarkable, given the consequences that swiftly ensued.[41]

President Truman, General Marshall and the joint chiefs of staff were agreed there must be no appeasement in Berlin but it took a little time to assess the magnitude of the problems involved in organising a massive airlift. In London Bevin emphasised to the American ambassador that the repercussions of withdrawal from Berlin would be catastrophic – 'We should not be able to hold western Germany if we quitted Berlin.'[42] Bevin consulted colleagues and officials and told them that Britain must contribute as effectively as possible to an airlift: 'He did not imagine that it would be possible to feed two million Germans, but he wanted to make a big display in order to keep up morale in Germany and perhaps lead the Russians to think that we were preparing to reinforce the Berlin garrison.'[43] The challenge inherent in organising an airlift on such a scale was huge. The quantities of vital commodities to be carried, the numbers of aircraft, the vagaries of the weather (especially in winter), and the density of population in west Berlin combined to raise grave doubts as to the success of the operation. Truman had no reservations upon attempting it: he believed in dealing powerfully with the Russians and realised that he could win the presidential election in November 1948 only by conveying decisive leadership to the American nation. By any criterion the airlift was an astonishing success and was responsible for the failure of the sustained Soviet endeavour to compel a western retreat. The airlift was begun on General Clay's instructions on 28 June 1948; the blockade lasted until 11 May 1949. According to figures provided by the British Air Ministry in May 1949, during the 318 days that the airlift had functioned, British and American aircraft made 195,530 flights to Berlin carrying 1,583,686 tons of food, coal and other goods (the standard airlift measure was the American short ton of 2,000 pounds weight). British aircraft fulfilled 63,612 flights and 369,347 tons and American aircraft 131,918 flights and 1,214,339 tons. British aircraft carried from Berlin approximately 30,000 tons and over 65,000 passengers. When the airlift commenced, the monthly total carried was 69,000 tons carried in 13,500 flights; in April 1949 the total carried was

235,360 tons in 26,000 flights. Britain dealt with about a quarter of the flights and had arranged the larger part of the ground organisation: six of the eight key airfields were situated in the British zone of Germany and the most significant airfield in Berlin was the RAF one at Gatow. Perspective on the nature of the operation was shown by the fact that the expectation at the end of January 1948 had been that approximately 750 tons a day would be carried but this was increased to 1,200 tons a day by the middle of August. By May 1949 the British contribution amounted to about 2,000 tons a day. The highest total carried by the British and Americans was achieved on 16 April 1949 with a figure of 12,940 tons.[44]

However, it took a lengthy period, essentially until the worst of the winter had passed before the full success of the airlift could be assured. The Soviet Union adopted a stance of being willing to discuss matters but not to the point of compromising sufficiently to achieve a settlement. In retrospect it is clear that this was designed to ensure the crisis did not escalate out of control but equally that western resolve was tested to the maximum extent through the duration of the blockade. The first important meeting in Moscow took place on 3 August 1948, when Stalin met western representatives. Stalin depicted himself as eminently reasonable and put the blame for the confrontation on western shoulders. He made no effort to conceal the fact that the political moves in west Germany indicating the intention to establish a state based at Frankfurt plus the decision to enforce currency reform were the causes of the crisis.[45] Stalin stressed there was no Soviet aim of expelling allied forces from Berlin. The western emissaries urged steps to resolve the currency impasse and the lifting of blockade restrictions to be followed by a four-power conference on the wider questions covering the future of Germany. Stalin welcomed the proposal to hold a conference but urged the political developments in west Germany be suspended and the new B mark in west Berlin abolished.[46] Near the end of the conversation he proposed the introduction of the Soviet Deutsche mark in West Berlin and the ending of transport restrictions; he was prepared to make the concession of no longer requiring the withdrawal of the political decisions regarding west Germany but he would place on record formally the Soviet government's wish that this be done.[47] The meeting ended on an amicable note. General Bedell Smith, the American ambassador in Moscow, felt it might be feasible to reach agreement on the basis suggested by Stalin: western policy over the currency issue had been confused and it was best to terminate it by accepting the Soviet currency provided the terms were clear and tolerable. On the political aspects, Bedell Smith deferred to his political masters in Washington but implied that agreement should be reached if this could be done without loss of face.[48]

The vital feature was whether the Soviet Union would not accept quadripartite control of currency in Berlin: sole Russian control was unacceptable. In subsequent talks with Molotov more difficulties were encountered, although these did not seem insurmountable. Agreement was reached on 30 August that the military governors in Berlin should examine suitable arrangements for ending the blockade and for implementing the Soviet currency in Berlin on a quadripartite basis. The military governors began a series of meetings on 31 August in Berlin but Marshal Sokolovsky proved obdurate and went back on undertakings given in the Moscow talks. Robert Murphy, Clay's political adviser, described the atmosphere on 7 September as deteriorating. It was obvious that Moscow had no intention of compromising and wished to possess sole control of currency. The Soviets were indeed creating tension in Berlin through the organisation of demonstrations aimed at preventing the city assembly from functioning.[49] Truman and Marshall decided that the talks had proved futile and that it was necessary to show that Soviet tactics would not be tolerated. Soon afterwards the Berlin question was raised in the UN Security Council at America's request; the Soviet Union objected and refused to participate in discussions on the subject.[50]

In early October Marshall, Bevin and the French Foreign Minister, Robert Schuman, met in Paris. Bevin reiterated how essential it was to be resolute; Russian actions in Hungary, Czechoslovakia and before that in Poland were intolerable:

> Until we had made Western Europe and Western Germany stronger we must hold on resolutely to the Berlin salient.
> ... At present ... nothing was sufficiently organised to prevent a Communist onrush into Western Europe. We must, therefore, continue with building up as rapidly as possible the economic and political strength of Western Europe behind the Berlin salient. We could do a great deal by resolute action within the next three or four months, whereas if we thought now in terms of retreat the effect would be disastrous.[51]

Marshall replied that the western position had been strengthened significantly in recent months and he alluded to the relevance of the atomic weapon:

> He did not like to lay too much stress on the atomic bomb but it was the atomic weapon which in his view enabled us to discount all questions of Soviet military action during the period of rebuilding. We should be guided by this important factor in considering every aspect of the atomic question. The Russians had previously thought that the American public would not permit the atom bomb to be used. They had now changed their minds and they were quite right to have done so. This was the principal factor militating against Soviet armed action.[52]

Marshall's comments should be placed in context by stating that contrary to the widely held belief at the time, the American B-29 planes sent to Britain during the Berlin crisis were not adapted to carrying atomic bombs. Furthermore the total American stockpile comprised fifty atomic bombs and some of these were subsequently discovered to be incapable of use.[53] In an election address to the American Legion on 18 October President Truman emphasised that America wished to avert war but not at the price of discredited policies associated with the name 'Munich'.[54]

All hinged on the ability of the airlift to cope with the winter weather in Germany. Prolonged bad weather would probably mean a western retreat, for it was recognised that the civilian populace could not be exposed to profound deprivation. Some difficulties had occurred in August as a result of shortages of certain commodites but the most dangerous period was in late December when fog threatened maintenance of flights.[55] However, the weather improved in January and the Russians were soon forced to accept that their gamble had failed; diplomacy had to extricate them as gracefully as possible from the predicament. The indication that the Soviet position was changing came in replies given by Stalin on 31 January to questions submitted by Kingsbury Smith, European director of the International News Services. Stalin did not refer to the currency question when commenting on how a settlement might be reached, thus revealing his willingness for a solution.[56] The State Department was waiting for a signal and now put a conciliatory procedure into effect. This consisted of arranging informal meetings between Philip Jessup, an able academic attached to the State Department, and Jacob Malik, the Soviet representative to the UN. This is particularly interesting in the Korean context for the avenue leading to the start of talks for a Korean armistice in the spring of 1951 were pursued in a similar fashion between Malik and George F. Kennan. Jessup met Malik on 15 February and inquired as to the significance of Stalin's replies to Kingsbury Smith: Malik confirmed that they connoted a change in the Soviet position and the negotiations were desired.[57] In ensuing discussions Jessup stated that while there was room for compromise, there could be no question of withdrawing the proposed establishment of a west German government. However, it should be feasible for a council of foreign ministers to be held before the new government was formally set up.[58]

Ernest Bevin was somewhat suspicious of the Jessup-Malik talks, feeling that the Soviet Union might be preparing a trap. He believed that the Russians were endeavouring to prevent ratification of the Atlantic pact by continental countries and hoped to delay moves leading to the strengthening of defences in western Europe. Bevin preferred to see the west German government actually in operation before talking further to the Russians.[59] Truman and Marshall were aware of the danger and considered Bevin's views too pessimistic: they wanted the blockade terminated as soon as possible, provided the Russians introduced no more complications. Jessup saw the British and French representatives to the UN, Cadogan and Chauvel, on 2 May. They approved the draft of a letter to Malik suggesting that the blockade be ended on 9 May and that a council of foreign ministers be held on 23 May. Malik agreed subject to preferring 12 May as the date for terminating the restrictions. This was accepted by the western envoys and a communiqué was circulated on 5 May stipulating that all blockade measures imposed by the Soviet Union since 1 March 1948 would be lifted on 12 May 1949; all counter-measures enforced by the western powers would similarly be lifted; and the council of foreign ministers would assemble in Paris on 23 May to discuss matters relating to Germany and Berlin, including currency questions. The Berlin blockade was concluded.

Fundamental differences over policies relating to Germany existed and inevitably so. However, the Soviet Union now tacitly conceded that while it could still embarrass the western powers in Berlin, it could not force them to leave without risking armed conflict. Berlin remained a focal point of future trouble, notably in 1961–62 with the construction of the odious wall, but the most serious confrontation had ended with limited agreement. Despite particularly provocative moments, as when Clay recommended sending an armed convoy from the western zones to Berlin and accepting the consequences – fortunately it was not implemented – and when a Soviet fighter shot down a British plane through the excessive zeal of the Russian pilot, both sides discerned the dangers clearly enough.[60] Truman, Marshall, the joint chiefs of staff and Stalin acted to prevent the crisis moving out of control. Ernest Bevin advocated a trenchant approach to the Soviet Union throughout, which reflected his ire at developments in central Europe in 1947–48 and his determination to see the Atlantic pact lead to a sustained American commitment to the defence of western Europe.[61] The Russian hope of thwarting the establishment of a west German state failed and steps leading to this were forwarded by the United States, Britain and France in May 1949.

The most significant developments in consolidating the relationship between the United States and western Europe occurred in 1948–49 with the conclusion of the North Atlantic Treaty Organisation (NATO) agreement. Truman, Marshall, the joint chiefs and the principal figures in the Democratic Party and in the moderate wing of the Republican Party accepted that traditional American views of the country's not embracing entangling alliances in peacetime should be jettisoned and that a positive American role should be fulfilled in Europe for many years to come. In 1947–48 this was a rather vague aspiration, since there was no specific American defence undertaking to Europe. Ernest Bevin was the principal architect of the NATO alliance; he believed that the sweeping rhetoric of the Truman Doctrine and Marshall Aid had to be followed by concrete American commitments, which would show the Soviet Union in absolutely unequivocal terms that an attempt to undermine the independence of western European countries would be met with force.[62] Bevin's view that an American commitment to Europe was indispensable to economic recovery and political stability was shared by the Conservative and Liberal parties and by the bulk of his own party outside the far left and fellow travellers: those of the centre-left who had harboured doubts originally changed their minds after the communist coup in Czechoslovakia. In March 1948 Bevin attended conferences in Paris and Brussels which provided for the setting up of the future Organisation for European Economic Cooperation (OEEC) and Western European Union (WEU). Bevin viewed these as preliminary and complementary steps to the attainment of a comprehensive security arrangement involving as many western European nations as possible, together with the United States.[63] He was wary, however, of the OEEC becoming a body that could dictate to its members as to their domestic economic and social policies, for this could affect the Labour government's plans and could militate against what he wished to achieve in the political and strategic spheres through alienating backbench Labour MPs.[64]

Negotiations to produce a NATO treaty took place in the second half of 1948. The chief difficulties were to achieve a definition of the American role which would satisfy both the European signatories and Congress; opponents of the treaty in the American Senate could be relied on to seize upon loose or imprecise language to castigate it. Equally Bevin was determined that the American commitment should be unambiguous. George Kennan contributed significantly with an able paper written in November 1948 and which influenced a working party on which he sat. Kennan stressed the psychological necessity for building self-confidence in western Europe and for demonstrating to the Soviet Union that the United States would not tolerate aggression. While there was a definite Soviet military threat to western Europe, the main Russian menace was political. It was hoped in Moscow that morale in the West could be insidiously undermined and this threat of creeping subversion halted. A treaty should be concluded rapidly but the military side of NATO should not be exaggerated; armed strength must be developed but only to the level where it reinforced the basic political message and not beyond.[65] The heart of the treaty comprised the definition of American military assistance and the circumstances in which this would occur. Article 4 as proposed stated that the signatories would confer whenever the territorial integrity, political independence or security of any of the parties was threatened and if a situation arose which threatened peace. Article 5 read:

> The Parties agree that an armed attack against one or more of them occurring within the area defined below shall be considered an attack against them all; and consequently that, if such an armed attack occurs, each of them in exercise of the right of individual or collective self-defence recognised by Article 51 of the UN Charter, will assist the party or parties so attacked by taking forthwith such military or other action, individually and in concert with the other parties, as may be necessary to restore and assure the security of the North Atlantic area.[66]

As Alan Bullock has rightly emphasised, this constituted the climax of Bevin's creative work as Foreign Secretary and one which proved an enduring pillar of British foreign policy and of the stability of western Europe.[67] There were still appreciable problems to be surmounted in the final stages of negotiations in Washington in the first three months of 1949. France, in particular, objected to the original American intention to exclude Italy from membership and to omit Algeria from the terms of the treaty. Dean Acheson, who had succeeded Marshall as Secretary of State in January 1949, handled the negotiations with consummate skill and ultimately accepted the two aspects on which the French felt so strongly. Norway and Denmark agreed to join the alliance but Sweden and Eire did not owing to the strength of the Swedish belief in neutrality and the Irish feeling over partition.[68] Apprehension over some unrest in Congress led Acheson to contemplate pulling back from reference to military action. On further reflection he decided to proceed regardless and the final form of words in Article 5 read:

> The Parties agree that an armed attack against one or more of them in Europe or North America shall be considered an attack against them all; and consequently they agree that, if such an armed attack occurs, each of them, in exercise of the right of individual or collective self-defence recognized by Article 51 of the Charter of the United Nations, will assist the Party or Parties so attacked by taking forthwith, individually and in concert with other Parties, such action as it deems necessary, including the use of armed force, to restore and maintain international peace and security.[69]

The treaty was approved overwhelmingly in the Senate; it was to last for a period of twenty years. Formal signatures by the respective foreign ministers took place in Washington on 4 April 1949.

In terms of assessing the offensive capabilities of the Soviet Union, American and British defence papers emphasised the might of conventional forces and the ability to expand on a sweeping scale if Russia took the decision to go to war. In July 1949 the Office of Intelligence Research within the Division of Research for Europe in the State Department submitted a report examining the relationship between domestic and foreign policies in Russia. Soviet military strength increased slightly in 1948–49 so that she possessed 24 armies (175 divisions) with 2.5 million troops plus 0.5 million state security troops ready for immediate action. Reserves of approximately 17 million men could be called on. From the latter 145 divisions and 8.5 million trained men could be mobilised in the field within 30 days so that within 240 days 193 additional divisions could be produced. Thus a total of divisional strength, in armies and reserve, amounted to 513. In the air Soviet strength was estimated at 17,000 but the bulk dated from the Second World War; it was believed that the Soviet air force experienced difficulties in providing engine and part replacements and lacked sufficient specialised personnel. However, it was capable of giving convincing support to a Soviet army intent on conquering Europe and could launch effective mass bomb attacks on Britain. The Soviet navy was much less developed and, with the exception of the submarine force, was not deemed a major threat. Inadequate intelligence was available to form an accurate impression of Soviet success in developing atomic weapons and guided missiles. In Europe Soviet expansion had been contained as a result of the political, economic and military initiatives fostered jointly by the United States and western Europe since 1947:

> Soviet capabilities for disruption and expansion have declined, but more in relative than absolute terms. This means that the efficacy of Soviet pressure at the present time is less dependent on Soviet capabilities than on the extent and force of current Western counter pressure. In short the USSR stands to gain by default if the Western powers, specifically the United States, are unable or unwilling to carry through their various programs directed toward achieving a greater political, economic, and military unity.[70]

The need for consistent, long-term American involvement in Europe was underlined.

In London the joint planning staff reported in March 1950 having revised their views in the light of exchanges with Washington in the autumn of 1949. At the beginning of 1950 the Soviet Union was not thought to have possessed more than ten atomic bombs and was anticipated to have a maximum of thirty by the end of 1950. If war came it might be preceded by a phase of diplomacy accompanied by growing tension. The West might have a few months' warning but war could equally occur with little or no warning. The joint intelligence committee envisaged that Soviet aims at the beginning of a conflict would include an offensive against western Europe, including Italy; an aerial bombardment against Britain; offensives in the Middle East, including Greece and Turkey; a campaign with limited objectives in the Far East; limited attacks against Canada and the United States; sea and air offensives; subversion and sabotage; and campaigns against Scandinavia and perhaps the Iberian peninsula. The joint intelligence committee contended that the Soviet Union had sufficient resources to pursue all the operations previously indicated. It was held that China might act opportunistically, whether or not manipulated by the Soviet Union. Allied strategy against Russia in a war commencing in 1950–51 should include a strategic air offensive including the use of atomic bombs; the retention of air bases and sea areas; the defence of other areas considered essential; the direction and control of sea and air communications.[71] Clearly the use of atomic weapons and dominance of the sea would be the strongest cards that could be played if war occurred. However, much guesswork was involved in weighing up the likelihood of Russia going to war. The joint intelligence committee, which advised the British chiefs of staff, believed that war could come sooner rather than later but Air Chief Marshal Sir John Slessor commented in a meeting on 22 March 1950 that the joint intelligence committee conceded that the evidence on which they based their report was slender. Slessor felt that a more carefully considered approach was required before advising the Cabinet that the planning date for a possible war should be brought forward.[72] In the last significant general discussion by the British defence chiefs before the Korean War started, held on 11 May 1950, it was recognised that there needed to be a change in emphasis on the relative importance of western Europe and the Middle East. In the past it had been thought that Britain and the United States could contemplate turning back a Russian invasion of western Europe from bases in Britain and thus regarding European defence separately from the defence of Britain. Now:

> The Chiefs of Staff ... considered that the defence of Western Europe must form part of the defence of the United Kingdom. The reason for this change in policy was that it was now considered that if Europe was overwhelmed, the United Kingdom would be threatened as never before and might well not survive. Moreover the effort required to liberate Europe once it had been overrun would be immense. A corollary to stepping up the importance of Western Europe was to lower somewhat the priority to be given to the defence of the Middle East. If we lost the Middle East we could still survive: if we lost Western Europe, we might well be defeated. It would not, however, be possible to win the war unless we held on to the Middle East or regained it.[73]

In Washington the feeling in the State Department early in 1950 was that while the West had broadly held its own in the Cold War, the initiative shown by America in Europe since 1947 had to some extent slowed down. Dean Acheson told colleagues at a meeting in the State Department held on 7 March 1950 that the momentum of the previous few years had been lost and a new approach was required to European problems. He felt that more could be achieved through NATO. Reference was made by others present to the future German relationship with NATO and to persuading the British to adopt a more realistic view of their role in the world given Britain's changed circumstances. Dean Rusk observed that the trouble with the British was that whenever one issue was settled they at once raised another. Rusk recommended that Acheson should ask Sir Oliver Franks how to break this vicious circle when he met the ambassador privately for dinner. Acheson asked Lewis Douglas, the ambassador in London, who could think imaginatively among British policy-makers. Douglas replied that neither Bevin nor Strang showed this quality but some officials in the Foreign Office could think along more original lines.[74] The developing consensus in Washington was that the Soviet Union was becoming more active. The new director of the policy planning staff, Paul Nitze, wrote that recent Soviet moves revealed greater militancy and boldness, which was new and bordered on recklessness. While these moves did not indicate a full-scale military onslaught within the near future:

> They do, however, suggest a greater willingness than in the past to undertake a course of action including a possible use of force in local areas which might lead to an accidental outbreak of general military conflict. Thus the chance of war through miscalculation is increased.[75]

The thorough reappraisal of the menace from the Soviet Union was effected early in 1950 in the preparation of the comprehensive report by the NSC, dated 14 April 1950, and known by the reference number assigned to it, NSC 68. It was prepared in response to a request from President Truman on 31 January and was sent to him on 7 April; he returned it five days later indicating his approval. It is an extremely lengthy document, extending to almost sixty pages in the published version.[76] The central message was that the Soviet Union was extremely powerful and was capable of inflicting great damage to the West; the dangers of subversion in particular had to be remembered. There was nothing new in the document and it reflected the culmination of the intelligence assessment or speculation over Soviet intentions pursued in the previous two years. It was a classic Cold War document in depicting the East versus West struggle as 'freedom' against 'slavery' and thus exemplified only too well how the Soviet Union was seen by most Americans. Cogent criticisms of NSC 68 were expressed by one American official, Schaub, the deputy chief of the Estimates Bureau of the Budget. In a memorandum dated 8 May he described NSC 68 as too simplistic; as an example he cited the fact that the murky nature of certain states with which the United States was involved was conveniently forgotten, although Indo-China or the Philippines could hardly be described as showing freedom at its best. Furthermore the report concentrated on a narrow definition of political freedom, ignoring the role of economic and social change. In Schaub's view far more thought was needed on the finer points of resisting and defeating communism instead of uttering rhetorical excesses.[77] These sentiments were convincing but out of tune with the times. From reflecting on the document, it is easy to comprehend why the Korean War was seen as the product of Machiavellian Soviet intrigue to embarrass the West and to assist in the Soviet aim of dominating Europe.

The contribution of European events to the perception of the Korean War and the response to it was that the United States and the Soviet Union saw Europe as the vital arena, which would be decisive in resolving who won the Cold War. This was an excessively Eurocentric view and seriously underestimated the importance of the world outside Europe, particularly China. As developments between 1945 and 1969 demonstrated with abundant clarity, neither the Americans nor the Russians understood the significance of developments in China. Each side was aware of the perils and in the case of the Berlin blockade eventually revealed more sense than might have been anticipated in extricating itself from it but there was no guarantee this would happen in the future. Stalin was kept well informed of western thinking by his highly placed spies, notably Guy Burgess, Donald Maclean and Kim Philby and perhaps by others. While it is obviously dangerous for important secrets to be conveyed swiftly to a hostile major power, it can also be argued that the effects militated against an adventurous policy, thus vindicating the view that the more countries know of each other's aims the better, provided the balance of information is not too one-sided. The degree of suspicion and animosity in Europe in June 1950 was so great as to magnify the developments in the Korean peninsula. The Soviet Union was not directly involved in Korea but Kim Il Sung was widely regarded as a Soviet stooge. North Korea had to be treated as if Stalin and not Kim had devised the attack on 25 June. Europe's battles were therefore fought on the battlefields of Korea but in a sense different from General MacArthur's use of the analogy: MacArthur wanted more resources devoted to Korea and believed that the contingency of the Soviet Union advancing in Europe was remote. To policy-makers in Washington and London the danger of a Soviet advance in Europe was very real. But a firm response in Korea was imperative.

# REFERENCES

1. For a cogent assessment of the Cold War in terms of move and counter-move, see Louis Halle, *The Cold War as History* (London 1967). The revisionist interpretation was originally expounded in terms of the animosity between East and West from 1917 in D. F. Fleming, *The Cold War and its Origins*, 2 vols (London 1961). See also Gabriel and Joyce Kolko, *The Limits of Power: The World and the United States Foreign Policy, 1945–1954* (London 1972).

2. On Stalin's character and career, see Isaac Deutscher, *Stalin: A Political Biography*, second edn (London 1967) and A. B. Ulam, *Stalin: The Man and his Era* (London 1974). For a revealing account of Stalin's cynical approach, see Milovan Djilas, *Conversations with Stalin* (London 1962).

3. For a general discussion of the problems as perceived by Truman, see H. S. Truman, *Memoirs: Year of Decisions, 1945* and *Years of Trial and Hope, 1946–52*, 2 vols, paperback edn (New York 1965). For an interesting if predictably sympathetic portrait, see Margaret Truman, *Harry S. Truman* (London 1973). The Democratic Party was weakened through dissent on the left and right: former Vice-President Henry Wallace criticised Truman's foreign policy for being too tough towards the Soviet Union and his domestic policy for not fulfilling the promises of the New Deal. Wallace stood in 1948 as the candidate of the Progressive Party. Governor Strom Thurmond of South Carolina criticised Truman for endorsing civil rights reforms and led a walkout from the Democratic convention in 1948 to stand as a Dixiecrat candidate.

4. Letter from Truman to John Nance Garner, 21 Sept. 1946, folder, Russia, 1945–48, PSF, box 187, Truman Papers, Truman Library.
5. For an account of Byrne's term of office and his relations with Truman, see R. L. Messer, *The End of an Alliance: James F. Byrnes, Roosevelt, Truman, and the Origins of the Cold War* (Chapel Hill, NC 1982).
6. See Alan Bullock, *The Life and Times of Ernest Bevin*, vol. III (London 1983), pp. 402–9.
7. See A. S. Milward, *The Reconstruction of Western Europe, 1945–51* (London 1984). For a lucid assessment of the background to, and character of, the Marshall Plan, see John Gimbel, *The Origins of the Marshall Plan* (Stanford, Calif. 1976).
8. For Anglo-American relations after 1945, see R. M. Hathaway, *Ambiguous Partnership: Britain and America, 1944–1947* (Guildford 1981), and Bullock, op. cit., III. See also L. S. Wittner, *American Intervention in Greece, 1943–1949* (Guildford 1982).
9. Permanent Under-Secretary's Committee, 'A third world power or Western consolidation', 9 May 1949, Prem. 8/1204.
10. For a careful examination of the making of the Czechoslovak crisis in 1948, see Martin Myant, *Socialism and Democracy in Czechoslovakia* (Cambridge 1981).
11. Ibid., p. 125.
12. Ibid., p. 129.
13. Ibid., p. 106.
14. *FRUS 1948* (4) p. 734, Bruins to Marshall, 28 Jan. 1948.
15. Ibid., p. 733.
16. Minute by P. F. Hancock, 13 Feb. 1948, on dispatch from Dixon to Bevin, 6 Feb. 1948, N1536/157/12, FO 371/71283.
17. Prague to FO, 11 Feb. 1948, and letter from Frank Roberts, Bevin's private secretary, to B. K. Trend (Treasury), 13 Feb. 1948, N1710/157/12G, ibid.
18. Myant, op. cit., pp. 198–9.
19. Ibid., p. 210.
20. Ibid.
21. Ibid., p. 207.
22. Bevin to Inverchapel (Washington), 25 Feb. 1948, N2181/157/12, FO 371/71284.
23. *FRUS 1948* (4) pp. 741–2, Steinhardt to Marshall, 27 Feb. 1948.
24. Myant, op. cit., p. 217.
25. *FRUS 1948* (4), pp. 754–5, Steinhardt to Marshall, 29 May 1948.
26. Prague to FO, 26 March 1948, N3685/157/12G, FO 371/71287.
27. Avi Shlaim, *The United States and the Berlin Blockade, 1948–1949: A Study in Crisis Decision-Making* (London 1983), pp. 19–20.
28. Ibid., pp. 137, 159.
29. Ibid., pp. 32–3.
30. Cited ibid., pp. 64–5, letter from Royall to H. L. Stimson, 21 April 1948.
31. Memorandum by Strang, 24 Feb. 1948, C1547/3/18/G, FO 371/70489.
32. Minute by Bevin, no date, on FO memorandum, 18 March 1948, C2319/3/18/G, FO 371/70490.
33. Minute by Strang, 28 April 1948, C3511/3/18, FO 371/70492.
34. Ibid.

35. Shlaim, op. cit., pp. 151–2.
36. Ibid., pp. 152–3.
37. Ibid., p. 154.
38. Ibid., p. 155.
39. Ibid., p. 156.
40. Ibid., p. 158.
41. Ibid., pp. 159–60.
42. Memorandum by Bevin, 26 June 1948, C5032/3/18/G, FO 371/70497.
43. Memorandum, 'Germany', 25 June 1948, C5094/3/18/G, ibid. Bevin consulted Hector McNeil, Minister of State at the FO, Arthur Henderson, Secretary of State for Air, General Brownjohn, Sir Ivone Kirkpatrick, Frank Roberts and Patrick Dean of the FO.
44. Statistics included in statement by Henderson at press conference, 11 May 1949, C4180/14/18, FO 371/76552.
45. *FRUS 1948* (2), pp. 999–1000, Bedell Smith to Marshall, 3 Aug. 1948.
46. Ibid., pp. 1003–4.
47. Ibid., p. 1005.
48. Ibid., p. 1006–7, Bedell Smith to Marshall, 3 Aug. 1948.
49. Ibid., pp. 1132–4, Murphy to Marshall, 7 Sept. 1948.
50. Ibid., pp. 1212–13, editorial note.
51. Extract from record of meeting in Paris between Bevin, Marshall and Schuman, 4 Oct. 1948, C8613/3/18/G, FO 371/70519.
52. Ibid.
53. Shlaim, op. cit., pp. 238–9.
54. Ibid., p. 292.
55. Ibid., p. 377, n. 191.
56. Ibid., p. 380.
57. *FRUS 1949* (3), pp. 695–8, memorandum by Jessup, 15 March 1949, referring back to meeting held on 15 Feb.
58. Ibid., p. 702, memorandum of conversations by Jessup, 21 March 1949.
59. Ibid., pp. 730–1, Douglas to Marshall, 25 Apr. 1949.
60. For a discussion of the aspects mentioned, see Shlaim, op. cit., pp. 130–1, 133–4 and 200–1.
61. For an assessment of Bevin's reactions to the Berlin blockade, see Bullock, op. cit., III, pp. 546–8, 557–9, 571–82, 606–7, 639 and 680.
62. Ibid., pp. 530–1.
63. Ibid., pp. 535–6.
64. Ibid., p. 535.
65. Ibid., pp. 644–5. For an illuminating insight into the treaty negotiations, see Nicholas Henderson, *The Birth of NATO* (London 1982).
66. Cited Bullock, op. cit., III, p. 645.
67. Ibid.
68. Ibid., p. 670.
69. Henderson, op. cit., p. 120.
70. 'Soviet internal situation: an analysis of the thesis that Soviet internal weaknesses constitute the determining factor in current Soviet foreign policy', Office of Intelligence Research, Division of Research for Europe, State Department, OIR, report number 4998, 1 July 1949, PSF file, folder, Russia, 1949–52, box 187, Truman Papers, Truman Library.

71. 'Plan Galloper', report of joint planning staff, 1 March 1950, JP(49)134 (Final), Defe 4/29.
72. Chiefs of staff conclusions, 22 March 1950, COS(50)47(3), Defe 4/30.
73. Chiefs of staff conclusions, 11 May 1950, COS(50)74(2), Defe 4/31.
74. Memorandum of conversation, 7 March 1950, folder of conversations, March 1950, box 65, Acheson Papers, Truman Library.
75. *FRUS 1950* (1), p. 146, study prepared by Nitze, 8 Feb. 1950.
76. Ibid., pp. 234–92, report of NSC, NSC 68.
77. Ibid., pp. 300–3, memorandum by Schaub to Lay, 8 May 1950.

*Chapter 7*

# THE OUTBREAK OF THE KOREAN WAR

The outbreak of the Korean War on 25 June 1950 saw the fusing of two crises in East Asia that had been linked but which had been handled separately by the United States to this point – developments in the Korean peninsula and in Taiwan. Some members of the UN, notably Great Britain, sought to maintain the distinction between the two: Britain supported the American reaction to events in Korea but had no wish to be dragged into conflict with China over Taiwan. This chapter examines the sequence of developments preceding and following the start of the Korean War. The contacts between South Korea and Taiwan will be considered first and the contribution made by the dispute over the future of Taiwan to the initial stages of fighting in Korea. From the summer of 1949 onwards there were frequent, enigmatic exchanges between Syngman Rhee's government and the declining Kuomintang regime in Taiwan. Chiang had visited Seoul in August 1949 for talks with Rhee; the Generalissimo had urged the conclusion of a Pacific pact involving South Korea, Taiwan and the Philippines to be underwritten if possible by the United States. Chiang wanted an understanding with the ROK providing for limited military cooperation with a contingency arrangement for Chiang to be given asylum in Seoul should the Chinese communists succeed in capturing Taiwan. The American State Department was aware of the general trend of Chiang's exchanges with the authorities in Seoul and Manila but was not conversant with all the details. Niles Bond, the officer mainly responsible for dealing with Korean matters in the State Department, wrote to John J. Muccio in Seoul on 1 June 1950 explaining that he had heard informally from the Navy Department that representatives of Chiang Kai-shek had opened negotiations with the South Korean and Philippines governments for asylum to be granted if Taiwan fell. It was understood that the Philippines was unwilling to cooperate and Bond commented to an emissary from the Navy Department:

> ... President Rhee would ... be loath to have such a conspicuous
> albatross as the Generalissimo hung about his neck. In reply to a further

question I added that I believed that it would be the Department's view that the Korean Government would be acting most unwisely were it to agree to accord asylum to the Generalissimo and that it should in no way be encouraged to do so.[1]

Bond requested Muccio to investigate and report back. Muccio replied on 23 June, just after the visit to Seoul of John Foster Dulles and John M. Allison from the State Department. Muccio began by remarking on Korean–Taiwanese contacts, 'There are indications that maneuverings have been going on but I have not been able to put my finger on anything concrete.'[2] Muccio had asked the acting Prime Minister of any approaches from Chiang and he had denied that any had occurred. Certain rumours had reached Muccio, although he had been unable to verify their accuracy. One was that Colonel Whang Woo, the Kuomintang's military attaché, had pursued inquiries on behalf of Chiang. The South Korean government had apparently refused to permit any Kuomintang group to be located in South Korea. A further rumour was that a Chinese consul-general had visited Seoul on the same basis. It was unclear who had been contacted in the South Korean government and Muccio thought it was probable that approaches would have been made to Korean leaders close to the Chinese, such as Lee Bum Suk, Shin Ik Hi or General Chi Chung Chun rather than to Rhee or the acting Prime Minister, Captain Sihn. Another report to Muccio had indicated that Chiang had offered to send rifles and ammunition to South Korea, apparently in exchange for Chiang being granted asylum. Muccio, Dulles and Allison met President Rhee and the Foreign Minister, Ben C. Limb, for discussions on 19 June: the significance of Dulles' visit in the Korean context will be considered later and for the moment only Taiwan will be considered. Rhee advocated a pact between anti-communist nations in the Pacific region but Dulles countered that formal pacts or alliances were not necessary for common action against an enemy. Dulles stated that American policy on Taiwan was being reviewed and that economic aid plus licences for exporting military equipment to Taiwan had been agreed before he left Washington. Dulles asked Rhee outright whether the ROK would allow Chiang and other high Kuomintang officers to settle in Seoul if Taiwan fell. Rhee held that every country should stand on its own feet; it was obvious that Rhee did not enthuse at Chiang's wish to find a safe haven in South Korea.[3] The exact nature of the discussions between the ROK and the Kuomintang remains murky and is a subject for legitimate speculation. Chiang was in a desperate situation; while the danger of Kuomintang troops in Taiwan defecting to the communists had subsided, he was faced with the likelihood of an invasion of Taiwan being attempted in August or September 1950. Chiang appeared doomed unless the United States intervened to save him or a third world war began in which circumstances all governments or areas hostile to communism could expect support. It could well be in Chiang's interest to encourage conflict in Korea, for American policy would probably change and Taiwan would benefit therefrom. There is no solid evidence pointing to Kuomintang complicity in the events immediately preceding the beginning of the Korean War. All that can be said is that it would be in Chiang's interest to stimulate South Korean belligerence.

General MacArthur became alarmed at the communist threat to Taiwan in the spring of 1950. This, too, is a murky topic in which much remains obscure. MacArthur had taken a deep interest in Taiwan in 1949–50 and had encouraged American and Japanese involvement in Taiwan.[4] MacArthur was in communication with the able American-educated Kuomintang general, Sun Li-jen, now commander-in-chief, Taiwan; Sun was regarded by many as the one slender hope of rescuing the Kuomintang in Taiwan and of giving the moribund regime a new lease of life.[5] Some felt that the United States might engineer a coup whereby Sun replaced Chiang Kai-shek and this might have happened but for the escalation of the Korean struggle into a major war. MacArthur expressed his views trenchantly in a memorandum dated 29 May and sent to the joint chiefs of staff. Information brought to his attention had shown Sino-Russian cooperation in the Shanghai and Peking areas and that Soviet jets had been sent to the Chinese communist air force. The problem of Taiwan had become an urgent one. MacArthur emphasised that the consequences of the capture of Taiwan would be grave. Such an eventuality would increase drastically the Soviet threat to the American military position in the western Pacific. If Soviet forces could use Taiwan, the Malay-Philippine-Japan shipping lanes could be cut and Japan isolated. Taiwan would give the Soviet Union the capability for operating against the central and southern flanks of the existing American strategic frontier of the littoral island chain from Hokkaido through to the Philippines. Soviet possession of air bases in northern Taiwan would greatly increase the Soviet air threat against Okinawa. Communist ability to intervene in South-East Asia would be facilitated through Soviet occupation of Taiwan. He stated in ringing terms:

> In the event of war between the United States and the USSR, Formosa's value to the Communists is the equivalent of an unsinkable aircraft carrier and submarine tender, ideally located to accomplish Soviet strategy as well as to checkmate the offensive capabilities of the central and southern positions of the FEC [Far East Command] front line. This unsinkable carrier-tender has the current capacity to operate ten air groups, and can readily be modified to accommodate twice that number. The Communist 'fleet' can be acquired and maintained at an incomparably lower cost to the USSR than could its equivalent of ten or twenty heavy aircraft carriers.[6]

MacArthur added that extensive reinforcements to American air strength would be imperative if Taiwan fell.

American policy towards Taiwan underwent a fundamental change in

May–June 1950: the joint chiefs of staff were fully aware of the arguments put forward by MacArthur and urged steps to neutralise Taiwan. President Truman and Secretary of State Dean Acheson were also reconsidering the issue. The reassessment was regarded as highly confidential in the State Department. The British ambassador, Sir Oliver Franks, met Acheson for one of their frequent private discussions after dinner on 5 June. Acheson was contemplating ways of denying Taiwan to the Chinese communists short of outright American military intervention in the island. The repercussions of the possible fall of Taiwan would be very serious in East and South-East Asia. Acheson had no solution in mind but it was clear that the Truman administration would seek to delay an attempt to invade Taiwan.[7] The British reaction was sombre: the permanent under-secretary at the Foreign Office minuted, 'There are the seeds of trouble here.'[8] On 22 June the British embassy confirmed that policy concerning Taiwan was being reappraised – 'Curiously enough no one in the State Department junior to Dean Rusk knows of this reconsideration, nor have they heard that Acheson had spoken to the Ambassador about Formosa.'[9] The British embassy was aware of consideration being given in the State Department to placing Taiwan under the control of MacArthur, as a reversion to Taiwan's undetermined status pending the conclusion of a Japanese peace treaty; the White House was said to be contemplating a declaration analogous to the Monroe Doctrine.[10] Intelligence from Taiwan on 13 June suggested that the Chinese communists might attack Taiwan in September with the invading forces coming from Amoy, Swatow and the Chusan islands. It seemed to be in the interest of the communists to attack Taiwan in 1950, although some observers believed an invasion was more likely in 1951.[11] An additional reason why Acheson was prepared to consider changing policy was his desire to secure bipartisan cooperation in Congress on matters relating to the Far East. Since the Republicans had criticised the administration's policy in this region for a lengthy period and had referred specifically to the importance of avoiding the fall of Taiwan, it followed that Acheson would have to placate his critics.[12] Franks believed the new attitude resulted from a combination of strategic and political pressures which had compelled Truman and Acheson to change line.[13]

When the Korean War began Chiang Kai-shek offered military assistance to South Korea. The Kuomintang Foreign Minister, George Yeh, plaintively commented that there were some effective fighting units in Taiwan despite the sad experiences in the mainland in 1948–49. He believed that the North Korean attack was an isolated probing tactic, although full Soviet prestige was almost certainly involved. He did not feel an attack on Taiwan was imminent.[14] Chiang Kai-shek was both reassured and alarmed at Truman's statement of 27 June in which he referred to Korea and Taiwan. Truman stated that the developments in Korea had raised the menace of wider aggression. A communist occupation of Taiwan would therefore be a threat to peace in the Pacific and could not be permitted:

> Accordingly I have ordered the Seventh Fleet to prevent any attack on Formosa. As a corollary of this action I am calling upon the Chinese Government on Formosa to cease all air and sea operations against the mainland. The Seventh Fleet will see that this is done. The determination of the future status of Formosa must await the restoration of security in the Pacific, a peace settlement with Japan, or consideration by the United Nations.[15]

Taiwan was protected against communist attack but equally the freedom of the Kuomintang government had been severely circum-scribed. It could not take action against China and the very future of the island was to be determined and conceivably on a basis contrary to the wishes of that government. Taiwan might be placed under MacArthur pending a Japanese peace settlement or under the UN prior to a decision that might lead to Taiwanese independence as advocated by Taiwanese autonomists. Truman and Acheson, long disillusioned with Chiang Kai-shek, had no intention on 27 June of committing themselves to propping him up for an indefinite period. They had acted because they had already decided before 25 June that Taiwan must not fall to the communists: the events in Korea became the occasion of announcing the new policy. For Truman and Acheson it was the easiest method of dealing with the dilemma confronting them but the combining of Taiwan and Korea created much difficulty in American relations with many other countries, including the Soviet Union, Britain, India and, most obviously, Communist China. Ironically it had the effect of underpinning Chiang Kai-shek for the rest of his life and of complicating American relations with Peking until the 1980s.

To turn now to the tortuous events in the Korean peninsula in June 1950. What exactly happened? Did North Korea launch a sudden, well-coordinated onslaught against South Korea as was generally believed? Or did South Korea attack first and thus provoke the conflict? It is impossible to determine with absolute accuracy precisely what occurred on 25 June 1950, since wildly divergent accounts were given by the two sides and their respective supporters. It is appropriate to begin with the report of UNCOK, since the task of this body was to observe the situation, particularly along the 38th parallel. The key report on behalf of UNCOK was submitted by two Australian military observers appointed in May, as a response to a request by UNCOK. The observers were Major F. S. B. Peach and Squadron Leader R. J. Rankin.[16] They devoted the period from 9 June to 23 June to inspecting ROK troops stationed along the parallel. Peach and Rankin stated that the ROK forces were organised 'entirely for defence' and were 'in no condition to carry out an attack on a large scale against the forces of the north'.[17]

South Korean troops were not concentrated and there was no massing at any point. In certain places the North Korean forces were effectively in possession of salients on the south side of the parallel and there was no indication that South Korean troops were about to act against them. Some South Korean troops were engaged in anti-guerrilla operations when guerrillas had infiltrated. The inadequate resources of the ROK army, in particular the absence of armour, air support and heavy artillery, rendered a South Korean invasion impossible in military terms. There were no signs that the ROK army was preparing an attack: their commanders demonstrated an attitude of 'vigilant defence'. As regards the position north of the parallel, civilians had recently been transferred from areas adjacent to the parallel northwards. A report that there was military activity near Chwiyari just north of the parallel, had been received. 'No report, however, had been received of any unusual activity on the part of the North Korean forces that would indicate any imminent change in the general situation of the parallel.'[18] Peach and Rankin submitted their report on 24 June and it was fundamental to the conclusion of UNCOK that North Korea was responsible for the military action that marked the beginning of the war. At 5 p.m. on 25 June the field observers had reported that North Korean forces had that morning mounted a surprise attack all along the 38th parallel. Kim Il Sung had claimed in a broadcast made on 26 June at 9.20 a.m. that South Korea had attacked the north in the section of Haeju, thus provoking counter-attacks. In the light of the report by Peach and Rankin, UNCOK unanimously rejected the North Korean contention and stated categorically that no offensive could possibly have been launched by South Korea; UNCOK continued:

> The invasion launched by the North Korean forces on 25 June cannot have been the result of a decision taken suddenly in order to repel a mere border attack or in retaliation for such an attack. Such an invasion involving amphibious landings and the use of considerable numbers of troops carefully trained for aggressive action and in relation to the area of great quantities of weapons and other war material, presupposes a long-premeditated, well prepared and well-timed plan of aggression. The subsequent steady advance of the North Korean forces supplies further evidence if further evidence is needed of the extensive nature of the planning and preparation for the aggression.
>
> It is the considered opinion of the commission that this planning and preparation were deliberate and an essential part of the policy of the North Korean authorities. The objective of this policy was to secure by force what could not be gained by any other means. In furtherance of this policy the North Korean authorities on 25 June initiated a war of aggression without provocation and without warning.[19]

The phraseology was emphatic but the fact remained that UNCOK was not clear exactly what had happened at the moment when fighting commenced. In addition, they side-stepped the question of the inflammatory rhetoric emanating from Rhee, revealing his ardent desire to unite the country, and ignored the provocation for which South Korea had been responsible on occasions in 1949–50 and which had worried KMAG.

What were the views of North Korea, the Soviet Union and China in June 1950? Who took the initiative in the chain of events? There is considerable obscurity over the decision-making process and the responsibilities of each. It was widely held in June–July 1950 that the Soviet Union had masterminded the North Korean attack and that Kim Il Sung was a puppet of Stalin's.[20] Few believed that Kim was sufficiently independent to seize the initiative himself. Some, subscribing to a monolithic, conspiratorial view of world communism, believed that China was supporting the Soviet Union in inspiring the North Korean attack; others maintained that China was not involved. Khruschev's reminiscences, if a reliable source, indicate that Kim Il Sung first proposed the attack and that Stalin acquiesced, as did Mao Tse-tung.[21] Bruce Cumings has investigated the evidence and maintains that North Korea was most probably the vital agent. Kim Il Sung was intensely nationalistic, proud, possessed of a mission to unify his country and contemptuous of opposition. The North Korean army had been strengthened through the entry of battle-hardened veterans who had fought with the Chinese communists and who constituted 80 per cent of the officers.[22] Cumings adduces a small but significant piece of information pointing to the likelihood of North Korea having launched the attack on 25 June: notebooks belonging to North Korean mechanics and technicians reveal that planes were being prepared for action in mid-June instead of undergoing the usual routine maintenance.[23] Cuming's thesis is convincing: Kim Il Sung wished to attack South Korea in fulfilment of his policy and that Stalin either acquiesced grudgingly or was not consulted at all.[24] Kim Il Sung was motivated not simply by determination to unite Korea but by the aim of ending political dependence upon the Soviet Union or China.

As for the Soviet Union, Stalin preferred to see the Korean peninsula ruled by a communist regime but it was not something he felt passionately about. Korea was important in that she bordered Soviet far eastern territories but it was almost certainly not a priority in Stalin's mind that Korea should be unified. Stalin was normally highly cautious in his international policy and was disinclined to gamble. Admittedly he could have reasoned that a Korean crisis might be worth the risk in terms of embarrassing the United States and that a North Korean attack might succeed at little cost. Stalin did not desire a major crisis in Korea and had no intention of involving the Soviet Union deeply in the peninsula's problems. This is borne out by his decision, evidently taken about a week after the Korean War began, to pull out Russian pilots and other advisers from North Korea so as to minimise the dangers of Soviet commitment.[25] It might be argued that Stalin would have gained from a diversionary war in the Far East, which could have hindered American efforts to rebuild western Europe. However, such a diversionary conflict could also unite Americans and lead to much increased defence expenditure; the latter indeed resulted. It is important to keep in mind the activities of Guy Burgess, Donald Maclean and Kim Philby.[26] Stalin received invaluable information from the highly placed spies and he must have been reasonably clear – or as clear as anyone was – on the likely trend of American policy-making. Policy document NSC 68, formally adopted in April 1950, and its strategy for American global containment of communism would surely have pointed to the probability of the United States reacting firmly to any crisis connoting a challenge to an American-supported regime.[27] On balance it is unlikely that the Soviet Union manipulated North Korea in June 1950 but it is still a possibility.

China had no motive for unleashing war in Korea. Chinese leaders had more than enough challenges with having to eliminate the last vestiges of opposition on the mainland, erect a viable political system and above all cope with the horrendous problems of the Chinese economy. Taiwan remained to be conquered, presumably in 1950 or 1951. Sino-American relations were bad but there was no reason for Mao Tse-tung to foster a Korean clash. Kim Il Sung was identified with a pro-Russian stance rather than one sympathetic to China and Mao would hardly benefit from strengthening Kim's authority. Naturally China was bound to be deeply concerned at war in Korea but there was little chance of China intervening while the purpose of the UN was to restore the status quo ante. Advancing beyond the 38th parallel would be another matter, however, and an approach towards the Yalu would be viewed by China as a direct threat and treated appropriately.

Now to consider the political situation in South Korea in June and developments in American policy-making. Syngman Rhee's support had waned in 1949–50 following the President's increasingly autocratic behaviour, the effects of inflation, and the revelations of corruption and incompetence in the administration. Rhee experienced a setback in the general election held on 30 May with those supporting him suffering appreciable losses.[28] The most striking feature was the large increase in the number of independents. There were various minor groups but the independents clearly constituted the key element. The British minister in Seoul summarised by predicting that some independents would subsequently join Rhee but that the defeat of men prominent in public life could only be interpreted 'as a demonstration of public feeling against the President and his associates and the Police'.[29] North Korea launched a propaganda campaign on 7 June with Pyongyang radio broadcasting an appeal from the Democratic Front for all Koreans – except Rhee's clique – to coalesce in support of unification: this would be achieved through holding a general election for the whole of Korea on 5 August with a new national legislature meeting in Seoul on 15 August; political leaders of north and south, again excluding Rhee and his close associates, would assemble to decide on arrangements for holding the election and UNCOK would be excluded from advising on the unification process.[30] Rhee was still confident of retaining control and the tone of his pronouncements on the future of Korea under his leadership did not change significantly. The nature of the assembly elected on 30 May pointed to Rhee encountering more problems with the body in future but the President revealed few signs of doubting his ability to surmount any problems.

Rhee's most significant engagement in mid-June was to receive an important American visitor, John Foster Dulles. Mystery surrounds the precise motives for Dulles's visit to Seoul. Dulles had accepted appointment in April 1950 as special consultant to the State Department with particular responsibility for handling the negotiations over the Japanese peace treaty. He was a firm advocate of resisting communism and his statements in Seoul were generally but not entirely encouraging to Rhee. The principal reason for Dulles's trip was to visit Tokyo for talks on the peace treaty and it was agreed after deliberations in the State Department that Dulles should go to Seoul. John J. Muccio had drawn attention to the feeling of isolation in South Korea and the absence of distinguished American visitors seemed to underline lack of interest in the fate of Korea. Given the tougher approach being adopted behind the scenes in Washington over Taiwan, a visit to Seoul was opportune. Dulles was accompanied by John M. Allison, a leading State Department official and a hardliner where encounters against communism were concerned. The South Korean assembly met on 19 June and was addressed by Dulles. He compared the Korean struggle for independence after colonial oppression to the American experience in escaping from British imperialism. The generosity of the United States in assisting peoples to secure and maintain their freedom was emphasised. He concluded, in the words of the British minister, 'with an eloquent assurance that the American people welcomed the Koreans as an equal partner in the great company of those who comprised the free World, a world which commanded vast moral and material power and in which any despotism which waged aggressive war doomed itself to unalterable disaster'.[31]

Dulles met Rhee for private talks on 19 June at the President's request. Rhee wanted greater American commitment in Korea and East Asia in total. Dulles regarded subversion as a more likely danger for South Korea than a direct North Korean attack; to combat subversion it was essential that governments took 'active steps to create conditions within their countries which would prohibit growth of communism'.[32] This required 'true allegiance to the principles of representative government and a real effort to self-control and hard work to create a stable economy and a government which deserved the support of its people ... '.[33] Dulles's public rhetoric conveyed the image of a more assertive American role which when taken in conjunction with his activity in working for a Japanese peace treaty, must have alarmed North Korea. In a famous photograph, afterwards produced in North Korean literature, Dulles was shown wearing his characteristic Homburg hat, peering intently across the 38th parallel at the communist hordes to the north. This was regarded in Pyongyang as demonstrating Dulles's aggressive intentions. Dulles's purpose certainly was to put more backbone into South Korea but he did not anticipate the developments that were shortly to take place. Alvary Gascoigne, head of the British liaison mission in Japan, reported to London on Dulles's return to Tokyo. Dulles described Syngman Rhee's mood as ebullient and said that far from passively awaiting an attack from North Korea, Rhee might instead take an initiative against the north. A British official in London commented with some embarrassment:

> It is quite clear that Mr Dulles had not the faintest inkling of what was impending. Read in the light of subsequent events, Mr Dulles's words seem unfortunate. It is true that Syngman Rhee who, although very reactionary is no realist, has talked in terms of solving the problem of Korean disunity by force. It is clear, however, that Mr Dulles merely meant to indicate that the South Koreans were in a buoyant frame of mind.[34]

The CIA produced a lengthy assessment of the capabilities of North Korea on 19 June, based on information made available on 15 May. It examined political, economic and strategic aspects. The chief points brought out were the degree of Soviet control, the disciplined character of the state with efficient armed forces; and that while factionalism existed, it did not represent a serious problem. The morale of North Korean troops was good. The ultimate objective of the Soviet Union was to unify the Korean peninsula under a communist government. The vulnerability of South Korea to a determined onslaught from the north was underlined, although it was felt that Soviet or Chinese participation would be necessary to ensure total military victory over the south.[35] To observers in Seoul on the eve of the war, all appeared relatively calm and there was no suggestion of imminent crisis. Holt, the British minister, wrote to the Foreign Office on 22 June that the most impressive occurrence had been the arrival of rain, which averted the threatened drought.[36] At 10 a.m. on 25 June John J. Muccio reported urgently to Washington that North Korean forces had invaded the south at several places that morning. Action had started at about 4 a.m. when Ongjin was attacked by North Korean artillery fire. Two hours later North Korean infantry began crossing the parallel in the vicinity of Ongjin and in the areas of Kaesong and Chunchon; an amphibious landing on the east coast south of Kangnung was also reported. Kaesong had apparently been captured at 9 a.m. and fighting was proceeding at the places indicated.[37] It should be pointed out that there was thirteen hours' difference in local time between Seoul and Washington; between the hours of 12 midnight and 1 p.m. Korea was one day ahead of Washington. Muccio's message sparked off hectic activity in Washington, New York and in world capitals. The United States faced the first real challenge of the Cold War, in terms of contemplating the use of appreciable numbers of American forces in a 'hot' war and one that could escalate into a far greater conflict involving the Soviet Union and (or) China.

President Truman was in Independence, Missouri, when the crisis broke and the immediate decisions were taken by Dean Acheson. The Secretary of State consulted the President by telephone and it was decided to raise the situation in the UN Security Council. In Tokyo General MacArthur was taken by surprise by the news of the North Korean advance and did not at first attach significance to it. MacArthur believed it was yet another of the numerous border incursions of the previous eighteen months and did not grasp the magnitude of the development. Dulles at once understood the implications, having only just returned from Seoul. There was no affection lost between MacArthur and Dulles, for each was suspicious of the other in the handling of the Japanese peace treaty and they represented diverging attitudes within the Republican Party. Dulles visited MacArthur late in the evening of the 25th, and impressed the gravity of it upon him.[38] Dulles and Allison recommended on 25 June that if necessary American forces should be deployed in Korea:

> To sit by while Korea is overrun by unprovoked armed attack would start disastrous chain of events heading most probably to world war. We suggest that Security Council might call for action on behalf of the organization under Article 106 by the five powers or such of them as are willing to respond.[39]

The Soviet Union had absented herself from meetings of the UN Security Council since January 1950, ostensibly because China was represented in the body by the defunct Kuomintang regime in Taiwan rather than by the Chinese communist government. Whether this was the reason for Soviet absence is a matter for conjecture. Bebler, the Yugoslav representative in the Security Council, believed Soviet behaviour was motivated by other considerations:

> Bebler had taken the line that the whole Korean incident had been engineered by the Russians in order thoroughly to embroil the United States with Communist China. Moscow was, according to Bebler, apprehensive of the growth of Communist China's power and determined not to have the latter in the United Nations. It was for this reason that the Russians had recognised Ho-Chi-minh [*sic*]. Now by prevailing on the United States to take action in respect of Formosa this had effectively

embroiled the Americans with the Chinese Communists and put a stop to any likelihood of the latter's early admission to the United Nations.[40]

Yugoslavia's relations with the Soviet Union were such that exaggeration or jaundiced interpretation could be expected, particularly as there were rumours of Russian troop movements in the Balkans.[41] However, it is likely that Stalin was not enthusiastic to see Mao Tse-tung's delegate participating in the Security Council openly. The Soviet absence was an immense bonus for Truman and Acheson in their decision to use the Security Council. American policy moved with rare speed, decisiveness and success in the initial phase of the Korean War. The Security Council adopted a resolution on 25 June by nine votes to nil with one abstention (Yugoslavia) and one not present (Soviet Union). This deplored the North Korean attack, termed the action a breach of the peace, and urged the cessation of hostilities with the withdrawal of North Korean forces to the 38th parallel.[42]

Truman returned to Washington by air on 25 June and was met at the airport by Acheson, Louis Johnson (Secretary of Defense) and James E. Webb (Assistant Secretary of State). According to Webb's retrospective account, they travelled from the airport in the same car as the President to facilitate discussion before an important meeting to be held over dinner at Blair House that evening. Webb stated that Truman's first remark was that he intended to act resolutely and uttered words to the effect, 'By God I'm going to let them have it.'[43] Johnson expressed full agreement but Webb stated that much thought had been devoted to the complexity of the crisis and it was essential for the President to consider the outcome before acting; Webb wrote that he spoke on these lines rather than Acheson because of the acrimonious relationship between Johnson and Acheson. When the party reached Blair House, Webb spoke privately to Truman before they joined the assembled guests for dinner. The recommendations of the State Department and the Pentagon were to eliminate as many North Korean tanks as possible through air attack, since the tanks were fast advancing on Seoul and Americans had to be evacuated from the city. The South Korean forces urgently required relief. The second recommendation was to use the Seventh Fleet to prevent an invasion of Taiwan. The third recommendation which, in the opinion of Acheson and certain others, would have to be implemented soon, was to send American military forces to South Korea to halt and reverse the North Korean advance.[44] The latter obviously had to be handled delicately at this time because the whole problem was under discussion in the UN. Those present at the dinner included the joint chiefs of staff. After the meal the major issues concerning Korea and Taiwan were debated. General Bradley did not believe the Soviet Union intended to begin a world war because she was not ready for it. He endorsed the actions recommended by Acheson, which included authorising MacArthur to supply Korea with arms and equipment under the terms of the existing aid programme and of dispatching the Seventh Fleet to prevent a Chinese invasion of Taiwan.

Louis Johnson raised the sensitive and highly important aspect of the relationship between Washington and General MacArthur: this soon became one of the major themes and controversies of the Korean War until MacArthur was ultimately dismissed by Truman. Johnson thought that instructions to MacArthur should be detailed 'so as not to give him too much discretion'.[45] Johnson held that 'there should not be a real delegation of Presidential authority to General MacArthur'.[46] However, other matters were so pressing that this was not pursued further. Johnson and the joint chiefs were opposed to using American ground troops in Korea; air and naval action could be taken but it would not be wise to deploy ground troops. Truman decided that MacArthur should send supplies to Korea together with a survey group. Elements of the American fleet were to be sent to Japanese waters; the air force should prepare a contingency plan for eliminating Soviet air bases in the Far East. The State and Defense departments should assess areas of the globe where Soviet action might take place.[47]

The United States embassy in Moscow recommended a firm response to the North Korean attack but did not think that the Soviet Union desired a general war.[48] In South Korea panic prevailed and Syngman Rhee apparently suffered a nervous breakdown. In the face of the drive south of the North Korean forces, Rhee was unable to discuss matters coherently and wished to leave Seoul for Taejon.[49] Everett Drumright, counsellor of the American embassy, wrote privately that Rhee had gone 'off his head' for a time but had quickly recovered.[50] The North Korean forces were superior in equipment and morale but the South Korean forces put up some resistance; as Muccio later observed, had they not done so, the North Koreans would have been in Seoul on the afternoon of 25 June rather than three days afterwards.[51] Truman and his advisers prepared the ground for dispatching United States forces to Korea under the authority of the UN. The President remarked that: 'he had done everything he could for five years to prevent this kind of situation. Now the situation is here and we must do whatever we can to meet it.'[52] Acheson began contacting America's allies to enlist their full support in the UN. His message to the British government stated that developments in Korea made clear that 'centrally directed Communist Imperialism has passed beyond subversion in seeking to conquer independent nations and now is resorting to armed aggression and war'.[53] Ernest Bevin was ill in hospital and Kenneth Younger, the Minister of State at the Foreign Office, handled day-to-day issues. The British response to the Korean crisis was to deplore the aggression that had occurred but there was no wish to become embroiled – or to see the United States deeply embroiled – in Korea when the most dangerous potential Soviet challenge was located in Europe.[54] The Foreign Office advised against including the reference to centrally directed communist imperialism since this would not permit the Soviet Union to undertake a diplomatic retreat should Stalin wish to do so.[55] The British representations succeeded and the reference was omitted from Truman's definition of American policy. Truman's statement of 27 June has already been cited in the context of policy over Taiwan. The paragraph dealing with Korea emphasised the true meaning of the fighting in the peninsula: 'The attack upon Korea makes it plain beyond all doubt that Communism has passed beyond the use of subversion to conquer independent nations and will now use armed invasion and war.'[56] On the same day the UN Security Council carried by seven votes to one (Yugoslavia opposing) and two members not voting (Egypt and India) with the Soviet Union still absent, a resolution condemning the breach of the peace, calling on North Korean forces to return to the 38th parallel, recognising that urgent military measures were necessary, and recommending member states to extend such assistance to South Korea as might be needed in order to repel the armed attack and restore peace.[57]

On 29 June MacArthur was instructed to use the naval and air resources of Far East Command to support the South Korean forces; to restrict the employment of the army to essential communications and service units; to defend Taiwan against attack and to ensure that Chiang Kai-shek's forces should not be used to attack the mainland; the Seventh Fleet would come under MacArthur's operational control; air operations could be extended to North Korea if and when this became necessary and such operations would concentrate on air bases, depots, tanks and other military targets (special care should be exercised to keep clear of the frontiers of Manchuria and the Soviet Union); munitions and supplies should be dispatched to Korea; the decision to commit American forces did not connote a decision to become involved in war with the Soviet Union but if the Russians intervened, then MacArthur's forces should defend themselves before reporting to Washington for further instructions.[58] MacArthur went to Korea and assessed the military position on 30 June. He reported that the South Korean forces were retreating in confusion and that the calibre of leadership had been poor. The South Korean army had been organised as a light defensive force and was faced by a challenge for which it was ill-equipped. Defensive preparations were inadequate and much equipment had been lost. The civilian population was tranquil but growing numbers of people were fleeing south to escape the North Koreans. Supplies were being maintained as best he could through the air-head at Suwon and the southern port of Pusan. It was imperative to stop the North Koreans and the answer was obvious:

> The only assurance for the holding of the present line, and the ability to regain later the lost ground is through the introduction of US ground combat forces into the Korean battle area. To continue to utilize the

forces of our air, and navy without an effective ground element cannot be decisive.[59]

Muccio's view was the same as MacArthur's. Muccio worked frantically to sustain South Korean morale but, in a telephone conversation on 30 June, he described the situation as desperate. He was unsure how long he could prop up the ROK government without tangible American assistance.[60] The ROK army had suffered 60 per cent casualties and had been reduced to a strength of 30,000 as against a North Korean strength of 100,000.[61]

The reaction of the Soviet Union was muted in the first ten days of the war. Stalin made no major statement and senior Soviet officials were reluctant to meet American and British diplomats. *Pravda* on 28 June published a front-page article stating that the imperialistic instigators of war had not stopped half-way in seeking to attain their aims. A provocative advance of South Korean troops had caused the conflict:

> Clique of Syngman Rhee entered on the road of military adventure. They counted in advance on military aid from their masters across the sea. Aggressive plans of their patrons now begin to show themselves. Truman had given orders to United States Air and Naval forces to give armed 'support' to South Korea and has ordered the 7th American Fleet to 'prevent an attack on Formosa', which constitutes an order for the occupation in effect, of part of the territory of China by American armed forces. This statement means that United States Government has undertaken direct acts of aggression. Have they not, however, gone too far? The American Government is grossly violating the constitution of United Nations and is acting as if United Nations did not exist. Question arises who authorised United States Government to take this step? In bringing its armed forces into action did the United States Government accord its policy with United Nations? Where and when did the Security Council take the decision freeing hands of United States Government to undertake actions in regard to Korea and China which Truman announced yesterday? In undertaking its openly aggressive acts it is evident that purpose of United States Government was to confront United Nations with a fait accompli.[62]

In the Soviet press reports were published on 29 June giving the reactions of North Korea and China, in addition to the Soviet Union. A communiqué issued by the North Korean army claimed victory in a rout of the South Korean forces. The People's Army was proceeding to liberate Chunchon, Honchen and areas to the south. Naval detachments were landed at Kannon and Semchon in the southern part of Kanwon province and had joined forces with guerrillas to liberate bordering areas. Further districts were in the process of being liberated. Seoul had been captured on 28 June at 11.30 a.m.; Kim Il Sung broadcast to congratulate the troops on their 'brilliant new victory' and to congratulate the inhabitants of Seoul on being freed from the yoke of

Syngman Rhee.[63] From New York Tass reported that the Korean crisis began with 'the adventurist attempt of the Syngman Rhee puppet clique directed by the USA, to invade the Korean People's Democratic Republic'.[64] This had been carefully prepared with the help of KMAG, more than 500 strong, commanded by Brigadier-General Roberts. Selective quotations from the American press underlined the dominant American impact on South Korea and Dulles's visit was emphasised. Rhee's past promises to unite Korea were cited, including a speech made by Rhee on 1 March 1950. Tass reported the comments of the Peking paper, *Jen Min Jih Pao*; the latter had published an editorial article headed 'The Korean people fighting against the invaders' and stated that the Korean People's Democratic Republic had been forced to respond to the aggression of Rhee's 'puppet troops'.[65] The Rhee clique was controlled by the United States and had 'made use of all barbarian stratagems possible for the persecution, arrest, murder and suppression of patriots and also to hinder and thwart the realisation of the proposals of the united democratic patriotic front for the peaceful unification of the country'.[66] Rhee and his followers were responsible for starting a civil war but fundamentally it was an American responsibility:

> The chief political intriguers and those responsible for the civil war are the American imperialists, and there is no need to declare that they have carried out the necessary preparations for the commencement of war.
>
> On June 19 State Department adviser Dulles, speaking to the so-called National Assembly of South Korea, openly announced the readiness of the USA to give all necessary moral and material support to South Korea, which is fighting against Communism.
>
> These facts are irrefutable proof that the American imperialists have incited the Syngman Rhee bloc in organising the civil war in Korea.[67]

The British Foreign Office believed that it was 'virtually certain that the Soviet Government had connived at if they have not instigated the aggression by the Communists of North Korea'.[68] It was most likely a probing act to see how the West responded; unless it was effectively opposed, it could stimulate Soviet initiatives elsewhere, as in Iran. The evaluations of George F. Kennan and Charles E. Bohlen, the two leading American authorities on Soviet policy-making, were similar. Bohlen told Kennan that it was 'a very clear case of typical Stalin methods whereby he initiates action not formally and directly involving the Soviet Union which he can and will press to the full if only weakness is encountered while leaving himself a way out without too direct loss of Soviet face if he considers the risks were becoming too great'.[69] The tone of the earlier statement in *Pravda* and of a subsequent statement on 29 June was interpreted by the American embassy in Moscow as meaning that the Soviet Union had adopted a waiting posture without committing herself too positively; the statements were ambiguous and seemed to offer scope for the Russians either to support North Korea or to avoid involvement. Admiral Kirk, the ambassador in Moscow, recommended a cautious approach, concentrating on refuting Soviet allegations against South Korea and stressing the UN dimension while seeing how matters evolved. [70] Kirk had met the elusive Andrei Gromyko, deputy Soviet Foreign Minister, on 29 June. Gromyko's comments were restricted to blaming South Korea for starting the war and pointing out that the Soviet Union had withdrawn forces from Korea before the United States. He reaffirmed the Soviet Union's traditional policy of non-interference in the affairs of other states.[71] While the situation was a delicate one, there was a possibility of eliciting Soviet cooperation and the British Foreign Office favoured standing firm but without antagonising the Russians. The British ambassador in Moscow, Sir David Kelly, sought to convince Gromyko of the merits of cooperation in defusing the Korean crisis. Gromyko told Kelly on 6 July that the Soviet government desired a peaceful solution and invited British reactions. Kelly replied that the Soviet Union could exert influence with North Korea to halt the bloodshed; the British wish was for the war to be stopped on the basis of reverting to the status quo ante. Gromyko nodded assent. Kelly inquired whether he could inform London that the Soviet Union would be willing to intervene diplomatically to achieve a settlement. Gromyko simply stated that the ambassador was aware of the Soviet position.[72] The British government urged the United States not to take action which might exacerbate matters and explained that British public opinion felt that the Russians themselves realised they had gone too far in Korea.[73]

The American embassy in Moscow believed that Russian ideas should be explored: the return of the North Koreans beyond the 38th parallel was fundamental and the United States could express the wish that all-Korea elections should be held, supervised by the UN.[74] Charles Bohlen's assessment was that Stalin faced a difficult choice now that American forces were fully committed in Korea. Once American power became effective the North Koreans would be forced to retreat and the issue of the 38th parallel would become a live one. Stalin would either have to allow American troops to cross the 38th parallel and thus tolerate an American presence close to Vladivostok and within easy bombing range of Khabarovsk, or of reoccupying North Korea with Soviet forces. It was unlikely that he would follow the latter course because it would increase the danger of direct Soviet conflict against the United States; in addition, the psychological repercussions in Asia would be undesirable. Stalin might be prepared to compromise through allowing a partial retreat with acceptance of the status quo ante. This would involve the retirement of North Korean forces and the departure of American forces; the latter would be unacceptable to the USA. What was all important was the speed of the United States military response in Korea.[75]

Acheson was cool in his reaction. The possibility of the Russians trying to sow dissent had to be borne in mind and it would not be wise to appear over-anxious or zealous. Acheson told the British that Sir David Kelly could pursue his discussions with Gromyko with the aim of securing a North Korean acceptance of the Security Council's resolution of 25 June. This would be without prejudice to the commitment of the UN to the peaceful unification of Korea on lines laid down by the UN General Assembly.[76] Ernest Bevin had been reflecting on Anglo-American relations in the light of Korea and decided to explain his views frankly to Acheson on 7 July, which were handed to the Secretary of State by Sir Oliver Franks the following afternoon. Bevin saw Taiwan and Chinese representation at the UN as stumbling-blocks, which should be removed. Over Korea the United States enjoyed the full support of world opinion, which could not be said of Taiwan. A number of countries, including India, believed that Taiwan should be taken over by the Chinese communist government eventually. In Bevin's opinion it was not sensible to muddle the clear-cut issue of aggression in Korea with the dubious matter of Taiwan. It would be best to play down the parts of President Truman's statement of 27 June referring to questions other than Korea. The Soviet attitude compelled consideration of the future of the Korean peninsula. It was possible that the Russians were endeavouring to exploit the existing divergences in Anglo-American policies to China; it was also possible that the Russians were hoping for a negative western approach on joint discussions. Another problem was that restoration of the status quo in Korea might simply result in a development such as had occurred in Czechoslovakia.[77]

Bevin's hope that Acheson would appreciate his frankness was reciprocated but Acheson's vigorous reaction was not palatable. Acheson responded on 10 July and made clear his resentment at Bevin's references to Taiwan and Communist China. Aggression in Korea represented the equivalent of German aggression in the 1930s. A strong reaction was essential to avert a repetition of the failures of the earlier decade. The Soviet Union could extricate herself from the dilemma she faced if she so wished. Russia had inspired the events in Korea and there was some evidence that China was involved in the fighting in Korea and elsewhere in Asia with serious implications for Britain in Hong Kong and Malaya. The Soviet Union had chosen to withdraw from the Security Council and this was not the responsibility of the Americans or British. On China Acheson said candidly he could see no way of reconciling the existing divergence between them. The United States could not recognise Peking because of the negative attitude shown to American nationals and interests; because China would not affirm international commitments; because she had recognised Ho Chi Minh and intervened in Indo-China; Peking was encouraging insurgents in the Philippines, Malaya, Burma and elsewhere; because China was working closely with the Soviet Union and had allowed Soviet penetration of

China; because Peking did not control the whole of China; and China was currently defying the UN by supporting North Korean aggression.[78] Acheson viewed China in classical Cold War terms and could discern the danger of dominoes toppling throughout South-East Asia and perhaps extending to India and Japan. He did not believe Chinese communist ambitions could be deflected through a temporary accommodation. Action had been taken on Taiwan to stabilise the situation and a longer-term solution would have to be worked out: this could occur through a Japanese peace treaty or through the good offices of the UN. Acheson instructed his ambassador in London to 'remind Bevin orally of grave doubts he himself expressed to me in private conversation in London as to wisdom of Britain's own China policy and ask him frankly what possible practical advantages he sees in trying to get Communist China into SC and return to SC of USSR in present situation'.[79] The Security Council had been able to act decisively only because of Russia's absence and a Soviet return would cause confusion. Acheson ended his instructions, 'I want you to leave him in no doubt of seriousness with which I view implications of his message and their possible effect on our whole future relationship.'[80]

Douglas visited Bevin in hospital on 11 July and communicated Acheson's message. Bevin was shaken by the acerbic nature of Acheson's remarks. He felt it was necessary to decide how to deal with any proposals the Soviet Union might produce and to consider the possibilities. He was vague on the advantages of having Communist China present in the Security Council. Bevin stated he had never doubted the wisdom or justice of the decision to recognise China but he had expressed doubts as to the outcome being what would be ideally wished. Douglas derived the impression Bevin had not grasped the full implications of the message and that possibly he had been pressured into sending it by his subordinates.[81] This was the first of the series of serious strains and tensions in Anglo-American relations during the Korean War and which resulted fundamentally from British reservations about the sweeping nature of American policy-making with the tendency to overreact in unduly emotional terms. Bevin was not dissatisfied at the exchanges between Gromyko and Kelly. His private secretary wrote that Bevin had not expected more and it would be necessary now to await developments; it was best to leave the Russians to make the next initiative. Bevin

> did not believe that Stalin wanted the situation in the Far East to develop in such a way as to cause the United States to build up tremendous forces there. It was possible that Mao Tse Tung [*sic*] wanted to try to involve Stalin in war with the United States, but he thought that Stalin would get out of this.[82]

The Soviet Union decided to return to the Security Council in August 1950, realising the foolishness of continued absence; the return was sweetened by the fact that it was the Soviet turn to chair the Security

Council and the chairman's role could be used to obstruct initiatives, as proved to be the case. No significant progress in American–Soviet relations in Korea was to be achieved until the spring of 1951 when George Kennan met Jacob Malik.

Finally to revert to developments in the UN and the formal establishment of the UN Command under General MacArthur. President Truman recalled in retirement that the most difficult decision of his presidency had been the commitment of American forces to the Korean campaign.[83] Truman possessed deep reserves of courage and tenacity and lived up to his favourite slogan of 'the buck stops here'. He was a man of straightforward, uncomplicated outlook and saw events in Korea as a flagrant act of aggression for which the Soviet Union was responsible. As with his colleagues, Truman was conscious of the mistakes made in dealing with Hitler in the 1930s and was determined not to repeat them. He would not preside over a 'far eastern Munich'. Truman did not wish to request a congressional declaration of war, for this might be time-consuming and could handicap his freedom of manœuvre. He carefully and stubbornly described the American role in Korea as part of a police operation under the authority of the UN. The UN was important because it meant that the United States would not be acting alone, that the principles of the UN Charter would be maintained, and that no encouragement would be given to right-wing, isolationist Republicans. The administration's decisive reaction to Korea was widely applauded in the country and there were few critics in Congress: Senator Robert A. Taft (Republican, Ohio) believed Truman should have brought the matter to Congress but there was no widespread dissatisfaction. The initial response of the American people in terms of correspondence to Truman revealed that up to and including 29 June letters ran ten to one in support of the President. More opposition was voiced in telegrams, however, where the total was 325 in support, 225 against with 125 classified as miscellaneous.[84] Truman held that General MacArthur should be appointed as the UN commander in Korea, since the United States would be contributing the vast majority of the UN forces and MacArthur was the greatest living American soldier with extensive experience of East Asia and the western Pacific. Truman was aware of MacArthur's tendency to act independently and of his political ambitions but believed these dangers could be controlled. There was indeed an added political bonus in having a right-wing Republican in command of the UN forces in Korea – so long, that is, as the appointment did not have a boomerang effect. MacArthur realised the immensity of the challenge but was confident he would succeed, given sufficient resources and freedom of action. What could be a more fitting climax for his military career than defeating communist aggression and perhaps rolling back communism out of Korea altogether? Furthermore, what could be a more appropriate way of launching a final attempt to secure the Republican presidential nomination in 1952?

John Foster Dulles exhibited little enthusiasm at MacArthur's proposed appointment. He wrote to Acheson on 7 July that he assumed the general would be designated for the post. Given the extreme gravity of the world situation, the necessity to prevent the Korean War becoming a world war and of preserving the support of the other members of the Security Council, and of other aspects drawn to the attention of Truman and Acheson previously:

> ... I suggest that the President might want to emphasise by personal message to General MacArthur the delicate nature of the responsibilities which he will now be carrying, not only on behalf of the United States but on behalf of the United Nations, and the importance of instructing his staff to comply scrupulously with political and military limitations and instructions which may be sent, the reasons for which may not always be immediately apparent, but which will often have behind them political considerations of gravity.[85]

MacArthur was not susceptible to hints or indeed to outright orders of which he disapproved and presidential authority could only be exercised over him with difficulty. Ultimately a confrontation with the White House was inevitable and there is little surprise at Truman's decision to dismiss MacArthur in April 1951, although respect for the President's courage is engendered. The UN Security Council carried a resolution on 7 July by seven votes to nil with three abstentions (Egypt, India and Yugoslavia) and one member absent (Soviet Union) welcoming support for the previous motions of 25 and 27 June recommending all members to supply military forces and other assistance; requesting the United States to appoint the commander of such forces, and to request the United States to furnish the Security Council with reports on developments.[86] Truman at once announced MacArthur's appointment, which was in addition to his existing appointments as SCAP and as commander-in-chief of United States forces in Korea. MacArthur responded with a fulsome message to Truman, thanking him most warmly for the confidence shown in him and promising complete loyalty to the President.[87]

Thus the events set in motion by Kim Il Sung's ardent wish to unify his country led to a situation whereby the UN was at war in Korea in a conflict of singularly unpredictable political and military character. Kim Il Sung and perhaps the Soviet Union had gambled on swift success with reluctant American acquiescence in the outcome. Instead the UN had endorsed the principle of containment in Korea, of no North Korean advance beyond the 38th parallel. What was not clear in July 1950 was whether the UN would proceed to endorse the principle of rolling back communism and of unifying the peninsula in accordance with UN policy as approved by the General Assembly in December 1948.

# REFERENCES

1. Letter from Bond to Muccio, 1 June 1950, State Department records, 795.00/1-750, RG59, box 4682, National Archives, Washington.
2. Letter from Muccio to Bond, 23 June 1950, ibid.
3. *FRUS 1950* (7), p. 109, memorandum by Allison, 19 June 1950.
4. See Chapter 5 above.
5. For MacArthur's interest in Taiwan, see W. W. Stueck, Jr, *The Road to Confrontation* (Chapel Hill, NC 1981), pp. 138–40, 150, and N. B. Tucker, *Patterns in the Dust* (Guildford 1983), p. 310, n. 39.
6. MacArthur to Department of Army, 29 May 1950, RG6, box 8, Formosa File, MacArthur Papers, MacArthur Memorial.
7. Letter from Franks to Dening, 7 June 1950, FC10345/9, FO 371/83320. Acheson thought highly of Sir Oliver Franks and had decided, soon after becoming Secretary of State, to meet the ambassador privately for informal 'off the record' discussions; see Dean Acheson, *Present at the Creation* (London 1970), p. 323.
8. Minute by Strang, 10 June 1950, FC10345/9, FO 371/83320.
9. Letter from Graves to Shattock, 22 June 1950, FC1345/12, FO 371/83320.
10. Ibid.
11. State Department to SCAP, 13 June 1950, relaying Taipei to Washington, 12 June 1950, RG6, box 80, Formosa File, MacArthur Memorial.
12. For Acheson's wish to promote a bipartisan policy, see dispatch from Franks to Bevin, 30 June 1950, FC10345/10, FO 371/83320.
13. Ibid.
14. Taipei to State Department, 26 June 1950, State Department records, 795.00/1-750, RG59, box 4682, National Archives.
15. *FRUS 1950* (7), p. 203, statement by Truman, 27 June 1950.
16. Robert O'Neill, *Australia in the Korean War*, vol. I, *Strategy and Diplomacy* (Canberra 1981), p. 12.
17. Ibid., p. 14.
18. Cited ibid.
19. *Report of the United Nations Commission on Korea: Covering the Period from 15 December 1949 to 4 September 1950*, General Assembly, Official Records: Fifth Session, Supplement no. 16 (A/1350) (New York 1950), p. 4. The report was signed by Arup Singh (Chairman) (India), A. B. Jamieson (*Rapporteur*) (Australia), Li Yu-wan (China, Kuomintang), Angel Gochez Marin (El Salvador), Henri Brionval (France), Benabe Africa (Philippines) and Kamil Idil (Turkey).
20. See G. F. Kennan, *Memoirs, 1925–1950* (London 1968), pp. 395, 486, and FO memorandum, 26 June 1950, FK1015/62, FO 371/84058.
21. N. S. Khruschev, *Reminiscences* (London 1971), pp. 367–9. The majority of authorities incline to accepting this source as genuine but the work should be used with caution.
22. Bruce Cumings, 'Introduction: the course of Korean–American relations, 1943–1953', in Cumings (ed.), *Child of Conflict: The Korean–American Relationship, 1943–1953* (London 1983), p. 39. Cumings states that a minimum of 30,000 troops were involved in the transfer from the Chinese to the North Korean army.

23. Ibid., pp. 40–1, n. 59.
24. Ibid., p. 41, n. 59, pp. 54–5. For further discussion of the circumstances of the beginning of the war, see Karunker Gupta, 'How did the Korean War begin?', *China Quarterly*, **8** (1972), 699–716. Gupta underlines the uncertainties over what occurred on 25 June and the possibilities of provocation from the ROK. See also R. R. Simmons, *The Strained Alliance: Peking, Pyongyang, Moscow, and the Politics of the Korean Civil War* (New York 1975): Simmons contends that Stalin had approved a North Korean attack but that this had been planned for August instead of June 1950 – Kim Il sung acted independently to advance the date.
25. See Khrushchev, op. cit., p. 370. See also BBC Monitoring, reported to FO, 24 Aug. 1950, FK10338/5, FO 371/84130. This was based on Central News from Korea and indicated that the Soviet Union had ordered withdrawal of all Soviet military advisers and tank teams from North Korea shortly after the UN decided on military aid for the ROK. Intelligence sources had checked the information and believed it to be genuine. The decision to withdraw all military advisers from North Korean battalions engaged in front-line operations was reportedly made about the eighth day of the war and coincided with the dispatch of armed forces to Korea. It was further indicated that tank teams were replaced by North Koreans. Intelligence sources revealed that there were fifteen Russian military advisers attached to each North Korean division and that tanks were manned by Russian veterans at the beginning of the invasion. The official Soviet view was that the North Koreans were doing well enough and could operate without Soviet participation.
26. Cumings in Cumings (ed.), p. 50. For a discussion of the activities of Burgess, Maclean and Philby, see Andrew Boyle, *The Climate of Treason: Five Who Spied for Russia* (London 1979).
27. NSC 68 revealed clearly the acceptance of the global communist threat and made clear the need to resist this menace by all appropriate means. For the text, see *FRUS 1950* (1), pp. 234–92.
28. As communicated in letter from Holt to Tomlinson, 7 June 1950, FK1015/12, FO 371/84056.
29. Ibid.
30. Letter from Holt to Tomlinson, 16 June 1950, FK1015/16, ibid.
31. Letter from Holt to Bevin, 20 June 1950, FK1015/79, FO 371/84059.
32. *FRUS 1950* (7), p. 108, memorandum by Allison, 19 June 1950.
33. Ibid.
34. Minute by Tomlinson, 5 July 1950, on dispatch from Gascoigne to Bevin, 22 June 1950, FJ1021/97, FO 371/83831.
35. *FRUS 1950* (7), pp. 109–21, memorandum by CIA, 19 June 1950.
36. Letter from Holt to Tomlinson, 22 June 1950, FK1017/23, FO 371/84077.
37. *FRUS 1950* (7), pp. 125–6, Muccio to Acheson, 25 June 1950.
38. Ibid., pp. 237–8, memorandum by Dulles, 29 June 1950, and J. M. Allison, *Ambassador from the Prairies*, paperback edn (Tokyo 1975), pp. 132, 134–5.
39. *FRUS 1950* (7), p. 140, Sebald to Acheson, 25 June 1950, enclosing views of Dulles and Allison.
40. Washington to FO, 29 June 1950, based on information given by Perkins

of the State Department to Hoyer Miller of the British embassy, FK1022/24, FO 371/84080.

41. Ibid.
42. *FRUS 1950* (7), pp. 155–6, resolution adopted by UN Security Council, 25 June 1950.
43. Letter from Webb to John W. Snyder, 25 April 1975, general correspondence, S, 1973–75, folder 2, Webb Papers, Truman Library.
44. Ibid.
45. *FRUS 1950* (7), p. 160, memorandum by Jessup, 25 June 1950.
46. Ibid.
47. Ibid.
48. Ibid, pp. 139–40, Kirk to Acheson, 25 June 1950.
49. Ibid., pp. 141–2, Muccio to Acheson, 26 June 1950.
50. Letter from Drumright to Allison, 8 July 1950, selected State Department records relating to the Korean War, box 4, Truman Papers, Truman Library.
51. Muccio Oral History, interview between Muccio and R. D. McKinzie, p. 11, copy in Truman Library.
52. *FRUS 1950* (7), p. 183, memorandum by Truman, 26 June 1950.
53. Ibid., pp. 186–7, Acheson to Douglas, 27 June 1950.
54. For British views, see Alan Bullock, *Life and Times of Ernest Bevin* vol. III (London 1983), pp. 790–3.
55. *FRUS 1950* (7), p. 187, n. 3.
56. Ibid., p. 202, statement by Truman, 27 June 1950.
57. Ibid., p. 211, resolution adopted by UN Security Council, 27 June 1950.
58. Ibid., pp. 240–1, joint chiefs of staff to MacArthur, 29 June 1950.
59. Ibid., p. 249, MacArthur to Acheson and joint chiefs of staff, 30 June 1950.
60. Ibid., pp. 254–5, Sebald to Acheson, 30 June 1950, summarising views of Muccio.
61. Ibid., p. 255, n.
62. Moscow to FO, 28 June 1950, enclosing summary of front-page article in *Pravda*, 28 June 1950, FK1015/52, FO 371/84057.
63. *Soviet Monitor*, 29 June 1950.
64. Ibid.
65. Ibid.
66. Ibid.
67. Ibid.
68. FO memorandum, 26 June 1950, prepared for Bevin, FK1015/62, FO 371/84058.
69. *FRUS 1950* (7), p. 174, Bruce (Paris) to Acheson, enclosing personal message from Bohlen for Kennan. For Kennan's views, see Kennan, op. cit., pp. 395, 486.
70. *FRUS 1950* (7), pp. 253–4, Kirk to Acheson, 30 June 1950.
71. Ibid., pp. 229–30, Kirk to Acheson, 29 June 1950.
72. Ibid., pp. 312–13, Kirk to Acheson, 7 July 1950.
73. Ibid., pp. 313–14, British embassy to State Department, 6 July 1950.
74. Ibid., pp. 315–16, Kirk to Acheson, 6 July 1950.
75. Ibid., pp. 325–7, memorandum by Bohlen, 7 July 1950.
76. Ibid., pp. 327–8, Acheson to Douglas, for communications to FO, 7 July 1950.

77. Ibid., pp. 329–30, message from Bevin to Franks, 7 July 1950, communicated to State Department, 8 July 1950.
78. Ibid., pp. 347–51, Acheson to Douglas, 10 July 1950, for communication to Bevin.
79. Ibid., pp. 351–2, Acheson to Douglas, 10 July 1950.
80. Ibid., p. 352.
81. Ibid., Douglas to Acheson, 11 July 1950.
82. Minute by Barclay, 12 July 1950, FK1022/96/G, FO 371/84085.
83. Film shown in the Truman Library in which the former President answered questions from school students on his career as President and the difficult decisions he had been faced with.
84. Memorandum by Hopkins for Ross, 29 June 1950, official file 471-B, box 1305, Truman Papers, Truman Library.
85. *FRUS 1950* (7), p. 328, memorandum from Dulles to Acheson, 7 July 1950.
86. Ibid., p. 329, resolution adopted by UN Security Council, 7 July 1950.
87. MacArthur to Truman, 11 July 1950, FECOM, general files, folder 4, RG6, box 8, MacArthur Papers, MacArthur Memorial.

# Chapter 8

# ROLLBACK AND CHINESE INTERVENTION IN KOREA

The development of the Korean War between July and November 1950 was largely dominated by General Douglas MacArthur. MacArthur restored confidence to the UN forces in the early part of this period, helped to stabilise the defence line in the Pusan redoubt before the dramatic events following the Inchon landing on 15 September and controlled the drive northwards, which culminated in the confrontation on the Yalu river, marking the decisive entry of China into the Korean conflict. The final phase of MacArthur's distinguished career remains extremely controversial because of the growing differences of opinion between the general and his superiors in Washington. The acrimony associated with his eventual dismissal by President Truman has obscured certain of the issues and the behaviour of the principals. MacArthur's supporters maintained that he had been made a scapegoat for the vacillation and timidity of Truman and the joint chiefs of staff. MacArthur's critics contended that he had pursued his own strategy with scant concern for constitutional proprieties. The allegations on both sides were exaggerated but each contained some validity. Part of the problem resulted from MacArthur's having too many commitments and responsibilities: he was simultaneously SCAP in Japan, commander-in-chief of American forces, and commander-in-chief of UN forces. He enjoyed immense prestige and power after many years of military service, concluding with his political role in Japan after 1945. Senior army officers had served under him and usually regarded him with awe. Politicians respected or feared him and were reluctant to challenge his authority.

MacArthur had freedom of manœuvre denied most commanders and he exploited that freedom for all it was worth. However, it was not simply a matter of MacArthur manipulating instructions and situations to his advantage; Truman and the joint chiefs often failed to provide instructions that were explicit enough and avoided ambiguity. The decision-makers in Washington on a number of occasions refrained from defining the objectives of policy clearly or emphatically because they were undecided themselves on crucial aspects. MacArthur stated to the Senate hearing on his dismissal, in May 1951, that, 'No more subordinate soldier has ever worn the American uniform than himself.'[1] There is ample evidence contradicting this sentiment but equally on various occasions MacArthur was permitted the freedom to interpret orders in the direction he desired. A series of incidents occurred between August 1950 and March 1951 in which MacArthur acted independently and some of his actions were disavowed. Only in April 1951 did Truman act vigorously and courageously to resolve the problem. MacArthur had considerable achievements to his credit in his handling of events between July and the beginning of October 1950 but he sadly squandered these by the extent of his miscalculations in late October and November 1950. The members of MacArthur's 'court' – his circle of close advisers – must bear much responsibility for the extent of the errors made, particularly over the likelihood of China entering into the war. His two principal aides were Generals Courtney Whitney and Charles Willoughby. They had served with MacArthur for many years and saw their functions as to protect the great commander from those who would waste his time or upset him. They were rivals in the customary bureaucratic jockeying surrounding a powerful figure whether in politics, the armed forces or business.[2] John J. Muccio, who saw much of MacArthur at this time, thought he possessed a great brain but had reached an age where he was no longer fully conversant with all significant aspects of the situation.[3]

Before discussing further the vital political questions from July to November 1950, it is necessary to summarise briefly the rapidly fluctuating military fortunes of the two sides (see Map 3). The North Korean forces advanced relentlessly during July until, in the last ten days of the month, they were threatening the south-eastern part of the peninsula, which included the important city of Taegu and the ports of Pusan and Masan. The UN command was represented by three American divisions; in addition, there were five South Korean divisions. The first American troops to be sent to Korea were thrust from the comparative luxury of life in Japan to the rigours of a Korean campaign for which they were ill-prepared physically and psychologically. The immediate prospect was grim with the danger of the UN being forced out of Korea before American reinforcements could arrive. MacArthur was faced with a profound challenge but to one of his vast experience the setbacks in Korea, serious as they were, could not compare with the Japanese onslaught he had been confronted with in 1942. The adversity he had suffered during the early stages of the Pacific War brought a sense of perspective and an appreciation of the ingredients required in organising the restoration of discipline and leadership. MacArthur's task was to stabilise the front and prepare the ground for the counter-attack. The vital moment came with his brilliantly conceived and implemented landing at Inchon on 15 September. The operation was an appreciable gamble and the joint chiefs were doubtful of its wisdom. MacArthur was supremely confident that the Inchon landing would succeed and would allow him to seize the initiative and to retain it. He was correct: the operation was a devastating achievement and sapped the morale of the North Koreans. The tables were turned and the UN forces steadily and then swiftly advanced north. By early October the UN forces on the eastern front had advanced beyond the 38th parallel (see Map 4). Nothing could stop MacArthur's men short of the intervention of China or the Soviet Union.

As regards his UN role, MacArthur enjoyed extensive freedom; he submitted reports to Washington where decisions were reached as to which should be submitted to the UN Secretary-General, Trygve Lie. The fact that the United States completely dominated the UN command facilitated MacArthur's activities. There were compelling political reasons for inducing or cajoling the member states of the UN to send forces to Korea. The Truman administration emphasised that the Korean conflict directly involved the world organisation for peace in repelling aggression. The argument could only be sustained convincingly if a number of countries participated under the UN flag. Hence the pressure applied by Truman and Acheson. Offers came but in limited numbers and with no guarantee that these could reach Korea rapidly. Britain offered naval assistance at the beginning of the war and this was promptly accepted by Truman, although Secretary of Defense Louis Johnson and the joint chiefs were less enthusiastic.[4] The Attlee government did not wish to commit British troops to Korea initially because British defences were fully stretched in Europe, Malaya and Hong Kong.[5] The Cabinet decided on 4 July that while it fully endorsed the American response in Korea, problems would be caused by the dispatch of troops; there was concern at the extent of the American commitment to Taiwan and possible implications for Britain and the UN.[6] It was made abundantly clear to Sir Oliver Franks, the ambassador in Washington, that continued refusal to provide troops would harm Anglo-American relations. Attlee brought the subject to the Defence Committee, which recommended to the Cabinet that notwithstanding the arguments on British commitments elsewhere, British land forces should be sent in order to consolidate Anglo-American friendship and to placate American public opinion.[7]

By 8 August Britain, New Zealand, the Netherlands, France and Canada had offered various combinations of naval and air assistance; military help had been promised by Britain, Australia, New Zealand, Thailand, Turkey and Taiwan (refused in the latter case for political reasons), and air assistance had been promised by South Africa, Belgium and Greece.[8] India offered an army hospital unit. Talks were proceeding with France, the Philippines and Pakistan regarding the possibility of sending troops. Ultimately fifteen nations in addition to the United States contributed armed assistance with a further five contributing medical units.[9] Sufficient credibility in the UN role was barely established in terms of the number of countries involved but this was no more than a veneer on the overwhelming American contribution. MacArthur did not care much about his responsibility to the UN; he regarded himself as an American commander fighting an American role in a war between the United States and international communism.

In terms of his military accomplishments between July and October 1950 MacArthur proved outstanding. He was a growing source of anxiety to Washington in the political sphere, however, and the first significant example concerned Taiwan during July and August 1950. MacArthur felt passionately that Taiwan must be denied to the Chinese communists for strategic and ideological reasons. MacArthur was well aware of political developments in Taiwan and was favourably disposed to Chiang Kai-shek. Truman and Acheson had been captivated in part by the strategic arguments for the importance of Taiwan but they were firmly opposed to a warm relationship with Chiang Kai-shek. They were contemplating the neutralisation of Taiwan, not an alliance with the decrepit Kuomintang, which they despised. MacArthur discerned the opportunity for cementing an American–Taiwanese understanding and worked to advance this aim. Chiang Kai-shek also appreciated the opportunity and offered to send some of his troops to Korea, despite the fact that a Chinese communist invasion of Taiwan was threatened imminently. It was a straightforward political ploy and treated accordingly in Washington: the offer was declined. MacArthur was prepared to contemplate utilising Chiang's forces through encouraging Chiang to launch an attack on the Chinese mainland, which would drive China from possible interest in assisting North Korea. Truman wrote to Acheson on 18 July that he had just read a message from MacArthur dated 16 July 'which has very dangerous implications'.[10] Truman asked Acheson to discuss the matter with the Secretary of Defense 'and instruct General MacArthur that an attack by the Chinese Nationalist Government on the Mainland will be considered an unfriendly act'.[11] American diplomats in Taiwan reported resentment in the Kuomintang government at the American refusal to accept troops for Korea and at the cavalier way in which Taiwan had been treated by the United States in the previous month.[12]

Chiang was anticipating that the Korean struggle would be transformed into a third world war in which eventuality all elements hostile to communism would be welcomed by the United States. The impression was conveyed in Taipei that the Kuomintang would not be sorry to see the United States defeated in Korea, as this would be poetic justice after the harsh criticisms expressed by the Truman administration of Chiang's regime. Indeed some Americans in Taiwan were wondering who was the real enemy – the United States government or the Chinese communists.[13] The Kuomintang authorities suppressed any dissent whether from native Taiwanese or refugees from the mainland with a firm hand. The atmosphere in Taiwan was one of apprehension and suspicion but the underlying feeling was that the worst was over in the sense that the Americans would not permit an invasion by the communists.[14] A significant proportion of the Kuomintang soldiers were ill, suffering from malaria, dysentery and malnutrition. The death rate was high and the army was short of medicine. The assessment of the American representative in Taipei was that in spite of poor health and detestation of Chiang Kai-shek, the officers and men would defend Taiwan because their dislike of the communists on the mainland now outweighed their dislike for their own leaders.[15] Strong reported further on 29 July that Chiang had resorted to the old tactic of seeking to play off MacArthur against Washington and the diplomats in Taipei: he recommended that a tough attitude should be pursued towards Chiang and that American policy-making should be properly coordinated to prevent Chiang's intrigues from achieving anything.[16] Strong ended pessimistically that previous reports indicating the Kuomintang was unlikely to hold Taiwan if attacked still held good.[17] Chiang moved sedulously by his long-accustomed methods to strengthen his control over the regime, and to preclude the contingency of a coup he advanced the position of his son, Chiang Ching-kuo, and Chen Cheng at the expense of the 'CC' clique.[18]

MacArthur determined to visit Taiwan personally to assess matters and to inject more confidence in Chiang's government. The State Department did not wish him to go, realising the political perils in so doing. The Defense Department felt less strongly. On 30 July authorisation was sent for MacArthur or one of his officers to visit Taiwan; the message stated, in ambiguous phraseology, that policy issues relating to Taiwan were currently being discussed between State and Defense pending the receipt of new instructions. MacArthur could send a senior officer on 31 July and go later himself. Alternatively if MacArthur believed it essential to go himself, he could do so.[19] Estimates had been made of the Chinese communist capability of mounting an attack and it was calculated that they could convey 200,000 armed troops from the mainland to Taiwan. The communists were deemed capable of taking Taiwan without excessive difficulty unless the United States intervened.[20] MacArthur seized his opportunity and departed for Taiwan at once to be greeted effusively by Chiang. MacArthur ignored American diplomats in Taipei and they were left in ignorance of many of the issues discussed on his trip.[21] MacArthur gave undertakings that aircraft would be supplied to Taiwan and arranged for runways to be lengthened to accommodate jet planes. Truman was unaware of the undertakings given by MacArthur.[22] Upon his return to Tokyo MacArthur reported on his two-day visit (31 July–1 August). There had been a valuable exchange of views with Chiang; the Kuomintang was anxious to cooperate with the United States. Chiang was in effective command of the government. MacArthur recommended that direct liaison between his command and Taipei should be established and that critical shortages of materials should be rectified. He had agreed with Chiang that the Far East Command Liaison Group should be established with Taiwan under his authority; this would examine the requirements of the Kuomintang forces. He had authorised periodic sweeps of the Seventh Fleet between Taiwan and the mainland, periodic reconnaissance flights over coastal areas of China, and familiarisation flights of small groups of American aviators.[23] Rumours quickly circulated that MacArthur had conducted talks of deep political significance and that he had acted independently of Washington. MacArthur issued an angry statement on 10 August denouncing critics of his visit and hoping the American people would not be misled by the 'sly insinuations' regarding his exchanges with Chiang.[24] MacArthur denied having discussed any political matters in Taipei. Answering questions during the Senate investigation in May 1951, he confirmed his strongly held opinion of Taiwan's value:

> I believe if you lost Formosa you lose the key to our littoral line of defense and encompass Truk. I believe the Philippines and Japan would be untenable from our military point of view. Formosa cannot be taken by Red China as long as the United States maintains control of the sea and or the air. ...
>
> I believe that from our standpoint we practically lose the Pacific Ocean if we give up or lose Formosa.[25]

When asked by Senator Estes Kefauver (Democrat, Tennessee) for his opinion of Chiang Kai-shek, MacArthur replied:

> I believe that to the average Asiatic Chiang Kai-shek stands out as the great symbol against communism. I believe that everyone opposed to communism has a sense of respect for the generalissimo in the Far East. Those that are inclined toward communism oppose him completely and absolutely, but he does stand as a symbol of an invincible determination to resist communism.[26]

MacArthur was not one to be discouraged by criticism. Soon after his controversial visit to Taiwan he dispatched a bold message to the American Veterans convention, meeting in Chicago, reiterating the value of Taiwan, the need to resist communism and pouring scorn on those who dissented from his views.[27] The message appeared in the press immediately and caused a furore in Washington. Dean Acheson was outraged at the general's trampling over delicate policy areas and in a direction not desired by the President and himself. Truman, already alerted to MacArthur's independent actions, instructed Secretary of Defense Louis Johnson to order MacArthur to withdraw the message. Johnson prevaricated and was reluctant to comply. Truman therefore personally wrote the message to MacArthur and told Johnson to send it.[28] It simply and clearly instructed the general to withdraw his statement, since it contained views not in harmony with the policy of the administration.[29] The Veterans had printed the message but agreed to cancel it, assuring MacArthur that they were with him 'to a man'.[30] There was no doubt that the administration was committed to preventing the Chinese communists from capturing Taiwan but Truman, Acheson and Dulles were contemplating neutralisation for the island, perhaps with the inhabitants deciding on their future through a plebiscite organised by the UN.[31] The President was irate at MacArthur's attitude but believed the general had to be supported in Korea at such a critical juncture.

In the political sphere the vital issue under consideration between July and September 1950 was whether or not UN forces should cross the 38th parallel, and, if so, what would be the fate of North Korea. At the beginning of the war the question had largely been put to one side, given the military exigencies and on the part of many, there was a vague understanding that the aim was to restore the status quo ante through driving the North Koreans beyond the 38th parallel. Cogent arguments could be found for advancing beyond the parallel and for not doing so. There could be no lasting solution of the Korean problem while the peninsula was divided into two states. The policy of the UN since 1947–48 had been to accomplish a unified Korea on the basis of freely arranged elections under UN auspices. The UN was indeed committed by past decisions and was in dispute with North Korea because of the refusal to permit UN supervision of the elections north of the 38th parallel. On the other hand, an attempt to unify Korea by force directed by the UN contained many dangers. Syngman Rhee could safely be relied on to cause maximum difficulty, since he had made no secret of his ambition to lead a unified Korea and only wanted the UN to function so long as it suited him. Major question marks surrounded the responses of the Soviet Union and China. Russia could argue that she had a residual right to assist North Korea or to reoccupy the area. China might intervene, since the disappearance of a communist state in Korea would threaten her frontiers. A sober examination of the situation and problems should have dictated caution once the parallel had been reached: the consequences of Russia or China entering the war were obviously extremely grave and a gamble ending in such an outcome should not have been risked. Predominant opinion in American and British policy-making circles supported crossing the parallel but with more serious doubts in Britain, which were soon to be accentuated.

Within the American bureaucracy basic disagreement existed between the main hawkish elements in the State Department led by John M. Allison and Dean Rusk, and the Policy Planning Staff, now headed by Paul Nitze but still deeply influenced by the views of Nitze's predecessor, George Kennan. Allison had argued strongly for crossing the parallel from early July onwards.[32] To his mind the North Koreans had fallen into a trap of their own creation and the opportunity to unite

Korea through the creation of an anti-communist state should be taken. The Policy Planning Staff favoured an agreement by North Korea to withdraw north of the parallel, to be followed by a negotiated settlement. Allison vehemently denounced such a response as craven:

> The aggressor would apparently be consulted on equal or nearly equal terms and the real aggressor, the Soviet Union, would presumably go unpunished in any way whatsoever. The aggressor would be informed that all he had to fear from aggression was being compelled to start over again.
> The North Korean regime is a creature of the Soviet Union set up in defiance of the will of the majority of the Korean people and in deliberate violation of three Resolutions passed in the General Assembly.[33]

Allison held there was serious danger of the South Korean people losing confidence in the United States unless a firm policy was followed. Furthermore it had to be understood that the communists were aiming to control Japan and that conquering Korea was the prelude to this development. Under no circumstances could the fall of Japan to communism be permitted. Allison accepted the possibility of war against the Soviet Union or China or both but he believed this had to be accepted:

> We should recognize that there is a grave danger of conflict with the USSR and the Chinese Communists whatever we do from now on – but I fail to see what advantage we gain by a compromise with clear moral principles and a shirking of our duty to make clear once and for all that aggression does not pay – that he who violates the decent opinions of mankind must take the consequences and that he who takes the sword will perish by the sword.[34]

The indications in late July and early August were that Russia and China were playing a watching game. The Soviet Union returned to the UN Security Council; Jacob Malik assumed the chair and worked to frustrate American intentions to strengthen the role of the UN in Korea. Acrimonious, tedious and repetitive propaganda exchanges between Malik and Warren Austin, the American delegate, occurred throughout August.[35] Russia was deeply committed to the North Korean cause but showed no inclination whatever to intervene directly in Korea. Soviet publications printed statements by Kim Il Sung, reports from Tass correspondents exposing odious American imperialism, and reproduced indignant motions from numerous 'peace bodies' condemning American aggression in Korea.[36] The Chinese response was similarly one of strong verbal condemnation of American actions. Chou En-lai's first response to the war had been a bitter denunciation of President Truman's statement of 27 June, but it is interesting that the strongest expression of opinion concerned Truman's references to Taiwan rather than Korea.[37] The British chargé d'affaires in Peking, John Hutchison, reported on 26 July that there were rumours of the dispatch of Chinese arms to the

Manchurian–Korean frontier and that 'volunteers' might be recruited from an international brigade to serve in Korea, but there was no solid evidence that the Chinese government was supporting North Korea with arms, men or supplies: he added his familiar plaintive qualification that his sources of information were extremely limited.[38] The official indications in Peking were that China had no intention of intervening in Korea. The weekly *World Culture* answered the question should the Soviet Union and China participate in the Korean War:

> China also has adopted the principles of non-intervention in Korea's domestic affairs ... the Soviet Union, each new democratic state, and all peace loving peoples in the world sympathise with Korean people's liberation movement but that does not imply that they should intervene with arms.[39]

Hutchison regarded the official line as very clear and this had been confirmed from another source, a junior member of the CCP.

The CIA reviewed the desirability of a military conquest of North Korea in a memorandum dated 18 August. In balanced manner it pointed out that such a course could have definite advantages but that grave risks were also entailed. Military success could not be guaranteed because the United States could count only on limited assistance from the members of the UN and the danger existed of China or Russia deciding to take military action in Korea. A further complication was the unpopular nature of Syngman Rhee's regime: to re-establish this and to extend its authority to the whole of Korea would be difficult, if not impossible. There could be permanent tension on the Korean borders even though Korea was unified, which might connote a permanent UN commitment.[40] George Kennan was about to leave the State Department at the end of August to take up an academic position, having become disillusioned by life in the bureaucracy.[41] He had fully supported the original decision to oppose North Korean aggression but experienced growing doubts as to where American policy was leading. In a memorandum dated 21 August Kennan observed that no clear, realistic policy had been devised in Korea and sections of public opinion in the United States were creating an emotional, moralistic situation, which contained the risk of real conflict with the Russians. The defects with policy as he saw them were that MacArthur possessed undue power and was not controlled effectively by Washington; policy towards China was involving conflict with other Asian states and with the British Commonwealth, the outcome being strengthening rather than weakening of links between Peking and Moscow; and the American intention to leave troops in Japan on a basis to be authorised by a Japanese peace treaty was undermining future relations with the Japanese people; the attainment of an agreement with Russia over Korea had been rendered far more difficult than it need otherwise be.[42] The aim should be to liquidate involvement on the Asian mainland speedily and on the most satisfactory terms possible. The long-term interests of the United States did not necessitate the existence of an anti-communist Korean regime throughout the Korean peninsula. It would be feasible to tolerate a Korea nominally independent but in practice responsive to Soviet influence, assuming this transition was accomplished gradually and not too emphatically, and provided the situation in Japan was stable. He summed up his approach:

> It is beyond our capabilities to keep Korea permanently out of the Soviet orbit. The Koreans cannot really maintain their own independence in the face of both Russian and Japanese pressures. From the standpoint of our own interests it is preferable that Japan should dominate Korea than that Russia should do so. But Japan at the moment is too weak to compete. We must hope that with the revival of her normal strength and prestige, Japan will regain her influence there. But the interval will probably be too long to be bridged over successfully by the expedients we have employed in the past or now have in contemplation. A period of Russian domination, while undesirable, is preferable to continued involvement in that unhappy area, as long as the means chosen to assert Soviet influence are not, as was the case with those resorted to in June of this year, ones calculated to throw panic and terror into other Asian peoples and thus to achieve for the Kremlin important successes, going far beyond the Korean area. But it is important that the nominal independence of Korea be preserved for it provides a flexible vehicle through which Japanese influence may someday gradually replace Soviet influence without creating undue international repercussions.[43]

Kennan urged an attempt be made to foster genuine diplomatic contact with the Soviet Union, on the precedent of the Malik–Jessup talks in 1949. The premisses would be American agreement to neutralisation and demilitarisation of Japan but with Japan possessing a strong police force while Russia would accept an end to the Korean War, including withdrawal of North Korean and American forces; a period of effective UN control over Korea would ensue for a minimum of one to two years. Taiwan should be handled with a plebiscite organised by the UN. Kennan's ideas were stimulating and there was much to be said for them. He looked rather too coldly at Korea, however, given the fact that American soldiers were dying in Korea at that moment as a consequence of what was believed to be Soviet-inspired aggression; it was unrealistic to talk of coming to accept a Korea susceptible to Soviet influence. The neutralisation of Japan, although advocated by MacArthur in former years, was not practicable now. Kennan's message that emotionalism should be controlled and diminished and that the obsession with the Soviet menace be put in perspective was entirely correct. However, as he recognised himself, it was unlikely to be achieved in the inflamed political atmosphere promoted by certain sections of the Republican Party for ulterior reasons.[44]

In September 1950 talks were planned between American, British and French foreign ministers. Preliminary consideration was given to the topics by representatives of the three countries in a meeting held in Washington on 30 August. The Americans recognised that a decisive watershed was approaching when decisions must be reached over crossing the 38th parallel and of determining the likely reactions of the Russians and Chinese to this development. The provisional American thinking was that the situation be closely monitored according to military achievements, that if the Soviet Union reoccupied North Korea, then UN forces should not cross the parallel pending further consideration in the Security Council; that UN forces should stay in South Korea for some time to come; and that the UN must not simply restore the Rhee government, which had displayed weakness and corruption. It was necessary to work out a carefully devised policy and allow existing passions to cool. The British attitude was that they concurred in the main in the American position but with differences of emphasis. It was important not to disguise the strong feelings aroused by the initial North Korean attack and equally important to carry Asian members of the UN in support of the policies to be decided. An early statement of UN aims was required. Rhee's regime had proved so unsatisfactory that a claim by the ROK to exercise sovereignty over North Korea could not be entertained. A possible solution could be found through holding free elections at the earliest date practicable to be authorised through a UN resolution. This would not commit the UN necessarily to crossing the 38th parallel: this decision could be taken at a later date. It was essential to commit the UN to the creation of a unified, genuinely democratic Korea.[45] Britain doubted whether crossing the parallel could be justified under the terms of the resolution of 27 June, since this was designed to repel the attack on South Korea. The Soviet Union was not likely to provoke a major war but might decide to reoccupy North Korea. The British believed that UNCOK, as constituted, was not a satisfactory body, and should be replaced by a new one representing particularly the Asian nations. The new commission would announce the decision to hold elections and arrange for UN forces to enter North Korea to supervise them. The elections should go forward in the liberated parts of Korea regardless of whether it was possible to hold them north of the 38th parallel.[46]

British references to Asian states and the need to mollify them resulted from the strength of feeling in India over the Korean conflict and the belief that India must be persuaded to support UN policy. The Attlee government's awareness of India's significance is explicable through the decision to grant India independence in 1947, a decision of which Attlee was justifiably proud. Attlee had close connections with India extending back to his membership of the Simon Commission in the late 1920s. Ernest Bevin was not as committed to India but wished to have Commonwealth support for Korean initiatives. Jawaharlal Nehru dominated Indian affairs and took a close interest in world affairs. Nehru believed the voice of the emergent nations must be heard and respected. He was critical of the United States because of the refusal to recognise Peking and because he believed the Truman administration viewed the world in too simplistic a way: in private he doubted the competence of Truman and Acheson.[47] Nehru sent a message to Attlee on 21 July, stressing the Asian perspective and the dangers of an inflexible, unsubtle handling of Korea by the United States.[48] The British feeling was that Nehru's advocacy of greater care and skill was warranted and that his opinions were 'moderate and sensible'.[49] American officials did not comprehend Nehru's reservations and his failure to condemn communism unequivocally.

The swift Indian recognition of the Chinese communist government led to greater warmth in their relations, notwithstanding areas of tension, such as Chinese policy towards Tibet. This enhanced the opportunities for the effervescent Indian ambassador in Peking, K. M. Panikkar. Panikkar was assessed by British diplomats earlier in 1950 as capable, lively and dynamic but not always consistent or wholly reliable. Panikkar's reports on the evolution of Chinese thinking on Korea assumed particular significance in September to November 1950, since there were no diplomatic relations between Peking and Washington and the British chargé d'affaires was effectively regarded as an outcast by the top Chinese leaders.[50] Panikkar's reports of his conversations with Chou En-lai and others were promptly conveyed to the British and American governments by the head of the Indian Ministry of External Relations, under Nehru, Sir Girja Bajpai. The British Foreign Office was closely interested in Panikkar's observations and believed he had to be viewed with some caution owing to his mercurial qualities. The State Department was more critical, suspecting him of undue sympathy for the Peking government. In September Panikkar's reports indicated that China was unlikely to intervene in Korea. On 20 September the American ambassador in New Delhi was notified of a meeting between Panikkar and Chou En-lai in which the latter had underlined the peaceful intentions of his government. China was not especially interested in Korea in Panikkar's opinion. Chinese interest in Korea had been more intense earlier on but had slackened in the previous two weeks. Panikkar's report was paraphrased by Bajpai in the words:

> In the circumstances direct participation of China in Korean fighting seems beyond range of possibility unless of course a world war starts as a result of UN forces passing beyond the 38th parallel and Soviet Union deciding directly to intervene. I am satisfied that China by herself will not interfere in the conflict and try to pull other chestnuts out of the fire.[51]

Panikkar believed that the success of the Inchon landing had confirmed Chinese scepticism over Soviet policy in Korea.[52] For the moment there seemed to be adequate confirmation of the improbability of Chinese intervention.

In Washington the debates over the wisdom of crossing the 38th parallel continued in September. The joint chiefs of staff, after consultation with MacArthur, and before the Inchon operation occurred, recommended that military action should be taken north of the parallel and these should be coordinated by South Korean forces on the assumption that the heart of the North Korean army would have been defeated south of the parallel. They were agreed that occupation of Korea by UN forces should be restricted to the chief cities south of the parallel and that occupation by UN forces should be terminated as soon as possible. MacArthur and Rhee had agreed that the ROK government should be re-established in Seoul and that Rhee would call a general election to fill vacant seats in the Korean assembly, which would be followed by the establishment of a single government for the whole of Korea.[53] Further consideration was given in the State Department to gathering support in the UN for a new resolution to provide for elections and a new commission to replace UNCOK. John Foster Dulles was critical of the belief that elections could be held in future throughout Korea. He did not think the UN forces would ever occupy the extreme northern provinces bordering on Vladivostok and Port Arthur and it would be foolish to commit the UN to an unattainable objective. As for India's attitude, Dulles was tempted to take the Indians at face value and tell them Korea was an Asiatic problem and they could decide on a suitable solution: forcing the Indians to accept responsibility would be the best way of educating them to the realities of world problems.[54] In general Dulles recommended an approach of allowing others to take the initiative for a time. Dean Acheson partially agreed but maintained, contrary to Dulles's view, that there was effective coordination between political and military objectives in Korea: if the United States was lucky and neither the Soviet Union nor China intervened in North Korea, MacArthur could implement political decisions. Dulles agreed that a UN resolution must be framed with unification in mind because this was consistent with the UN presence in Korea. He warned presciently of the perils:

> He [Dulles] went on to say that from our overall strategic position, we should not commit ourselves to a war deep in Asia against the Chinese Communists and the Soviets.[55]

The great success of the Inchon landing now brought about a mood of euphoria in Washington and in this atmosphere the decision to cross the 38th parallel was taken. The draft prepared for MacArthur by the joint chiefs on 26 September stated that he should ascertain carefully whether there was a Chinese or Russian threat to the UN operations, in which case the position must be reported at once to Washington. MacArthur's military objective was the destruction of North Korean forces and he could conduct military, naval and air operations north of the 38th parallel. This was on the basis that there was no major involvement in Korea by Chinese or Russian forces. MacArthur's men were not to cross the Manchurian or Soviet borders with Korea under any circumstances and non-Korean ground forces were not to be used in the north-east provinces, on the Soviet border or along the Manchurian border. Air or naval action was not to be taken against Manchuria or Soviet territory.[56] General George Marshall had by this time replaced Louis Johnson as Secretary of Defense; Johnson was dismissed by Truman because of his persistent bickering with Acheson and his opposition to various aspects of policy. Marshall was in poor health and only accepted office again as a result of the Korean situation and his own potent sense of duty. He was vastly experienced and widely respected – except by Senator McCarthy and some of his supporters – and a definite source of stability to the administration. However, Marshall had been out of office since the end of 1948 and was not conversant with the tortuous development of policy. In particular, he was not familiar with the differences of opinion that had already arisen between Washington and MacArthur. Marshall did not become fully aware of the difficulties until he read through past papers at the end of March and beginning of April 1951 and reached the conclusion that President Truman was wholly justified in recalling MacArthur. Marshall sent an unfortunately worded instruction to MacArthur on 29 September:

> We want you to feel unhampered tactically and strategically to proceed north of 38th parallel. Announcement above referred to may precipitate embarrassment in UN where evident desire is not to be confronted with necessity of a vote on passage of 38th parallel, rather to find you have found it militarily necessary to do so.[57]

MacArthur later claimed this allowed him to operate as he thought best in pursuing activities north of the 38th parallel. Marshall's instruction was too vague and injudicious.

The First Committee of the UN General Assembly met on 30 September. A Soviet proposal to invite representatives from North and South Korea to take part in the debate was rejected by 46–6 with 7 abstentions. A resolution proposed by Kuomintang China inviting a South Korean representative only to participate was carried by 50–5 with 5 abstentions. During the debate the American delegate, Austin, described the 38th parallel as an artificial line without merit and advocated a unified, independent Korea.[58] Acheson took the view that the UN forces were fully entitled to cross the 38th parallel, as this was in keeping with the resolution of 27 June.[59] The British Foreign Office now accepted this opinion, which had previously been doubted.[60] However, in late September there were definite indications that the Chinese attitude was changing, as it was realised in Peking that the 38th parallel might well be crossed in the near future. Bajpai told Henderson, the

American ambassador in Delhi, that China might act if UN forces crossed the parallel and that a world war could result.[61] Panikkar's reports were conveyed to the British who passed them on urgently to Washington on 27 September. Panikkar had spoken to General Nieh Jung-chen, chief of staff of the Chinese army under Chu Teh. Nieh condemned American .air incursions into Manchuria, which had included bombing of Chinese territory; China would not tolerate such behaviour. Panikkar had seen Chou En-lai on 21 September and had deduced then that China would adopt a more aggressive policy. Nehru had urged restraint on both sides.[62] The British felt Panikkar's appraisals had to be viewed with caution, given his volatile and not always reliable nature. At the same time, the warnings must be given serious consideration.[63] The foolishness of American pilots in bombing areas in Manchuria and occasionally in Siberia antagonised China and the Soviet Union. Chou En-lai addressed an emphatic protest to Trygve Lie on 24 September for submission to the Security Council and General Assembly. Chou drew attention to several incidents in which Chinese territory had been bombed, causing injury to citizens and the destruction of property. Chou recalled protests he had addressed on 27 and 30 August and on 10 September over violations of Chinese air space and attacks on Chinese territory. Chou commented:

> The new criminal act by planes of the aggressive forces of the United States in Korea proves that the number of instances of provocative actions expressed in the violation of the Chinese air frontiers by the aggressive forces of the United States in Korea, is constantly growing and more clearly than ever before exposes the determination of the United States of America to extend the aggressive war against Korea, to carry out armed aggression against Taiwan and still far extend its aggression against China.[64]

Chou protested bitterly at the fact that China was represented by the completely discredited regime of Chiang Kai-shek. He warned the members of the UN that if they continued to support American imperialism in Korea, they themselves would suffer the consequences. Peace in the Far East could only be restored by the withdrawal of 'American aggressive forces' from Korea.

In American and British policy-making bodies the most perceptive warning of the consequences of pushing north beyond the 38th parallel came from the British chiefs of staff. It is fascinating to reflect that, contrary to the public image, defence chiefs are frequently reluctant to support courses of action that will precipitate wider conflict and entail the acceptance of greater commitments. At the beginning of the Korean War the American joint chiefs of staff had been most reluctant to send ground forces to Korea. The British chiefs of staff appreciated the dangers inherent in the development of the Korean operation better than their counterparts in Washington or the British Foreign Office. This is attributable principally to the acumen of the Chief of the Air Staff, Air Chief Marshal Sir John Slessor. During the first nine months of the war Slessor made cogent observations on the trend of American policy and the confusion within it. Admiral Lord Fraser, the First Sea Lord, agreed with Slessor but expressed himself less trenchantly. Field Marshal Sir William Slim, Chief of the Imperial General Staff, vacillated but came down in support of Slessor. The latter drafted a memorandum on 14 September for his colleagues in which he wrote that reports from Air Vice-Marshal Bouchier, attached to MacArthur's headquarters, strengthened his feeling that the Americans were unclear as to what their aims were in Korea. Slessor feared that victory in rescuing South Korea paradoxically could result in 'extended and indefinite commitments and even in the worst case, involve serious risks of a clash with Russia and Communist China'.[65] Politically the UN's action in Korea was intended to achieve an independent, unified and democratic Korea, although Slessor was sceptical as to how far any Korean regime must meet the criterion of 'democratic' and how any state could be with the Soviet Union and China on the borders.

It was clear that neither the United States nor Britain wished to be committed to retaining large forces in Korea for an indefinite period. Europe was the priority and it would be dangerous to be diverted to East Asia. No doubt some forces would have to be kept in Korea at the end of the war to obviate a future attack and to ensure the situation was no worse than it had been on 23 June 1950. There was little point in sending UN forces north of the 38th parallel with the possible exception of South Korean troops. Slessor could see no logic in accepting the responsibilities inherent in the occupation of North Korea. Such an occupation would involve contentious political decisions on the future of North Korea, an appreciable increase in the forces required in North Korea to preserve order and guard against a Chinese or Russian attack. Slessor proposed that a resolution be put to the UN General Assembly calling for national elections in Korea supervised by the UN; North Korea should be instructed to send representatives to Seoul to meet the Truce Commission; a new UN commission should subsequently supervise the elections and would have to enter North Korea for this purpose possibly accompanied by South Korean troops; no other UN troops should enter North Korea; if the North Korean government refused to cooperate, the UN should accept the position rather than coerce North Korea; South Korea must be transformed into a more attractive state through improved political, economic and social standards:

> Synghman [*sic*] Rhee and co. must not have a free hand to misgovern the place as they did before; land reforms etc. should be enforced and the UN Commission will have to remain in S. Korea for a long time.[66]

Slessor believed that the UN could be proud of having defeated clear aggression and of restoring the status quo ante: if the latter could not be improved upon, owing to the obduracy of the North Koreans, so be it.

When the chiefs of staff met on 20 September Slessor advanced his analysis persuasively. Fraser stated that the UN forces should move as far north as was necessary to prevent the North Koreans organising a further attack.[67] Marshal of the Royal Air Force Lord Tedder, usually present in Washington for coordinating purposes, agreed with Slessor and was worried at the economic devastation of Korea. Slim concurred and thought the UN forces should not cross the parallel. The committee was unanimous as to the great desirability of reducing commitments in Korea as soon as practicable so as to concentrate on the most vital areas. General MacArthur must be told unambiguously what to do – 'Unless instructions were issued to General MacArthur there was a grave danger of forces being moved forward into North Korea without the implications of such action having been fully studied. One result of such action might be to provoke the Russians or Chinese Communists to invade North Korea.'[68] The chiefs of staff returned to the subject at three successive meetings in early October with a representative of the Foreign Office present. On 3 October Slim argued that if it was decided to occupy the whole of Korea, the UN command would need only to possess enough forces to combat guerrilla activity in the whole area. If the UN forces stopped at the 38th parallel, it would be necessary to meet the guerrilla menace and a possible renewed conventional attack from North Korea. Lord Fraser again adopted the line that action north of the parallel should be determined by the situation at the time of the advance and that MacArthur's forces should advance no more than was essential. Slessor reiterated most convincingly the views expressed in his earlier memorandum.[69]

On 4 October the committee discussed a telegram from Bouchier indicating the operations MacArthur intended to pursue north of the parallel. Fraser said the UN would be accused of aggression if its forces advanced beyond the parallel; there was apparently no military necessity to cross the parallel because it would take three to four months for the North Koreans to re-equip themselves. Advancing beyond the parallel would most likely lead to an extension of the war and a more critical attitude might be adopted by India and other countries in South-East Asia.[70] Slim agreed with Fraser but provided a muddled response. He recognised that the Chinese were so frightened of American intentions that they might intervene. Equally the Americans could not be intimidated by China. The South Koreans should be allowed to cross the parallel but there was no need for UN troops to do so, at least in the next ten to fourteen days. The North Koreans should be given the opportunity to surrender in which case the UN forces would stay south of the parallel. If the North Koreans proved obdurate, MacArthur's forces could proceed north. An offer to discuss matters could be made to Peking. Slessor was absent and his deputy emphasised the parallel should only be crossed if unavoidable to conclude military operations.[71] The Foreign Office's representative commented on the opposition building up in the UN to any operations north of the parallel; the Foreign Secretary wished to invite Chinese communist representatives to the UN General Assembly in New York and was urging this upon the United States. The information at the disposal of the Foreign Office pointed to military columns being in the process of moving from Manchuria into North Korea.[72]

In Tokyo Alvary Gascoigne, head of the liaison mission, saw MacArthur on the evening of 3 October. The general dismissed Chou En-lai's warning to Panikkar as 'pure bluff'.[73] If the Chinese had been serious, they would not have issued a warning in this manner. MacArthur was extremely complacent about any threat from China or the Soviet Union, which remained true down to the massive Chinese onslaught in late November:

> In any case MacArthur claimed he had plenty of troops [to deal] adequately with the Chinese and even with the Russians if they should prove so foolish as to enter the arena at this stage. The Chinese, he said, had neither troops nor equipment nor air power to take him on – if the Chinese had come in three weeks ago it might have been another matter. . . .
> If the Chinese came in, MacArthur would immediately unleash his air force against towns in Manchuria and North China including Peking – he knew Chou must know that, and must realise his (MacArthur's) vastly greater potential in the air, on the ground, and on the sea. Chou's statement to Pannikar [*sic*] was just blackmail.[74]

The British embassy in Washington reported on 4 October that, contrary to the impression conveyed by Dean Rusk a short time before, MacArthur's instructions were opaque and dealt largely with surrender terms to be conveyed to North Korea.[75] The alarm felt by the chiefs of staff hardened and their fears were conveyed to Clement Attlee and Emanuel Shinwell, the Minister of Defence, who were attending the Labour Party conference in Margate. Intelligence reports had reached London via Burma to the effect that China would definitely intervene if the UN forces traversed the 38th parallel. Sir Roger Makins communicated Ernest Bevin's anxiety. Lord Fraser firmly stated the views of the chiefs of staff that the dangers implicit in moving into North Korea were not worth the risks involved: as the Americans were determined to go ahead, a further appeal should be made by the UN to Pyongyang. If China intervened, great care should be exercised not to exacerbate problems by such actions as bombing cities in Manchuria.[76]

British apprehension was conveyed to Washington on 6 October and again on 12 October.[77] Bevin stressed the importance of acting with discretion to consolidate the military successes and of not adopting a bellicose approach to China. Meanwhile a resolution of the UN General Assembly, approved on 7 October, had established a new commission to replace UNCOK with a membership comprising Australia, Chile, the Netherlands, Pakistan, the Philippines, Thailand and Turkey. This was known as the United Nations Commission for the Unification and Rehabilitation of Korea (UNCURK). The terms of reference were to take over from UNCOK, to pursue the UN's aim of a unified, independent and democratic government for the whole of Korea; to exercise responsibilities in handling relief and rehabilitation on a basis to be decided; that an interim committee be formed pending the new commission's arrival in Korea; and requiring it to submit regular reports to the General Assembly.[78] China issued an official statement on 10 October in reply to the UN resolution. The latter was described as 'entirely illegal' and contrary to the views of the majority of the world's population.[79] The resolution was seen in Peking as authorising the advance of American forces with the aim of expanding the war in Korea. The aspects urging rehabilitation and democracy were dismissed as a façade to cover aggression. The United States had manipulated the vote in the UN and this did not represent a genuine free expression of opinion – 'For instance, the vote of the Chiang Kai-shek brigands is simply a ghostly mockery.'[80] The population of the countries supporting the resolution was estimated at 660 million as against 722 million in the five countries opposing it, headed by the Soviet Union. With the addition of the seven abstentions and a reserved vote, a total figure of 1,196 million was arrived at. Therefore the Americans and their supporters represented a minority of the UN. Emphasis was placed on the Asian dimension: India was very critical of American policy and other Asian nations deprecated American dominance. China desired a peaceful solution in Korea but this could only be attained on the lines advocated by the Soviet Union. The climax was a denunciation of hostile American actions affecting Chinese territory and people and a warning that China would soon act:

> The American war of invasion in Korea had been a serious menace to the security of China from its very start. The American invading forces in Korea have on several occasions violated the territorial air of China and strafed and bombed Chinese people and have violated the rights of a Chinese merchantman to sail the high seas and conducted forced search. Its attempts to enlarge the war in the east are known to everybody.
>
> Now the American forces are attempting to cross the 38th parallel on a large scale, the Chinese people cannot stand by idle with regard to such a serious situation created by the invasion of Korea by the United States and its accomplice countries and to the dangerous trend towards extending war.[81]

It was possible to regard the Chinese words as blustering rhetoric not likely to lead to concrete action. This was MacArthur's view and the attitude of many in Washington. In London there was a more sober attitude and a growing feeling that the Chinese might mean what they had stated.

President Truman decided at the beginning of October to fly to the western Pacific to meet General MacArthur. Much controversy has surrounded the motives for the President's mission. Was it attributable to doubts entertained at the White House regarding MacArthur's strategy? Was it due to Truman's wish to seize the headlines in the press and assist beleaguered Democrats in the forthcoming November elections? Was it all a cunning Machiavellian ploy to outmanœuvre MacArthur and put the blame on his shoulders for any setbacks that might occur? Truman and MacArthur had not met; amazingly MacArthur had not visited the United States since 1938. Truman had wanted him to return in 1948 for discussions on the future of Japan but MacArthur maintained he was too busy. MacArthur did not wish to meet Truman, for he always believed in keeping Washington personnel at a distance and this included the President. Truman's decision to travel so far to meet a general, no matter how distinguished, outraged some Americans including Dean Acheson: the Secretary of State regularly visited Europe but never travelled to Tokyo, believing it best to avoid the court of the American 'emperor' in Tokyo. Truman was a shrewd politician and obtained what he wanted from the meeting. John J. Muccio travelled on the same plane as MacArthur to Wake island and has testified to the general's ire at having to leave his responsibilities in Tokyo even for a brief period, in order to see the President.[82]

Part of the controversy over the encounter surrounds the notes taken surreptitiously by Vernice Anderson, Philip Jessup's secretary. MacArthur was to state subsequently that he had been unaware that notes were being taken and his followers raged at the dishonesty of Truman in having the words of their hero somewhat embarrassingly recorded for posterity. MacArthur must have been naïve if he believed that no record would be made of such an important meeting. Vernice Anderson has stated that she took notes by accident, being present in an adjoining room to the one where the meeting was taking place; as she could hear the proceedings, she automatically started taking notes, since Philip Jessup always liked full records to be kept during his frequent travels. Her notes while full were not verbatim and she denied General Courtney Whitney's allegation that she lurked in the background and peeped through a keyhole.[83] As Miss Anderson points out, notes were taken by several of those present at the meeting and used in the record produced. Those present, in addition to Truman and MacArthur, were Admiral Radford, General Bradley, Ambassador Muccio, Secretary of the Army Frank Pace, Ambassador Jessup, Assistant Secretary Rusk, Harriman, Colonels Hamblen and Matthews plus General Whitney.[84]

The discussion was of a discursive nature and covered various aspects of the campaign. MacArthur stated that he had full support from Washington and had no complaints. Truman asked him for his assessment of the likelihood of Chinese or Russian intervention. MacArthur thought there was little chance of either intervening. The

Chinese had 300,000 men in Manchuria of which approximately one-third were distributed along the Yalu river. The Chinese were hampered by the absence of an air force. American air superiority was such that the Chinese would be massacred if they advanced towards Pyongyang. The Russians were in a different category, for they possessed a reasonably efficient air force with excellent pilots equipped with modern planes. The Russians could put 1,000 planes in the air with between 200 and 300 more from the Soviet fleet. MacArthur was nevertheless confident of American superiority in the air. He stated there were no Russian ground troops immediately available for North Korea and it would take six weeks to transfer a division by which time winter would have arrived. In reply to another question from Truman, MacArthur urged the conclusion of a Japanese peace treaty: the Soviet Union and China should be invited and if they declined, the treaty should be concluded without them.[85] Truman inquired about the feasibility of negotiating a Pacific pact analogous to NATO. MacArthur thought this would be 'tremendous' but very difficult to achieve because of the lack of homogeneity in the Pacific.[86] On Taiwan Truman said he had spoken fully to MacArthur in private and they were entirely in agreement. MacArthur agreed with Bradley that the calibre of troops provided by some of the UN states in Korea was bad. He wished to remove non-Korean forces from Korea as soon as he could once the military operations had been successfully terminated.[87]

Truman had a lengthy private discussion with MacArthur of which no record has apparently been kept. Truman did draft a few notes in his own hand five weeks afterwards in which he wrote that MacArthur had apologised for his message to the Veterans in August and hoped it had not embarrassed the President. MacArthur told him he had no political ambitions as regards the Republican presidential nomination in 1952 and that the politicians had made a 'chimp' of him in 1948.[88] MacArthur regarded the meeting as a waste of time and evidently wondered what Truman's motive had been. It is most likely that the President's visit was occasioned by his wish to hear MacArthur commit himself on the state of the war and particularly on the contingency of Chinese or Russian intervention: should matters become difficult, MacArthur's statement could be released to the press just as Truman did later authorise the record being leaked to a journalist, Tony Leviero.[89] A further motive was probably to gain some favourable publicity for the congressional elections but little was accomplished here when the results were known: the Republicans made significant gains at Democratic expense.

It became clear in the second half of October that China was intervening in the Korean War; the extent of Chinese activity was uncertain, however, and it was a subject for speculation as to whether China was engaging in an extension of diplomatic blackmail or whether China intended this as the first phase of action which would be followed if necessary by a second devastating phase. MacArthur ignored the limited forms of Chinese action and pressed ahead determined to end the campaign on a glorious note of triumph as quickly as he could. This is best illustrated by examining a map (see Map 4). On 5 October the UN forces in western Korea were still south of the 38th parallel but in eastern Korea the UN troops had advanced well beyond the parallel, above the port of Kansong. By 19 October they were on the outskirts of Pyongyang in the west while in the east they had taken the port of Hungnam and were moving towards Iwon. The advance was then far more rapid in the west so that Chosan, near the Yalu, was reached on 26 October. In the east progress was slower and Hyesanjin (on the Yalu) and Chongjin on the Soviet border reached by 24 November.

Chinese intervention in Korea was initially unobtrusive and then increased appreciably. The first signs of the Chinese presence appeared in early October but it was not until the last ten days of the month that confirmation of significant numbers was obtained. Just as Truman maintained that the UN was implementing police action rather than waging war in Korea, so the Chinese government maintained that Chinese troops in Korea were 'volunteers'. It was not the concept of volunteers as recalled from the Spanish Civil War (1936–39), however; many of the Chinese who fought in Korea had been in the Kuomintang armies until 1948 and a significant proportion refused to return to China after serving as POWs. The use of the term 'volunteers' was designed to minimise the international complications and to obviate a formal declaration of war.[90] On 24 October MacArthur ended restrictions on the use of UN troops in North Korea and instructed his ground commanders to proceed, utilising all personnel, until the northern borders of Korea were reached. He defended his action when queried from Washington on the basis of military necessity because the South Korean troops were incapable of dealing with the situation on their own. The joint chiefs of staff asked whether this was compatible with the directive of 27 September and MacArthur contended that his action was reconcilable with the terms of General Marshall's telegram of 29 September.[91] On 25 October ROK forces clashed with appreciable numbers of Chinese troops at Onjong: the second regiment of the sixth division was effectively eliminated in bitter fighting on 25–26 October. Four other ROK regiments were defeated in the same region shortly afterwards.

On 27 October information received from Hong Kong indicated that a Chinese observation group was in Korea; apparently there were two divisions of Chinese troops in Korea and those captured claimed to be in the North Korean army. It was thought that China did not intend to dispatch large numbers to Korea.[92] Two days later it emerged that five prisoners identified as Chinese had been captured in the area of the Eighth Army and a further two prisoners in the area of the X Corps. All wore full or partial North Korean uniforms. There was no indication of sizeable numbers of Chinese troops.[93] The CIA believed a total of between 15,000 and 20,000 Chinese troops was operating in task force units while the parent units stayed in Manchuria. Soviet-type jet aircraft were reported to be in the Antung–Sinunju area. The Chinese aim, according to the CIA, was to create a cordon sanitaire south of the Yalu river in order to guarantee the security of the Manchurian border from UN forces and to protect the flow of electric power from the important Suiho hydroelectric system serving the vital industrial base in Manchuria. Subsequently it was discovered that six Chinese armies comprising eighteeen divisions had moved into Korea during the month of October with a nominal strength of 180,000.[94]

A Chinese declaration was issued on 4 November warning that the security of China was threatened by the actions of the imperialists, led by the United States. Aggressive measures adversely affecting the Chinese people were recalled, including deaths and injuries to Chinese nationals with the destruction of property. Previous Chinese warnings had been ignored, the 38th parallel had been crossed, and large numbers of UN troops were advancing towards the Yalu and Tumen rivers, thus threatening China's north-eastern border. The close relationship between China and North Korea was stated more clearly than before and the gravity with which Peking viewed the position was conveyed:

> Just as with the Japanese imperialists in the past, the main objective of United States aggression on Korea is not Korea itself, but China. History shows us that the existence of the Korean People's Republic and its fall and the security or danger of China are closely intertwined. The one cannot be safeguarded without the other. It is not only a moral duty that the people of China should support the Korean people's war against America, but it is closely related to the direct interest of all the Chinese people and is determined by the necessity of self defence. To save our neighbour, to save ourselves, to defend our fatherland, we must support the people of Korea.
>
> Throughout the country the Chinese people are enthusiastically volunteering to resist American aggression, aid Korea, protect their homes and defend their country.[95]

Chou En-lai's statement that the Chinese people would not submit to foreign aggression or to their neighbours being invaded was quoted together with a reiteration of the Chinese wish to see the Korean struggle ended by agreement. Such an outcome could not be secured, given American policy, and China was left with no choice:

> Thus we have been forced to realise that if lovers of peace in the world desire to have peace, they must use positive action to resist atrocities and halt aggression. It is only resistance that can possibly teach the imperialists a lesson and settle in a just way the question of independence and liberation in Korea and other areas according to the will of the people. .... [96]

The *Peking People's Daily* on 13 November published an interminable editorial, comparing Japanese and American imperialism and their effects on East Asia since 1868. The essence of the belligerence displayed by the United States was attributed to the crisis faced by world capitalism as a consequence of the Second World War. A dramatic advance had been registered in the sharp decline of capitalism with the emergence of many 'people's democracies' headed by the Soviet Union. The 'tycoons of American capitalism' had sought to escape the crisis confronting them through the pursuance of aggressive policies.[97] The role of the Soviet Union was harder to determine and the old argument as to whether Peking and Moscow functioned as one or as rivals resurfaced. *The Times* adopted the view in a leader published on 10 November that there were significant divergences between China and Russia and these should be exploited rather than consolidated.[98] The British Foreign Office dissented in the form of minutes by G. G. Buzzard and A. A. E. Franklin: the Soviet Union and China worked closely together and it was futile to seek differences between them.[99] John Hutchison, the chargé d'affaires in Peking, believed that the recent Chinese statements should be accepted as wholly genuine but Buzzard drew attention to the high propaganda content in all communist statements.[100]

British fears over the danger of conducting bombing operations in the vicinity of the Yalu were conveyed to Washington. The joint chiefs of staff instructed MacArthur on 6 November to defer plans for bombing targets within 5 miles (8 km) of the Manchurian border and requested an explanation as to why MacArthur had ordered the bombing of Yalu river bridges.[101] MacArthur's attention was drawn to the promise to consult Britain before pursuing bombing raids in sensitive areas. The situation was visibly deteriorating and in retrospect it is surprising that more strenuous efforts were not made in Washington to avert the collision with China. Aerial reconnaissance on 8 November revealed large numbers of Chinese vehicles crossing the Yalu; approximately 700 vehicles were involved.[102] John Paton Davies of the Policy Planning Staff had already urged the war be localised and that China must be kept out of it: he feared the approach of a third world war if his advice was disregarded.[103] The planning adviser in the Bureau of Far Eastern Affairs, Emmerson, examined the possible use of the atomic bomb against China and recommended that it should be used only as a last resort; from a practical viewpoint he believed that China offered few suitable targets because of her scattered cities, low level of industrialisation, and immensity. The peculiar horror of atomic warfare meant that the impact on world public opinion was a major consideration.[104] The CIA estimated on 8 November that Chinese military strength in Manchuria totalled approximately 700,000, of which at least 200,000 comprised regular field forces; the Chinese would not have acted without prior agreement with Moscow and the intervention might even be directed by the Russians.[105] Britain had for some weeks contemplated halting MacArthur's advance and the creation of a demilitarised zone. MacArthur did not take kindly to interference with the completion of his operations and argued strongly for continuing without hesitation. He castigated the reported British plan as redolent of appeasement and in keeping with British behaviour at Munich in 1938. MacArthur brushed aside the accumulating evidence of Chinese intentions:

> To give up any portion of North Korea to the aggression of the Chinese Communists would be the greatest defeat of the free world in recent times. Indeed to yield to so immoral a proposition would bankrupt our leadership and influence in Asia and render untenable our position both politically and militarily.[106]

Ernest Bevin formally proposed the establishment of a demilitarised zone on 13 November. He thought an appropriate resolution for the UN should be devised, declaring such a zone to exist on a line extending roughly from Hungnam in the east to Chogju in the west to the Manchurian–Siberian–Korean frontier. The zone would be created as a temporary arrangement and the past commitments of the UN would be reiterated. Admittedly there would be considerable difficulty in deciding administrative arrangements for the zone but an attempt should be made to reach an agreement with the North Korean government with the latter laying down its arms and accepting a temporary administration under UN authority.[107] Tentative efforts were made by the State Department to sound out the Chinese through the Swedish ambassador in Peking.[108] President Truman made conciliatory remarks at a press confidence on 16 November and stressed that he had no desire for conflict with China.[109]

The obstacle was the adamant attitude of General MacArthur and the inability of the administration in Washington to curb him. MacArthur pressed ahead oblivious of the nemesis that was so soon to overtake him. He was confident of complete success and contemptuous of China and the Soviet Union. MacArthur's own intelligence was defective and this has been explained on the grounds of General Willoughby's innate belief that the Chinese were inferior.[110] MacArthur's view was that the Chinese would only intervene to a limited extent: Bouchier, the British defence representative attached to his staff, informed London on 13 November that the Chinese contribution to North Korea totalled about 90,000 of which probably 50,000 had advanced on the two fronts and had engaged the UN forces. Bouchier tended to echo MacArthur's opinions and described the military position as satisfactory and 'much more hopeful than is probably presented in other parts of the world'.[111]

The failure of Washington to act led Bevin to decide on a direct approach to the Chinese government through Hutchison in Peking. Difficulties existed in applying this approach, for senior Chinese leaders had refrained from contacting the British embassy. Bevin decided not to propose a demilitarised zone formally but that if an opportunity arose when Hutchison spoke to a Chinese representative, it could be mentioned informally.[112] Hutchison saw the Chinese Vice Foreign Minister, Chang Han-fu, on 23 November and handed him a message, stressing its urgency. Hutchison then spoke, as instructed, in a personal capacity. He referred to the dangerous implications of the current crisis and the manifest fears in Peking that Chinese territory was about to be attacked. The most sensible method of removing Chinese apprehension was to establish a demilitarised zone on the Korean side of the frontier. Chang inquired as to what precisely was meant by a demilitarised zone and how order would be maintained. Hutchison defined the zone as a kind of 'cushion'; further thought would have to be given to the administration of the zone but the local North Korean authorities could perhaps accept responsibility.[113] The United States opposed putting forward the proposal officially owing to doubts over North Korea's attitude and the suspicions that it could stimulate communist recalcitrance.[114] The anxieties of members of the UN were considered at a high level in Washington, including Dean Acheson and the joint chiefs of staff; it was decided to inform MacArthur of the concern but not to change his mission in a radical way. MacArthur was informed that support had been voiced for the demilitarised zone; the consensus in Washington was that action should be pursued immediately to agree with other governments on plans to achieve a unified Korea and to avoid expansion of the war.[115] It was necessary to allay Chinese and Russian concern over a threat to Manchuria and Siberia.

MacArthur replied that it would be impossible to halt his offensive and any lack of resolution would have detrimental effects on morale in South Korea and encourage aggression elsewhere in the world. There had always been a possibility of Chinese intervention and this would have been more dangerous in July and August when UN forces were restricted to the Pusan area. His aims were to conclude the war speedily, return American forces to Japan and POWs to their home countries, and foster unification of Korea through the assistance of UNCURK.[116] MacArthur's forces were divided into two and he surprisingly made no effort to regroup in preparation for a Chinese attack. After the decisive Chinese action in later October and early November, the Chinese refrained from advancing further, most likely in the hope that a compromise would be reached whereby MacArthur's troops stopped their advance. When this did not materialise MacArthur showed every prospect of fulfilling his mission. MacArthur erroneously believed at the time he commenced his final offensive on 24 November that the enemy forces consisted of 83,000 North Koreans and between 40,000 and 71,000 Chinese. In reality the opposing Chinese comprised approximately 300,000 most of whom had moved into Korea in previous weeks without being detected by American intelligence in the rugged terrain. The full impact of Chinese intervention hit MacArthur's exposed forces on 25 November, thus making mockery of MacArthur's disregard for China. MacArthur communicated the transformation of the situation in graphic terms:

> All hope of localization of the Korean conflict to enemy forces composed of North Korean troops with alien token elements can now be completely abandoned. The Chinese military forces are committed in North Korea in great and ever increasing strength. No pretext of minor support under the guise of volunteerism or other subterfuge now has the slightest validity. We face an entirely new war.[117]

The story of the origins of the Korean War therefore ends with China's entry into the war. No hope existed of terminating the war quickly and it was a very difficult conflict of far more dangerous potential. Chinese participation could have been averted by the adoption of more sensitive, realistic policies. This would have necessitated a more clear-cut understanding than existed in Washington and the application of limitations upon General MacArthur's freedom of action. The Truman administration, despite its reservations over MacArthur's behaviour, was the prisoner of the general's immense prestige and kudos after Inchon. However, beyond the issue of personalities is that of American policy towards China. The refusal of the United States to contemplate recognition and Chinese membership of the UN and the growing American determination to prevent the Peking government from securing control of Taiwan contributed powerfully to the intense fear of ultimate American intentions. China had her share of responsibility, too, for the state of Sino-American relations, since the new government was suspicious and fundamentally isolationist. The emotional, inflamed state of American public opinion, the mordant partisan attacks on Truman and Acheson, had created an atmosphere where conciliation was difficult or impossible to implement. No one in Washington wished to be accused of appeasing the 'Reds'. The events unfolded with the inexorability of a Greek tragedy.

# REFERENCES

1.  *Military Situation in the Far East and ... Relief of General of the Army Douglas MacArthur, Hearings of the Armed Services and Foreign Relations Committee, US Senate*, part 1, p. 27, 3 May 1951, statement by MacArthur. Throughout his testimony MacArthur reiterated his acceptance of the President's authority and his respect for the constitution.
2.  John J. Muccio believed MacArthur was hemmed in by the rivalry of Whitney and Willoughby and that they prevented him receiving the intelligence he needed, see Muccio Oral History, p. 71, interview between Muccio and Jerry N. Hess, 10 and 17 Feb. 1971, Truman Library.

3.  Ibid., p. 72.
4.  David Rees, *Korea: The Limited War* (London 1964), pp. 24–5, and Robert O' Neill, *Australia in the Korean War, 1950–53*, vol. I, *Strategy and Diplomacy* (Canberra 1981), pp. 50–2.
5.  Minutes of staff conference chaired by Emanuel Shinwell, Minister of Defence, 10 July 1950, COS(50)104(1), Defe 4/33. Shinwell welcomed evidence that 'the Korean affair was not distracting American attention from the vital European theatre'.
6.  British Cabinet conclusions, 4 July 1950, 42(50)3, Cab. 128/8.
7.  Ibid., 25 July 1950, 50(59)3.
8.  *FRUS 1950* (7), p. 545, memorandum by Merchant to Rusk, 8 August 1950.
9.  See Appendix for list of countries and casualties.
10. Letter from Truman to Acheson, 18 July 1950, selected records relating to the Korean War, folder 1, 'Neutralisation of Formosa', box 6, Truman Papers, Truman Library.
11. Ibid.
12. Strong (Taipei) to Acheson, 21 July 1950, ibid.
13. Ibid.
14. Ibid.
15. Strong to Acheson, 29 July 1950, ibid.
16. Strong to Acheson, 29 July 1950, second message, ibid.
17. Ibid.
18. Strong to Acheson, 30 July 1950, ibid.
19. Department of Army to MacArthur, 30 July 1950, RG9, box 43 *JCS* File, MacArthur Papers. MacArthur Memorial.
20. Department of Army to MacArthur, 29 July, ibid.
21. Strong to Acheson, 3 August 1950, selected records relating to the Korean War, folder 1, box 6, Truman Papers, Truman Library.
22. Ibid.
23. MacArthur to Department of the Army, 7 Aug. 1950, RG9, box 43, *JCS* outgoing File, MacArthur Papers, MacArthur Memorial.
24. MacArthur to Department of the Army, 10 Aug. 1950, RG6, box 8, Formosa File, MacArthur Papers, MacArthur Memorial.
25. *Military Situation in the Far East*, 1, pp. 52–3.
26. Ibid., p. 111.
27. MacArthur to Clyde A. Lewis, C-in-C, Veterans of Foreign Wars of the United States, 20 Aug. 1950, RG6, box 8, MacArthur Papers, MacArthur Memorial.
28. Johnson to MacArthur, 26 Aug. 1950, ibid.
29. For Acheson's view of the problems involved in dealing with MacArthur, see Dean Acheson, *Present at the Creation* (London 1970), pp. 422, 518ff.
30. Lewis to MacArthur, 27 Aug. 1950, RG6, box 8, MacArthur Papers, Formosa File, MacArthur Memorial.
31. *FRUS 1950* (6), pp. 347–51, memorandum from Howe to Armstrong, 31 May 1950, enclosing extract from draft memorandum by Rusk, 30 May 1950.
32. *FRUS 1950* (7) p. 272, memorandum by Allison, 1 July 1950.
33. Ibid., p. 459, memorandum by Allison to Nitze, 24 July 1950. Allison was director of the Office of North-East Asian Affairs and Nitze was director of the Policy Planning Staff.

34. Ibid., p. 461.
35. See *United Nations Security Council Official Records, Fifth Year, 1950*, no. 22, 1 Aug. 1950, pp. 12–21; no. 23, 2 Aug., pp. 14–19; no. 24, 3 Aug, pp. 1–10, 13–19; no. 25, 4 Aug., pp. 1–17; no. 26, 8 Aug., pp. 8–21; no. 27, 10 Aug., pp. 3–15; no. 28, 11 Aug., pp. 1–4, 11–20; no. 29, 14 Aug., pp. 14–16; no. 30, 17 Aug., pp. 16–19; no. 31, 22 Aug., pp. 1–16, 26–35; no. 32, 25 Aug., pp. 1–9; no. 33, 29 Aug., pp. 1–8.
36. See *Soviet Monitor*, 19 July 1950, where a fervent appeal was printed from Kim Il Sung, urging the South Koreans to overthrow the American presence, and ibid., 25 July 1950, printing Tass reports on the military successes of the North Korean army and the corruption of the South Korean regime in July 1950.
37. See A. S. Whiting, *China crosses the Yalu: the decision to enter the Korean War* (New York 1960), pp. 54–58, for a discussion of Chinese attitudes in July, 1950.
38. Peking to FO, 26 July 1950, FK1022/247, FO 371/84093.
39. Ibid.
40. *FRUS 1950* (7), pp. 600–3, memorandum prepared by CIA, 18 Aug. 1950.
41. See G. F. Kennan, *Memoirs, 1925–1950* (London 1968), pp. 426–7, 466, for Kennan's developing dissatisfaction with what could be achieved in the State Department.
42. *FRUS 1950* (7), pp. 623–4, memorandum by Kennan, 21 Aug. 1950.
43. Ibid., p. 625.
44. Ibid., p. 628.
45. Ibid., pp. 667–71, US delegation minutes, preliminary conversations for September foreign ministers meeting, 30 Aug. 1950.
46. Ibid., pp. 670–1.
47. See CIA memorandum by Hillenkoetter, 'Observations of Pandit Nehru on international affairs with particular reference to India's relations with the United States, Great Britain and the Soviet Union'. 20 Dec. 1949, PSF files, box 249, folder CIA Intelligence, Truman Papers, Truman Library. The original source of the information is not indicated. Nehru's views were stated thus: 'Nehru's impression of President Truman was that of a placed in a role far superior to his capacities. Equally mediocre was his view of Secretary of State Dean Acheson. Nehru had a very unfavourable impression of the Department of State, which he described as uncertain, confused, superficial, too much inclined to improvisations and at the same time pretentious and arrogant.'
48. Message from Nehru to Attlee, 21 July 1950, FK1022/281/G, FO 371/89095.
49. Letter from Strang to Franks, 10 Aug. 1950, ibid.
50. See Peking to FO, 23 May 1950, for the views of Hutchison with minutes by A. A. E. Franklin, 26 May 1950, and Esler Dening, 30 May 1950, FC1909/8, FO 371/83558. See also notes from Commonwealth Relations Office to FO, 27 Oct. 1950, for a 'Biographical note and personality sketch of Pannikar [*sic*] Indian ambassador to China', FC1909/13, ibid.
51. *FRUS 1950* (7), p. 742, Henderson to Acheson, 20 Sept. 1950.
52. Ibid., p. 743, Henderson to Acheson, 20 Sept. 1950.
53. Ibid., pp. 707–8, memorandum by joint chiefs of staff, 7 Sept. 1950.
54. Ibid., p. 746, minutes of fourth meeting of US delegation to UN General Assembly, 21 Sept. 1950.

55. Ibid., p. 747.
56. Ibid., pp. 781–2, Webb to US mission at UN, 27 Sept. 1950.
57. Ibid., p. 826, Marshall to MacArthur, 29 Sept. 1950.
58. Ibid., p. 830, editorial note.
59. Ibid., p. 833, minutes of eleventh meeting of US delegation to UN General Assembly, 2 Oct. 1950. Acheson was replying to a question from Senator Henry Cabot Lodge (Republican, Massachusetts), a member of the delegation.
60. FO memorandum by Shattock, no date, ?October 1950, FK1022/393/G, FO 371/84099.
61. *FRUS 1950* (7), pp. 790–2, Henderson to Acheson, 27 Sept. 1950.
62. Ibid., pp. 793–4, memorandum by Merchant, 27 Sept. 1950.
63. Ibid., p. 794. Hubert Graves of the British embassy in Washington expressed the reservations over Panikkar's character.
64. *Soviet News*, 27 Sept. 1950, reproducing text of Chou En-lai's protest, 24 Sept. 1950.
65. 'Policy following an enemy defeat in S. Korea', note by Slessor, 14 Sept. 1950, appendix to confidential annexe, chiefs of staff minutes, COS(50) 142(8), Defe 4/36.
66. Ibid.
67. Chiefs of staff minutes, 20 Sept. 1950, ibid.
68. Ibid.
69. Chiefs of staff minutes, confidential annexe, 3 Oct. 1950, COS(50)160(2), Defe 4/36.
70. Chiefs of staff minutes, confidential annexe, 4 Oct. 1950, COS(50)161(1), ibid.
71. Ibid.
72. Ibid.
73. Tokyo to FO 3 Oct. 1950, FK1022/373/G, FO 371/84099.
74. Ibid.
75. Washington to FO 4 Oct. 1950, FK1022/389, ibid.
76. Chiefs of staff minutes, confidential annexe, 5 Oct. 1950, COS(50)162(1), ibid.
77. *FRUS 1950* (7), pp. 893–7, memorandum by Rusk, 6 Oct. 1950, and pp. 930–2, memorandum by Jessup, 12 Oct. 1950, enclosing message from Bevin to Franks, 11 Oct. 1950.
78. Ibid., pp. 904–6, resolution adopted by UN General Assembly, 7 Oct. 1950.
79. Peking to FO, 12 Oct. 1950, enclosing statement issued on 10 Oct., FK1022/430, FO 371/84101.
80. Ibid.
81. Ibid.
82. Muccio Oral History, pp. 80, 84, and Ambassador Muccio's reiteration to the author, 15 March 1982.
83. Vernice Anderson Oral History, pp. 46–7, 52, 55, interview between Anderson and Jerry N. Hess, 1971, copy in Truman Library.
84. *FRUS 1950* (7), pp. 948–60, for the record compiled by General Bradley on the basis of notes taken by various of those present.
85. Ibid., p. 954.
86. Ibid., p. 956.
87. Ibid., pp. 958–9.

88. Notes by Truman on Wake Island meeting, 25 Nov. 1950, PSF files, 'Longhand Notes' file, 1945–1955, box 263, Truman Papers, Truman Library.

89. R. J. Donovan, *Tumultuous Years: The Presidency of Harry S. Truman, 1949–1953* (London 1982), p. 369.

90. For an account of Chinese policy, see Whiting, op. cit., pp. 116–30.

91. *FRUS 1950* (7), pp. 995–6, editorial note.

92. Ibid., pp. 1003–4, Wilkinson (consul-general, Hong Kong) to Acheson, 27 Oct. 1950.

93. Ibid., pp. 1013–14, Drumright to Acheson, 29 Oct. 1950.

94. Ibid., pp. 1025–6, memorandum by Bedell Smith to Truman, 1 Nov. 1950. For a discussion of Chinese military intervention, see J. F. Schnabel and R. J. Watson, *The History of the Joint Chiefs of Staff: The Joint Chiefs and National Policy*, vol. III (Wilmington, Del. 1979), pp. 277–87.

95. FO to New York (for British delegation to UN), 7 Nov. 1950, enclosing Chinese statement, 4 Nov., FK1023/92, FO 371/84113.

96. Ibid.

97. Peking to FO, 13 Nov. 1950, FK1023/100, FO 371/84114.

98. *The Times*, 10 Nov. 1950.

99. FO minutes by Buzzard, 10 Nov. and Franklin, 13 Nov. 1950, FK1023/82, FO 371/84113.

100. Peking to FO, 7 Nov. 1950, with minutes by Buzzard, 8 Nov. 1950, FK1023/102, FO 371/84114.

101. *FRUS 1950* (7), pp. 1057–8, joint chiefs of staff to MacArthur, 6 Nov. 1950.

102. Ibid., p. 1095, Drumright to Acheson, 8 Nov. 1950.

103. Ibid., p. 1083, draft memorandum by Davies, 7 Nov. 1950.

104. Ibid., pp. 1098–1100, memorandum by Emmerson, 8 Nov. 1950.

105. Ibid., pp. 1101–6, memorandum by CIA, 8 Nov. 1950.

106. Ibid., pp. 1107–10, MacArthur to joint chiefs of staff, 9 Nov. 1950.

107. Ibid., pp. 1138–40, British embassy to State Department, 13 Nov. 1950.

108. Ibid., pp. 1141–2, memorandum by Rusk, 13 Nov. 1950.

109. Ibid., p. 1161, editorial note.

110. Muccio Oral History, p. 73, where Muccio commented that Willoughy disliked the Chinese and showed disdain for their capabilities. This arose from his brief acquaintance with China many years before. For comments on Willoughby's role, see William Manchester, *American Caesar* (London 1979), pp. 608, 613.

111. Bouchier to chiefs of state, 13 Nov. 1950, FK1015/296/G, FO 371/84072.

112. *FRUS 1950* (7), pp. 1173–5, British embassy to State Department, enclosing message from Bevin to Franks, 17 Nov. 1950.

113. Peking to FO, 23 Nov. 1950, FK1023/150, FO 371/84117.

114. *FRUS 1950* (7), pp. 1228–9, Acheson to embassy in London, 24 Nov. 1950.

115. Ibid., pp. 1222–4, Collins to MacArthur, 24 Nov. 1950.

116. Ibid., pp. 1231–3, MacArthur to joint chiefs of staff, 25 Nov. 1950.

117. Ibid., p. 1237, MacArthur to joint chiefs of staff, 28 Nov. 1950.

# CONCLUSION

The Korean War was a peculiar struggle in which the first year of the conflict saw rapid tergiversations with the success of the initial North Korean advance, then the equally dramatic UN counter-attack and eclipse of the North Koreans, followed by the intervention of China and the forcing back of UN forces, and finally the relative stabilisation of the military conduct of the war after the failure of the last major Chinese offensive, launched in April 1951.[1] It was clear in June 1951 that the war would not end in a military victory for either side; a political solution would have to be found. It took two years to reach this solution and even then it was impossible to negotiate a general settlement: futile meetings of the armistice commission have continued to assemble regularly for ritualistic, propagandistic denunciation of each other but without solid evidence that a more encouraging turn of events was likely. The period of maximum uncertainty was in December 1950 and January 1951 when morale in the UN was low and speculation mounted as to the possible courses of action that could be followed by the United States. President Truman's allusion to contingency planning involving the atomic weapon at a press conference held in late November 1950 stimulated a flurry of anxiety and activity of which the most tangible instance was the decision of the British Prime Minister, Clement Attlee, to fly to Washington for talks with Truman in early December. The talks were held in a tense atmosphere and Attlee conveyed unmistakably the concern in western Europe and in the UN over the objectives of American policy and the role of General MacArthur. The urgent task of rebuilding western Europe politically and economically and of ensuring that Soviet aggression in Europe could be repelled must be reiterated. Attlee underlined the fears in Europe that MacArthur wielded excessive power and that this had not so far been curbed.[2]

Truman stated there would be no retreat in the American determination to defeat aggression but it was obvious that American leaders were still reeling from the shock of the Chinese onslaught and that no one could forecast how American policy would evolve. The situation could have developed in several different directions. The UN forces could try to stabilise their lines after significant retreat and prepare themselves for a renewed offensive with limited aims. In association with the latter or distinct from it, an attempt could be launched to secure a negotiated termination. Alternatively American troops could be withdrawn from Korea and an economic blockade of China organised with the possibility of using the atomic weapon against selected Chinese cities, as contemplated by MacArthur. American hatred of China attained violent proportions, accentuated by the acrid nature of political disputes in Congress and McCarthyite condemnation of the administration for the loss of China. The British government was so alarmed as to send Air Chief Marshal Sir John Slessor to Washington in the middle of January 1951; it was imperative to obtain assurances that the United States would not withdraw from Korea or take drastic action against China. Slessor was told by General Omar Bradley that American troops would stay in Korea but Bradley did not hide his personal preference for seeing American forces extricated from a theatre that was not essential to the contest between communism and the 'free world'.[3] The United States insisted that the UN General Assembly should condemn China for her aggression in Korea. Britain and other members of the UN were apprehensive that this could lead to a full-scale economic blockade with the danger of escalation into a war embracing the whole of the Far East.[4] Anglo-American relations were strained considerably because of the American zeal for securing a motion castigating China. At one point it looked as though Britain might oppose an American-sponsored motion but, after further exchanges and after the Chinese government repudiated Indian efforts to produce a moderate motion, Britain supported the United States in the motion carried in the UN General Assembly on 1 February 1951.

In January and February 1951 it became clear that, serious as the military position of the UN forces was, it was less grave than the utterances of MacArthur had indicated in December 1950. The joint chiefs of staff took steps to strengthen their control of the military campaign and developed direct communication with General Matthew B. Ridgway, who had taken command after the death of General Walton Walker in December. MacArthur was in process of being bypassed and his power was declining. This did not lessen MacArthur's capacity for causing trouble and the long-simmering dispute between MacArthur and his superiors in Washington came to a head in March and April. Truman and Acheson were contemplating an attempt to open communication with Peking and to start the process leading to a political solution in Korea. MacArthur deliberately cut across this strategy, having seen a copy of the statement, threatening an extension of the war unless the Chinese negotiated but also conveying his willingness to meet the commander-in-chief of the Chinese forces.

Truman was incensed and probably reached his private decision to recall the obdurate general at this time.

The culmination to MacArthur's cavalier behaviour came when his letter to the Republican minority leader in the House of Representatives, Joseph W. Martin of Massachusetts, was made public in early April; in this communication MacArthur conveyed with crystal clarity his distaste for the Asian policies of the Truman administration and that he favoured a more resolute approach to punish China. Most likely MacArthur believed the President would draw back from removing him from his posts but equally MacArthur did not appear to care what happened. He had always been extremely self-centred and vain; he regarded Truman with contempt and perhaps felt that a confrontation with Truman, whose popularity was declining, could help to carry him to the Republican presidential nomination in 1952. Truman rose to the great challenges of his presidency and he did not shirk from dismissing the soldier with the highest prestige and longest record of service in the United States army. The President consulted General George Marshall, the Secretary of Defense, and the joint chiefs of staff. All agreed that MacArthur must be recalled, Marshall concluding after a perusal of the papers detailing exchanges with MacArthur over the years, that his recall was long overdue. The mechanics of conveying the news to MacArthur himself was unfortunately bungled because of fears that the press would publish the information prematurely. There was some truth in MacArthur's allegation that he had been dismissed as a result of diplomatic representations by western governments, particularly Britain. Attlee, Bevin, the British chiefs of staff (especially Slessor) and Sir Oliver Franks had each conveyed alarm at what Franks termed 'MacArthuritis'; MacArthur's apparently infinite talent for making controversial public announcements not discussed with the members of the UN participating in operations – or indeed with Washington – led the British to fear that MacArthur could, through injudicious action, involve the UN in war against China and possibly with the Soviet Union.[5] It would be wrong to state that MacArthur was recalled because of British representations in themselves but these contributed more than Truman and Acheson admitted to the accumulating disillusionment with him in Washington. The decision caused tremendous emotion and debate and MacArthur received a magnificent welcome on his return to the home country he had not seen for thirteen years. However, the excitement soon subsided and the administration's skill in depicting the crisis as a constitutional confrontation between an elected president and a recalcitrant general eventually succeeded in diminishing positive support for MacArthur. The general's own political ambitions were frustrated and his political contribution to the Republican convention in 1952 was confined to delivering the keynote address before the convention nominated his rival, General Dwight D. Eisenhower, as the presidentia candidate.

In April 1951 the Chinese launched a ferocious attack in what proved to be the last major endeavour to end the war by military means. The timing of the attack came as a surprise, since it occurred some six weeks sooner than anticipated, indicating that the defects in intelligence were not all to be attributed to MacArthur and his circle. Once the attack was contained signs of a desire for compromise emerged. The Soviet Union had been unhappy with the long-term implications of the fighting in Korea, since the UN had originally condemned North Korea and intervened. Stalin was prepared to tolerate a short war from which North Korea emerged victorious but was unwilling to allow a protracted conflict in which China would have a more insistent voice in deciding the outcome. It is probable that the Soviet Union exerted pressure in Pyongyang and Peking and obtained grudging consent to a bid for peace being made. The United States was similarly anxious to explore paths that could extricate the UN from Korea; George F. Kennan, who had left the State Department at the end of August 1950 to pursue an academic career, acted as intermediary in confidential discussions with Jacob Malik, the Soviet delegate to the UN. The important signal came with a radio broadcast delivered by Malik on 23 June 1951 in which, amid the customary verbiage, was a statement that the Soviet Union desired a peaceful resolution of world problems.[6] It had not seemed possible that the war could be brought to an end within the near future. Contacts were opened with North Korea and China and the first discussions commenced in July 1951. The atmosphere in which the exchanges occurred was not only frigid but highly acrimonious. North Korea and China had no intention of compromising on fundamentals and were most likely less anxious for a settlement than Russia. China had wanted the UN to recognise that Peking and not Taiwan should occupy the seat in the UN Security Council belonging to China and that the United States should desist from protecting Taiwan. This remained a stumbling-block, although the talks centred on issues directly related to the war in Korea.

Contrary to the sanguine hope in Washington that the peace talks could be concluded relatively quickly, they proved to be extremely protracted and contentious. North Korea and China believed time was on their side; their forces could remain where they were indefinitely and periodic forays could be undertaken to emphasise that they had no intention of making major concessions. American public opinion and the members of the UN might well tire of the stalemate and favour further concessions to escape from Korea. South Korea was not happy with the opening of peace talks because Syngman Rhee was as dedicated as before to unifying Korea; this could only be achieved through force and Rhee trumpeted a vehemently anti-communist line calculated to appeal to a significant segment of American opinion. Rhee remained a veritable thorn in the side of the United States to the conclusion of the war and beyond. One of the most difficult issues encountered in the talks revolved around the fate of prisoners of war. Few would have believed in

July 1951 that it would take exactly two years to achieve an end to the war and even then without a genuine settlement of the problems dividing Korea. Both sides contributed to this prolonged exchange: the United States was often simplistic and impatient and the Chinese and North Koreans too rigid and obdurate. It would be naïve to think that the savagery unleashed in 1950–51 could be suddenly halted but equally it was not necessary for the process to be so extended.

The truce talks were initially conducted at Kaesong, which proved an undesirable venue as it was within territory occupied by the communist forces; the atmosphere was menacing and intimidating and General Ridgway subsequently admitted that he had erred in accepting Kaesong. The talks were moved to Panmunjom in October 1951: the political climate was not better but it was a more suitable setting than Kaesong. There were various problems to be resolved – arrangements over inspections and troop replacements, the supervision of airfields and participation in an international supervisory commission.[7] Progress was slowly made in these areas so that in May 1952 one major problem remained, the thorny matter of the repatriation of prisoners of war (POWs). This proved extremely intractable and again each side shared responsibility for this situation. China and North Korea demanded that all POWs should be returned: international law and precedent pointed in this direction. International agreements stated that POWs on each side should be returned at the close of the conflict. In 1945 the United States and Britain forcibly returned White Russian POWs to the Soviet Union to placate Stalin; many went to labour camps and to their deaths.[8] The assumption in international understandings had been that the matter would be essentially straightforward and the contingency of POWs bitterly opposing the governments ruling their countries had not been recognised. A considerable proportion of Chinese POWs had served in the Kuomintang forces until 1948–49 and some disliked Chinese communism; now the opportunity had come for them to avoid returning to China and instead to go to Taiwan. Some of the North Koreans conscripted had no love for Kim Il Sung's government and similarly wished to remain in South Korea. Dean Acheson at first showed some signs of vacillation, discerning that an acrimonious dispute would render the conclusion of an agreement far more difficult. President Truman viewed it in clear moral terms. It would be wholly wrong to compel POWs to return to torture and death; furthermore the free world could derive valuable propaganda from the situation. American policy was predicated upon voluntary repatriation and both Truman and Acheson adhered to this approach, as did Eisenhower and Dulles when the new administration took office in January 1953.

In July 1951 it was not thought that significant numbers would be unwilling to return. At the beginning of 1952 it was estimated that between 10 and 25 per cent would not want to go back; this was a serious underestimate.[9] In private United States officials reckoned that the numbers returning would comprise approximately 116,000 of 132,000 POWs and 18,000 of 38,000 civilians; about 28,000 POWs and 30,000 civilians would oppose returning but it was thought that only around 16,000 POWs and 20,000 civilians might resist repatriation by force.[10] Statements made at Panmunjom indicated that approximately 116,000 would be willing to return. In reality about 70,000 only wished to go back (5,000 out of 21,000 Chinese; 54,000 out of 96,000 North Koreans; 4,000 out of 15,000 South Koreans; and 7,500 of 38,000 civilians).[11] The communist response was predictably bitter: accusations were hurled that great pressure had been applied to POWs to produce this result and that the United States had been deliberately misleading. Undoubtedly there was partial validity in the accusations because the Americans had implemented a programme to indoctrinate POWs. More significant was the fact that Kuomintang soldiers were employed as prison guards where Chinese prisoners were held and they were responsible, together with the hierarchy of prisoners within the camps, for using brutality and intimidation to coerce POWs to declare against returning.[12]

The exchanges at Panmunjom in the summer of 1952 appeared to show that North Korea was more willing to compromise than China. Meanwhile the United States was faced with growing dissatisfaction among its allies at the inability to end the war. India advocated an armistice, the return of POWs on each side wishing to return, and the setting up of a commission to determine the fate of the remainder: Krisna Menon, the Indian representative at the UN, put forward the proposal skilfully and imprecisely.[13] The Truman administration regarded the proposal with hostility, since POWs refusing to return would stay in prison camps. It appeared as though the United States would be involved in difficulty and isolation, as their allies sympathised with the Indian motion. The Americans were then paradoxically assisted by the Soviet Union, which condemned the Indian proposal. Acheson then cleverly exploited the situation by securing an amendment to the Indian resolution to the effect that POWs unwilling to return would be freed by the commission approximately four months after the armistice.[14] The reasons why the Soviet Union pursued this line at the UN remain a matter for conjecture and probably resulted from a belief that the Menon proposal could act as a boomerang subsequently for the Soviet Union and China if it was accepted that communist POWs need not be returned at the termination of conflict.

The talks dragged on interminably with no sign of progress being made. Fighting of a sporadic and sometimes intensive character flared periodically. The United States used intensive conventional bombing of North Korea in a bid to force the communist countries to concede a negotiating basis acceptable to the Americans. Weariness with the stalemate in Korea grew in the United States and in western Europe. The popularity of the Truman administration further waned in the midst of the economic problems produced by the war and the bitter Republican censure of the administration for the bellicosity shown by Communist China. Truman had considered withdrawing from the contest for the Democratic nomination since 1950 if not sooner. Early in 1952 he finally made his decision and announced that he would not accept renomination.[15] This left the field wide open in both parties, for there was no outstanding candidate in either party around whom either the Democrats or the Republicans could unite. The Democrats nominated the earnest, cultivated liberal from Illinois, Governor Adlai Stevenson. The Republicans nominated General Dwight Eisenhower after a tough battle at the convention in which the moderate Eisenhower defeated the standard bearer of the right wing, Senator Robert A. Taft of Ohio. Eisenhower had not been involved in domestic politics before the beginning of 1952 and had been considered a possible contender for the Democratic nomination in 1948 and, looking ahead, for 1952. Eisenhower had the excellent credentials of his distinguished wartime command in Europe and of having served as chief of staff of the army after the war. After a brief, unhappy spell as president of Columbia University he was recalled to become the first commander of NATO in western Europe in 1951. He was an admirable choice for the Republican Party, since he was well known, popular, deeply experienced in foreign and defence issues; for Republican moderates he was the only man who could prevent Taft from gaining the nomination.[16]

The Truman administration ended its term weary and frustrated at the inability to conclude the war. This reaction was well illustrated when Anthony Eden informed Cabinet colleagues in December 1952 of an encounter in which Dean Acheson, appearing evidently the worse for drink after a party, attacked British views over Korea as put forward by the British Minister of State at the Foreign Office, Selwyn Lloyd. Acheson had been more obdurate than the American military and 'more royalist than the "royalists" '; he revealed an obsession with India and a suspicion of Indian efforts to promote progress in Korea.[17] Acheson was usually arrogant in his behaviour but he had been under great pressure for a long time because of the mordant partisan attacks made upon him. The presidential election had resulted in a smashing victory for Eisenhower whose wide appeal and avuncular character could not be matched by Stevenson. Furthermore the Democrats had been in office for twenty years and it was time for a change. Eisenhower had no brilliant ideas for tackling the Korean stalemate; however, he made one bold statement during the campaign in which he pledged that, if elected, he would visit Korea promptly to assess the position for himself. He redeemed this promise immediately in December 1952 and became more closely acquainted with the military and political realities.

Upon assuming office in January 1953 Eisenhower was confronted with the same difficulties as his predecessor. China and North Korea seemed no more willing to come to terms. Eisenhower's Secretary of State, John Foster Dulles, had made stirring speeches during the campaign on the need to roll back communism, despite the consequences of attempting to do so in Korea in October 1950. Eisenhower took the crucial decisions in foreign policy and acted as a check on the exuberance of his Secretary of State; Eisenhower has come to be assessed more favourably in the field of foreign policy.[18] The President was determined to end the Korean conflict and let it be known that unless this occurred, the United States might use the atomic weapon. Whether this threat swayed the decision or whether China and North Korea had grudgingly recognised that the war should be terminated is uncertain. The death of Stalin may well have contributed to a less rigid attitude among the communist states. Eisenhower's eagerness to end the war did not please Syngman Rhee, who proved extremely obstructive in the final phase in 1953. Eisenhower was exasperated with him and warned of serious consequences unless South Korea cooperated.[19] Thought was given to encouraging a coup in Seoul to remove Rhee. In July 1953 the Korean War ended with agreement on the demarcation line between the two Korean states with provision for regular meetings of the armistice commission at Panmunjom, and with a full settlement of the Korean problem including reunification to be arrived at subsequently. The demarcation line was some distance to the north of the 38th parallel in the east and centre but to the west was drawn below the parallel so that the town of Kansong was now in the south and Kaesong was in the north (see Map 2). The number of POWs accepting repatriation comprised 82,500 (including 6,700 Chinese) and about 50,000 (including 14,700 Chinese) decided not to return.[20]

Dulles informed the British in July 1953 that he hoped Korea could be unified within five to ten years as a neutral state.[21] The hope was not borne out. In economic terms Korea changed enormously in the years ahead with appreciable economic growth in North and South Korea; this was particularly marked in South Korea where the economy developed with remarkable speed in the later 1970s and early 1980s to the point where she rivalled Japan in shipbuilding, cars and electrical goods. Politically, however, no significant progress had been made in surmounting the division. For most of the period since 1953 relations have been tense and vituperative with mutual insults hurled and periodic threats from Kim Il Sung to attack the south. Kim consolidated his power base ruthlessly during the 1950s through removing his opponents in the indigenous and Yenan factions of the party. Pak Hon-yong, the North Korean Foreign Minister, was arrested immediately after the end of the war, accused of plotting with the United States, and executed two years later. The Yenan faction was purged in the later 1950s. Kim ruled supreme and prepared for his son, Kim Jong Il, to succeed him. In international relations Kim Il Sung pursued a shrewd policy of establishing the full independence of North Korea and of avoiding reliance upon Moscow or Peking. Although the Russians had helped to install him in power originally, Kim's relations with the Soviet Union were often strained. If anything his relations with Peking were rather warmer, although also subject to considerable coolness at times. The cult of the personality flourished as the thoughts of Kim Il Sung were elevated to a status of equality with Stalin and Mao Tse-tung. In South Korea Syngman Rhee remained in power until 1960. By then he was senile and his regime was distinguished by extensive brutality and corruption. Large-scale demonstrations with encouragement from the American CIA brought his rule to an end. A brief experiment in liberal government in 1960–61 was followed by a military coup and the ascendancy of the military, which has lasted since 1961. While there have been signs of developing maturity in South Korean politics, the hopes that a political system analogous to that in Japan could materialise have not been borne out. Economic success, if maintained, may bring about viable democratic government in the ROK.

Is there any likelihood of the division of Korea being ended? The most crucial question here is what will happen in North Korea after the departure of Kim Il Sung. It is possible that the North Korean army might loom large in decision-making or take full power itself. Alternatively Kim Jong Il may continue his father's regime on a similar basis. Whatever transpires in the political evolution of the two Korean states, it appears unlikely that a unified Korea can be achieved in the foreseeable future. The sharp ideological split and the power of vested interests in both Korean states renders unification improbable. The United States still has a sizeable force in South Korea under UN authority; Jimmy Carter talked of withdrawing these troops in his presidential campaign in 1976 but refrained from doing so when faced with the realities of office. Such action would have had a destabilising effect and could create a situation not dissimilar to that of 1948–50. The United States is likely to be committed to Korea for a long time to come.

Finally why did the Korean War occur? Most wars take place because of a mixture of aggression or perceived aggression and of miscalculation. Usually muddle is more conspicuous that malevolence but the latter should not be discounted. Korea was in a chronically unstable position from 1945 to 1950. There were deep social divisions within the country, accelerated and brought to a climax by the Japanese colonial occupation from 1910 to 1945. Left to her own devices Korea would probably have become a radical and very possibly communist state but one that would not have been subservient to the Soviet Union or China. The intervention of the United States and the Soviet Union ensured that a unified Korea finding her own salvation would not be the outcome. The United States did not wish to see South Korea incorporated within the communist sphere but would not make the defence of the ROK a priority before June 1950. The Soviet Union believed that sooner or later South Korea would fall into the communist camp and perhaps felt the risk of North Korean action could be accepted in June 1950, although it is impossible to say with certainty what the Russian attitude was. China was not deeply involved before June or even October 1950 and then acted because of the American threat to Manchuria. Historians have emphasised that the events of June 1950 must be seen in the context of the endemic civil war in the Korean peninsula since August 1945. We do not know precisely what happened before the outbreak of the open, large-scale conflict in June 1950. It is likely that North Korea took the initiative in advancing but Bruce Cumings is surely right in stressing that this action has to be understood in terms of the bitter hostility between the two Korean states and that South Korea had done much to provoke the north.[22] Kim Il Sung certainly erred in his gamble and Syngman Rhee had erred equally in his shrill boasts between 1948 and 1950. Responsibility for the outbreak and escalation of the war has to be shared widely. North and South Korea had inflamed matters, as had the United States and the Soviet Union. China could have acted with more consistency and effect in the nature of the warnings forwarded in September and October 1950. Korea was a victim of her own murderous internal animosities and of the mutual suspicion and hatred of the superpowers in the Cold War.

# REFERENCES

1.  For a lucid narrative of the war, see David Rees, *Korea: The Limited War* (London 1964).
2.  For the British record of the talks between Truman and Attlee, see Prem. 8/1200. For the American record, see *FRUS 1950* (7) pp. 1361–77, 1382–6, 1390–1408, 1435–42, 1449–79.
3.  Slessor reported to the Cabinet on his discussions on 22 January, see Cabinet conclusions 5(51)3, 22 Jan. 1951, Cab. 128/19.
4.  Cabinet conclusions, 4(51)5, 18 Jan. 1951, ibid. Ernest Bevin observed in Cabinet that the enforcement of drastic sanctions would bring the increased risk of general war in the Far East. This opinion had been endorsed by the Commonwealth prime ministers: condemnation of China should be restricted to Chinese actions in Korea.
5.  For a discussion of British views see Peter Lowe, 'Great Britain, Japan, and the Korean War, 1950–1', in John Chapman and David Steeds (eds), *Proceedings of the British Association for Japanese Studies*, IX (1984), 98–111.
6.  For the relevant extract from the broadcast, of 23 June 1951, see *FRUS 1951* (7), editorial note. For the private discussions between Kennan and Malik, see ibid., pp. 507–11, Kennan to Matthews, 5 June 1951, pp. 536–8, letter from Kennan to Acheson, 20 June 1951, and pp. 551–2, Kirk to Acheson, 25 June 1951.
7.  B. J. Bernstein, 'The struggle over the Korean armistice: prisoners of repatriation', in Bruce Cumings (ed.), *Child of Conflict* (London 1983), p. 262.

8.  On this aspect see Nikolai Tolstoy, *Victims of Yalta* (London 1977).
9.  Bernstein in Cumings (ed.), p. 275.
10. Ibid., p. 284.
11. Ibid.
12. Ibid., p. 285.
13. Ibid., p. 301. See also Roger Bullen, 'Great Britain, the United States and the Indian armistice resolution on the Korean War, November 1952', in Ian Nish (ed.), *Aspects of Anglo-Korean Relations* (London 1984), pp. 27–44.
14. Bernstein in Cumings (ed.), p. 306.
15. See handwritten note by Truman, 16 April 1950, 'Longhand Notes' file, 1945–1955, PSF files, Truman Papers, Truman Library, in which the President wrote that he would not be a candidate for the Democratic nomination and that Governor Adlai Stevenson appeared a suitable choice.
16. For an important biography of Eisenhower, see Stephen Ambrose, *Eisenhower: The Soldier, 1890–1952* and *Eisenhower: The President, 1952–1969* (London 1983–84).
17. See memorandum by Eden, dealing with proceedings at the seventh session of the UN General Assembly, 15 Dec. 1952, CC (52) 441, Cab. 129/57.
18. See R. A. Divine, *Eisenhower and the Cold War* (Oxford 1981) and Ambrose, *Eisenhower: The President.*
19. Writing in his diary Eisenhower condemned Rhee as a most unsatisfactory ally, 24 July 1953, in R. H. Ferrell (ed.), *The Eisenhower Diaries* (London 1981), p. 248.
20. Bernstein in Cumings (ed.), p. 307.
21. Cabinet conclusions, 21 July 1953, CC53(44) 4, Cab. 128/26, part 2.
22. Cumings, 'Introduction', in Cumings (ed.), pp. 40–1.

# APPENDIX

## (A) UNITED NATIONS FORCE CONTRIBUTIONS IN THE KOREAN WAR

(Source: Robert O'Neill, *Australia in the Korean War*, I, Canberra, 1981 p. 462.)

*Australia:* Two infantry battalions, part of the First Commonwealth Division, two destroyers or frigates, one aircraft carrier and a fighter squadron.
*Belgium:* One infantry battalion.
*Canada:* One reinforced infantry brigade, including tank and artillery forces, part of the First Commonwealth Division, three destroyers and a squadron of transport aircraft.
*Colombia:* One infantry battalion and a frigate.
*Ethiopia:* One infantry battalion.
*France:* One reinforced infantry battalion.
*Greece:* One infantry battalion and transport aircraft.
*Luxembourg:* One infantry platoon.
*Netherlands:* One infantry battalion and naval forces.
*New Zealand:* One regiment of artillery, part of the First Commonwealth Division.
*Philippines:* One infantry battalion and one company of tanks.
*Thailand:* One infantry battalion, naval forces, air and naval transports.
*Turkey:* One infantry brigade.
*Union of South Africa:* One fighter squadron.
*United Kingdom:* Two infantry brigades, one armoured regiment, one and a half artillery regiments, one and a half engineer regiments and supporting ground forces, all part of the First Commonwealth Division; the Far Eastern fleet; and Sunderland aircraft of the RAF.
*United States of America:* The Eighth Army of six army divisions and one marine division, Naval Forces Far East (three task forces), and Far East Air Forces (three air forces).
*Medical Units:* Denmark, Italy, India, Norway and Sweden.

# (B) CASUALTIES OF THE KOREAN WAR

(Source: based on official UN publications and reproduced in David Rees, *Korea: The Limited War*, London, 1964, pp. 460–1.)

Republic of Korea (South Korea) – 1,313,836 (estimated)
Approximate breakdown of 300,000 authenticated casualties: Killed 47,000; Wounded 183,000; Missing and POW 70,000

United States – 142,091
Deaths – 33,629; Killed in action 23,300; Wounded in action, 105,785; Missing in action, 5,866; Captured or interned, 7,140

UN (excluding USA) – 17,260
Killed 3,194; Wounded 11,297; Missing and POW 2,769

Estimates of communist casualties – between 1,500,000 and 2,000,000
China approximately 900,000; Democratic People's Republic of Korea (North Korea), 520,000; Civilian casualties in DPRK estimated at about 1 million.

# SELECT BIBLIOGRAPHY

## (A) MANUSCRIPT SOURCES

### BRITAIN

*Cambridge*
*Churchill College, Cambridge*
Attlee Papers
Philip Noel-Baker Papers
Slim Papers

*London*
*British Library of Political and Economic Science*
Dalton Diaries and Papers

*Public Record Office, Kew*
(a) *Cabinet Office*
   Cab 128, Cabinet conclusions, 1948–53
   Cab 129, Cabinet memoranda, 1948–53
   Cab 131, Defence Committee
   Cab 134, Far Eastern (Official) Committee; China and South-East Asia
   Committee
(b) *Ministry of Defence*
   Defe 4, Chiefs of Staff minutes, 1947–51
   Defe 5, Chiefs of Staff memoranda, 1947–51
(c) *Foreign Office*
   FO 371, records relating to Korea, 1945–50
   records relating to China, 1948–50
   records relating to Japan, 1948–50
   records relating to Germany (Berlin Blockade), 1948–9
   records relating to Czechoslovakia, 1948
   records relating to Soviet Union, 1948–50
   records relating to United Nations, 1948–50
   records relating to United States, 1948–50

(d)  *Prime Minister's Office*
Prem 8
(e)  *Private papers*
FO 800, Bevin Papers

*Royal Commonwealth Society*
Malcolm MacDonald Papers

*Private possession*
Kenneth Younger Diaries (Lady Younger, in temporary possession of Professor Geoffrey Warner)

## Manchester
*Private possession*
Raymond Streat Papers (in possession of Sir George Kenyon)

## Oxford
*Western Manuscripts Department, Bodleian Library*
Attlee Papers

## UNITED STATES

### Independence, Missouri
*Harry S. Truman Library*
Dean Acheson Papers
George M. Elsey Papers
Edgar A. J. Johnson Papers
Thayer Papers
Harry S. Truman Papers: Foreign Affairs files; Official Files: Selected Records relating to Korean War, Department of Defense, Department of State; President's Secretary's Files: various, including CIA memoranda and reports, 1950–1, and papers dealing with Korean War; General Files; Post-Presidential Files
James E. Webb Papers
Oral Histories: Vernice Anderson; Niles W. Bond; Matthew J. Connelly; George M. Elsey; Livingston Merchant; John J. Muccio (two separate interviews with Jerry N. Hess, 1971, and R. D. McKinzie, 1976); Charles S. Murphy; Robert G. Nixon; Arthur D. Ringwalt.

### Norfolk, Virginia
*Douglas MacArthur Memorial*
Douglas MacArthur Papers
Charles Willoughby Papers

### Washington, District of Columbia
*National Archives*
Record Group 59, Decimal Files, 795, 1950, Korea; Record Group 218, Joint Chiefs of Staff Files, Decimal Files 091, 092, 1948–51, relating to Soviet

Union and eastern Europe, UN Command Operations in Korea, Wake Island conference, Asia, Australia, Formosa, Korea, Omar Bradley Papers, North Atlantic Treaty, China, Indo-China, MacArthur Hearings. Record Group 319, Army Operations, General, 1950–51, Decimal Files 091, Korea, 1950–51

James F. Schnabel and Robert J. Watson, *The History of Joint Chiefs of Staff: The Joint Chiefs of Staff and National Policy*, vol. III, *The Korean War*, part 1. Historical Division, Joint Secretariat, Joint Chiefs of Staff, April 1978.

## (B) PRINTED DOCUMENTARY COLLECTIONS, DIARIES AND MEMOIRS

Margaret Carlyle (ed.), *Documents on International Affairs, 1947–8, 1949–50*. London 1952–53.

*Foreign Relations of the United States*. Washington, DC. Selected volumes, 1945–51.

*Military Situation in the Far East. Hearings before the Committee on Armed Services and the Committee on Foreign Relations, United States Senate, 82nd Congress, First Session. To Conduct an Inquiry into the Military Situation in the Far East and the Facts Surrounding the Relief of General of the Army Douglas MacArthur from his Assignment in that Area.* 5 parts. Washington, DC 1951.

Dae-sook Suh, *Documents of Korean Communism, 1918–1948*. Princeton, NJ 1970.

*United Nations, Security Council Official Records*. Fifth year, 1950. New York 1950.

United Nations, *Report of the United Nations Commission on Korea: Covering the Period from 15 December 1949 to 4 September 1950*. New York 1950.

Acheson, Dean, *Present at the Creation: My Years in the State Department*. London 1970.

Allison, J. M., *Ambassador from the Prairies* (Paperback edn). Tokyo 1975.

Ferrell, R. H. (ed.), *The Eisenhower Diaries*. London 1981.

Franks, Oliver, *American Impressions*. Oration delivered at London School of Economics, 11 December 1953.

Gayn, Mark, *Japan Diary* (Paperback edn). Tokyo 1981.

Kennan, G. F., *Memoirs, 1925–1950*. London 1968.

Khruschev, N. S., *Khruschev Remembers*. London 1971.

MacArthur, Douglas, *Reminiscences*. London 1964.

Ridgway, Matthew, *The War in Korea*. London 1967.

Sebald, W. J., with Russell Brines, *With MacArthur in Japan: A Personal History of the Occupation*. London 1967.

Truman, Harry, *Memoirs: Year of Decisions, 1945*; and *Years of Trial and Hope, 1946–1952* (Paperback edn). New York 1965.

Vandenberg, A. H., Jr (ed.), *The Private Papers of Senator Vandenberg*. London 1953.

# (C) ADDITIONAL READING

Allen, G. C., *A Short Economic History of Modern Japan* (4th edn). London 1981.

Anderson, T. H., *The United States, Great Britain and the Cold War, 1944–1947*. London 1981.

Becker, J. H., *Winds of History: The German Years of Lucius Dubignon Clay*. London 1983.

Bernstein, B. J., 'The perils and politics of surrender: ending the war with Japan', *Pacific Historical Review*, **46** (Feb. 1977), 1–28.

Bernstein, B. J., 'New light on the Korean War', *The International History Review*, III (2) (April 1981), 256–77.

Blum, R. M., *Drawing the Line: the Origin of the American Containment Policy in East Asia*. London 1982.

Borg, Dorothy, and Waldo Heinrichs (eds), *Uncertain Years: Chinese–American Relations, 1947–1950*. London 1980.

Buckley, Roger, *Occupation Diplomacy: Britain, the United States, and Japan, 1945–1952*. Cambridge 1982.

Bullen, Roger, 'Great Britain, the United States and the Indian armistice resolution on the Korean War, November 1952', pp. 27–44, in Ian Nish (ed.), *Aspects of Anglo-Korean Relations*. London 1984.

Bullock, Alan, *Life and Times of Ernest Bevin*, vol. III. London 1983.

Burkman, T. W. (ed.), *The Occupation of Japan: The International Proceedings of 5th Symposium sponsored by the MacArthur Memorial, 21–22 October 1982*. Norfolk, Va. 1984.

Calvocoressi, Peter (ed.), *Survey of International Affairs 1947–1948, 1949–50*. London 1952–53.

Carlton, David, *Anthony Eden: A Biography*. London 1981.

Cohen, W. I. (ed.), *New Frontiers in American–East Asian Relations: Essays presented to Dorothy Borg*. New York 1983.

Cumings, Bruce (ed.), *The Origins of the Korean War: Liberation and the Emergence of Separate Regimes, 1945–1947*. Guildford 1981.

Cumings, Bruce (ed.), *Child of Conflict: The Korean–American Relationship, 1943–1953*. London 1983.

Daniels, Gordon, 'Britain's view of post-war Japan', pp. 257–77, in Ian Nish (ed.), *Anglo-Japanese Alienation, 1919–1952*. Cambridge 1982.

Deutscher, Issac, *Stalin: A Political Biography* (2nd edn). London 1967.

Divine, R. A., *Eisenhower and the Cold War*. Oxford 1981.

Djilas, Milovan, *Conversations with Stalin*. London 1962.

Donovan, R. J., *Tumultuous Years: The Presidency of Harry S. Truman, 1949–53*. London 1982.

Douglas, Roy, *From War to Cold War, 1942–1948*. London 1983.

Dower, J. W., *Empire and Aftermath: Yoshida Shigeru and the Japanese Experience, 1878–1954*. London 1979.

Drifte, Reinhard, *The Security Factor in Japan's Foreign Policy, 1945–1952*. Ripe, East Sussex 1983.

Farrar, P. N., 'Britain's proposal for a buffer zone south of the Yalu in November 1950', *Journal of Contemporary History*, **18** (2) (April 1983), 327–51.

Gillin, D. G., with Charles Etter, 'Staying on: Japanese soldiers and civilians in China, 1945–1949', *Journal of Asian Studies*, XLII (May 1983), 497–518.

Gimbel, John, *The Origins of the Marshall Plan*. Stanford, Calif. 1976.

Gordenker, Leon, *The United Nations and the Peaceful Unification of Korea: The Politics of Field Operations, 1947–1950*. The Hague 1959.

Grajdanzev, A. J., *Modern Korea*. New York 1944.

Grupta, Karunker, 'How did the Korean War begin?', *China Quarterly* 8 (1972) 699–716.

Hathaway, R. M., *Ambiguous Partnership: Britain and America, 1944–1947*. Guildford 1981.

Harris, Kenneth, *Attlee*. London 1982.

Henderson, Gregory, *Korea: The Politics of the Vortex*. Cambridge, Mass. 1968.

Henderson, Nicholas, *The Birth of Nato*. London 1982.

Higgins, Trumbull, *Korea and the Fall of MacArthur*. New York 1960.

Kim, Ilpyong J., *Communist Politics in North Korea*. London 1975.

Kim, Joungwon A., *Divided Korea: The Politics of Development, 1945–1972*. London 1976.

Kolko, Joyce and Gabriel, *The Limits of Power: The World and the United States Foreign Policy, 1945–1954*. London 1972.

Long, E. R., 'Earl Warren and the politics of anti-communism', *Pacific Historical Review,* **51** (1) (Feb. 1982), 51–70.

Lowe, Peter, 'Great Britain, Japan, and the Korean War, 1950–1', in John Chapman and David Steeds (eds), *Proceedings of the British Association for Japanese Studies*, IX (1984), 98–111.

Lowe, Peter, 'British attitudes to General MacArthur and Japan, 1948–1950', in Gordon Daniels (ed.), *Europe Interprets Japan*. Tenterden, Kent 1984.

Luard, Evan, *A History of the United Nations*, vol. I, *The Years of Western Dominance, 1945—1955*. London 1982.

McCormack, Gavin, 'The reunification of Korea: problems and prospects', *Pacific Affairs,* **55** (1) (Spring 1982), 5–31.

Messer, R. L., *The End of an Alliance: James F. Byrnes, Roosevelt, Truman, and the Origins of the Cold War*. Chapel Hill, NC 1982.

Milward, A. S., *The Reconstruction of Western Europe, 1945–51*. London 1984.

Morgan, K. O., *Labour in Power, 1945–1951*. Oxford 1984.

Myant, Martin, *Socialism and Democracy in Czechoslovakia, 1945–1948*. Cambridge 1981.

Myers, R. H. and M. R. Peattie (eds), *The Japanese Colonial Empire, 1895–1945*. Guildford 1984.

Nagai, Y. and A. Iriye (eds), *The Origins of the Cold War in Asia*. Tokyo 1977.

Nish, Ian, *The Origins of the Russo-Japanese War*. London 1985.

Oliver, R. T., *Syngman Rhee: The Man behind the Myth*. New York 1955.

O'Neill, Robert, *Australia in the Korean War, 1950–1953*, vol. I, *Strategy and Diplomacy*. Canberra 1981.

Ovendale, Ritchie, 'Britain, the USA and the European Cold War, 1945–8', *History,* **67** (220) (June 1982), 217–36.

Ovendale, Ritchie, 'Britain, the United States and the Cold War in SE Asia, 1945–50', *International Affairs,* **58** (3) (Summer 1982), 447–64.

Paige, G. D., *The Korean Decision*. London 1968.

Reardon-Anderson, James, *Yenan and the Great Powers: The Origins of Chinese Communist Policy, 1944–46*. London 1980.

Rees, David, *Korea: The Limited War*. London 1964.

Scalapino, R. A. (ed.), *North Korea To-Day*. London 1963.

Scalapino, R. A. and Chong-sik Lee, *Communism in Korea*, 2 parts. London 1972.

Schnabel, J. F., *United States Army in the Korean War. Policy and Direction: the First Year*. Washington 1972.

Schram, S. R., *Mao Zedong: A Preliminary Reassessment*. Hong Kong 1983.

Shlaim, Avi, *The United States and the Berlin Blockade, 1948–1949: A Study in Crisis Decision-Making*. London 1983.

Simmons, R. R., *The Strained alliance*. New York 1975.

Stueck, W. W. Jr, *The Road to Confrontation: American Policy Towards China and Korea, 1947–1950*. Chapel Hill, NC 1981.

Suh, Dae-sook, *The Korean Communist Movement, 1918–1948*. Princeton, NJ 1967.

Thorne, Christopher, *Allies of a Kind: The United States, Britain and the War Against Japan, 1941–1945*. London 1978.

Thorne, Christopher, *The Issue of War: States, Societies, and the Far Eastern Conflict of 1941–1945*. London 1985.

Tucker, N. B., *Patterns in the Dusk: Chinese–American Relations and the Recognition Controversy, 1949–1950*. New York 1983.

Ulam, A. B., *Stalin: The Man and his Era*. London 1974.

Whiting, A. S., *China Crosses the Yalu: The Decision to Enter the Korean War*. New York 1960.

Wilson, Dick, *Chou: The Story of Zhou Enlai, 1898–1976*. London 1984.

Wittner, L. S., *American Intervention in Greece, 1943–1949*. Guildford 1982.

Wolf, D. C., '"To secure a conveniences": Britain recognise China – 1950', *Journal of Contemporary History*, **18** (2) (April 1983), 299–326.

Yoshitsu, Michael, *Japan and the San Francisco Settlement*. New York 1983.

# MAPS

225

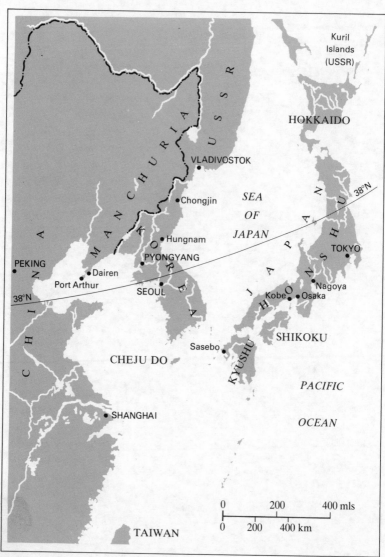

Map 1  Korea and neighbouring areas

Map 2   Korea, the 38th Parallel, and Demarcation Line, 1953

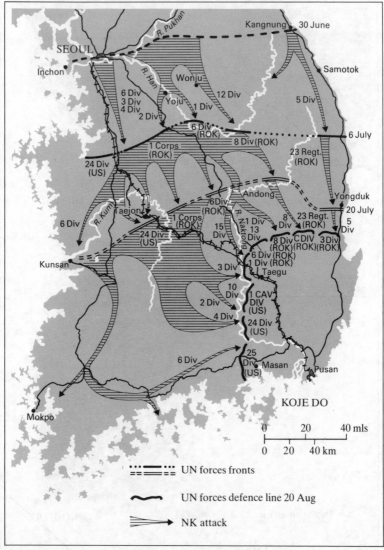

Map 3   The North Korean advance July–September 1950

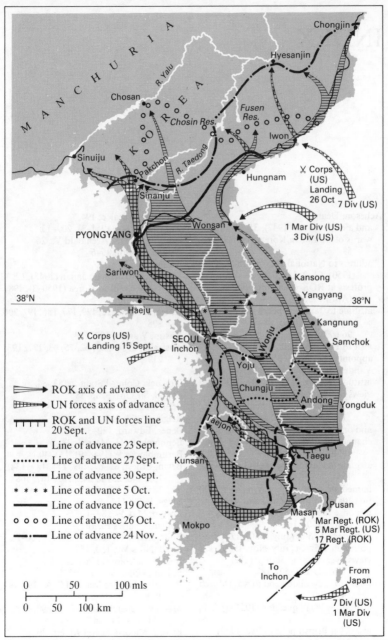

Map 4   The UN Command's counter-attack, September to November 1950

229

# INDEX

Acheson, Dean
  and aid for Korea (1947), 31
  warns of trouble in Korea (April 1949),
    59
  address to National Press Club (Jan.
    1950), 61–2, 119, 120
  protests at ROK economic policy
    (April 1950), 65
  attitude to Japanese peace treaty
    (1949–50), 81, 85, 88–9, 90, 95 n44,
    96 n73
  visit to London (May 1950), 90
  appointed Secretary of State (1949), 105
  Vandenberg's opinion of, 105–6
  attitude to China (1949), 109, 110–11
  views on recognition of Chinese
    Communist government, 112–13,
    117
  and origins of NATO, 142
  changes views over Taiwan (May–June
    1950), 153, 154
  attitude to Chiang Kai-shek (June 1950),
    154
  immediate response to war in Korea, 160
  first Blair House meeting and, 161
  response to Anglo-Soviet exchanges
    (July 1950), 167–8
  attitude to China (July 1950), 178
  policy on Taiwan (July–Nov. 1950), 178
  views over crossing 38th parallel
    (Sept.–Oct. 1950), 187
  hopes for negotiated end to war (March
    1951), 207
  attitude to POW question (1951–3), 210,
    211
  attack on British policy (Dec. 1952),
    212
  Eden's criticisms of, 212
Allison, John M., 151, 158, 181–2
Anderson, Vernice, 194
Armistice talks (1951–3), 209–13
Arnold, General Archibald V., 26
Ashida Hitoshi, 85–6
Atomic bombs
  decision to drop on Japan (1945), 12, 13
  possible use of in Korea (1950–3), 198,
    206, 213
Attlee, Clement, 12, 129, 177, 185, 192, 206,
  208
Austin, Warren, 182, 188
Australia, 37, 44, 45, 62, 75, 93, 177, 193,
  217

Babcock, Colonel Stanton, 83, 84
Bajpai, Sir Girja, 186, 188
Bebler, Alex, 160–1
Belgium, 177, 217
Benes, Edward, 130–3
Benninghoff, H. Merrell, 23
Berlin blockade (1948–9), 133–40
Bevin, Ernest, 83, 87, 109, 111, 129, 134,
  139, 140–2, 148 n43, 162, 167, 168,
  185, 192, 199, 208
Biggs, E. T., 114
Bishop, Max W., 80–1
Bohlen, Charles E., 165
Bolte, Major-General Charles L., 66–7
Bond, Niles W., 150, 151
Bonesteel, Colonel Charles, 14
Borton, Hugh, 29
Bouchier, Air Vice-Marshal C. A., 190, 191,
  199
Bradley, General Omar N., 85, 90, 118,
  161, 194, 195, 207
Brown, Major-General Albert, 30
Brownjohn, Major-General N. C. D., 148
  n43
Bunce, Arthur, 30, 64

Burgess, Guy, 146, 157
Burma, xii, 118, 129, 167
Butler, R. A., 30-1
Butterworth, W. Walton, 47, 48, 82, 89,
   111, 112, 118
Buzzard, G. G., 198
Byrnes, James F., 13, 23, 27, 128

Cabot, John, 108-9
Cadogan, Sir Alexander, 139
Cairo conference (1943), 10
Canada, 37, 44, 45, 143, 177, 217
Chang Han-fu, 200
Chang, John M., 62
Chauvel, Jean, 139
Cheju island, 2, 57, 58
Chen Cheng, 179
Chennault, General Claire L., 115
Chiang Ching-kuo, 179
Chiang Kai-shek, Generalissimo
   and Cairo conference (1943), 10
   attitude to internal situation, 98, 100
   policy towards Soviet Union, 99-100
   refers to Korea (Oct. 1948), 102
   resigns as president, 102
   attitude to MacArthur, 115
   retreats to Taiwan, 113
   attitude to Rhee, 150-2, 153
   Acheson's censure of, 154
   relations with ROK, 150-3
   threat to Taiwan and, 152
   offers military help to ROK, 153
   MacArthur's visit to see (July–Aug.
      1950), 179-81
   hopes for third world war, 178
Chile, 193
China, *see also* Taiwan
   Cairo conference (1943) and, 10
   Yalta agreement (1945) and, 10
   Chapter 5, *passim*
   American wish for coalition
      government, 99, 101
   Soviet policy towards, 99-100
   decline of Kuomintang, 101-4
   CCP (Chinese Communist Party)
      statements, 100, 103-4, 108
   recognition issue and, 105-13
   ECA (Economic Co-operation
      Administration) and, 107
   Kuomintang retreat to Taiwan, 113
   fate of Taiwan and, 113-19, 152-4,
      178-80
   reaction to Korean War (June–July
      1950), 157, 182-3
   Indian relations with, 167, 186-7, 188-9
   intervention in Korea, 189-201

   policy towards Korean War (1950-3),
      189, 207, 208-15
Chou En-lai, 108, 120, 182, 189, 192, 197
Churchill, Winston S., 128
Clay, General Lucius D., 134-40
Clubb, O. Edmund, 100, 101
Collins, General J. Lawton, 85, 118
Connally, Senator Tom, 62
Cooke, Alistair, 101
Coulter, General John B., 47
Czechoslovakia, 130-3 138, 167

*Daily Mail*, 81
Davies, John Paton, 198
Dean, Patrick, 148 n43
Dening, Sir Esler, 27, 82, 83, 120
Dewey, Governor Thomas E., 85, 89, 101,
   110, 128
Dixon, Sir Pierson, 131-2
Douglas, Lewis, 132, 144, 168
Drumright, Everett, 63, 162
Dulles, John Foster, 37, 89, 91, 96 n73,
   128, 151, 158-60, 170, 187, 212-13
Dunn, James, 14

Eden, Anthony (1st Earl of Avon), 212
Egypt, 163, 170
Eichelberger, General Robert, 86
Eisenhower, General Dwight D., 208, 212,
   213
El Salvador, 37

Ferguson, Brigadier A. K., 79
Formosa, *see* Taiwan
Forrestal, James, 81, 115
France, 37, 44, 45, 177
Franklin, A. A. E., 198
Franks, Sir Oliver, 65, 95 n44, 144, 153,
   167, 177, 208
Fraser, Admiral Lord, 191

Gascoigne, Sir Alvary, 73, 78, 83, 87, 90-1,
   114, 159, 192
Germany, 9, 133-40
Goodfellow, M. Preston, 25, 41 n43
Gottwald, Clement, 131
Great Britain
   Hyde Park agreement (1944), 12
   Potsdam conference (1945) and, 12
   trusteeship in Korea and, 24
   views on Korea (1945-7), 25, 27, 29
   views on Korea (1948-50), 45, 46, 50-2
   attitude to Japanese recovery, 74-6, 81,
      86-7, 93
   desire for Japanese peace treaty, 82-3,
      90-1

Bevin's discussions with Acheson (May 1950), 90
attitude to Chinese developments (1948–9), 103, 114
exchanges with USA over recognition (1949), 104–6, 109–13
response of Attlee government to USA, 126, 128–30
rejects 'third power' concept, 130
views over Czechoslovakia (1948), 131–3
policy regarding Berlin blockade (1948–9), 133–40
construction of NATO alliance and, 140–2
assessment of Soviet power, 142–4
attitude over Taiwan (June 1950), 153
response to start of Korean war, 158–9, 162–3, 165
attempt to negotiate with Soviet Union (July 1950), 166–9
Acheson's acrimonious message to, 167–8
contributes to UN forces in Korea, 177
foreign ministers conference (Sept. 1950) and, 185
concern to keep Indian support, 185–6
attitude to crossing 38th parallel (Sept.–Oct. 1950), 188–92
opposition of chiefs of staff to crossing 38th parallel, 189–92
urges cautious policy to China, 199–200
warns against bombing operations, 198
MacArthur's criticism of (Nov. 1950), 199
proposes demilitarised zone, 199–200
Attlee's visit to Washington (Dec. 1950), 206
concern over motion condemning China, 207
contributes to removal of MacArthur, 208
Greece, 31, 128, 143
Gromyko, Andrei, 166, 168

Harriman, W. Averell, 194
Henderson, Arthur, 148 n43
Henderson, Loy, 188
Hillenkoetter, Admiral Roscoe H., 115, 203 n47
Hodge, General John Reed, x, 15, 21–37, 44, 45, 46
Holt, Captain Vyvyan, 159
Ho Hon, 22, 28
Hoffman, Paul, 107
Hoover, Herbert, 118

Howley, Colonel Frank, 135
Huang, Peter K., 114
Hull, Cordell, 9, 16 n27
Hungary, 37, 138
Hutchison, John C., 112, 182, 200
Huston, Cloyce K., 83

Iberian peninsula, 143
Ikeda Hayato, 89–90
India, 10, 36, 44, 45, 75, 163, 167, 168, 170, 185
Indo-China, xii, 118, 167
Inverchapel, 1st Baron, 31
Italy, 143
Ito Hirobumi, Prince, 2
*Izvestia*, 54

Jackson, S. H., 44, 45, 48
Jacobs, Joseph E., 44–5
Japan
  ambitions of in Korea, 1–2
  colonial policy towards Korea, 3–5
  end of Pacific war and, 11–14, 20
  Chapter 4, *passim*
  and Taiwan, 113–15
  start of Korean war and, 183
  Kennan's suggestions concerning (Aug. 1950), 183–4
*Jen Min Jih Pao*, 165
Jessup, Philip C., 63, 85, 117, 139, 184, 194
Johnson, Louis, 83, 85, 88, 90, 95 n44, 117, 161, 162, 167, 177, 180, 188
Joint Commission, U.S.-Soviet, 26–7, 32–6
Judd, Walter, 101

Kelly, Sir David, 120, 166, 168
Kennan, George F., 36, 77–80, 104, 105, 139, 141, 165, 169, 181, 183–4, 209
Kermode, D. W., 29, 30, 45
Kevauver, Senator Estes, 180
Khruschev, Nikita S., 51, 156
Kim Il Sung
  early career of, 8–9, 38
  fervent nationalism of, 38, 170
  and NKIPC, 50
  establishment of DPRK and, 50–1, 56
  outbreak of Korean war and, 156–7, 215
  Soviet and Chinese policies towards, 156–7
  policies after Korean war, 213–14
Kim Jong Il, 213
Kim Ku, 5–6, 24, 25, 32
Kim Kyu-sik, 22, 28
Kim Tu-bong, 39

Kirk, Admiral Alan, 166
Kirkpatrick, Sir Ivone, 148 n43
Knowland, Senator William F., 65, 118
Korea (before 1948)
  political and geographical character of, 2
  annexation of by Japan, 2–3
  impact of Japanese colonialism on, 3–5
  anti-Japanese resistance movements
    and, 5–9
  end of Pacific war and, 11–15
  Chapters 2 and 3, *passim*
  Hodge's policy towards south, 21–37,
    44–6
  CPKI (Committee for the Preparation of
    Korean Independence), 21–2
  KPR (Korean People's Republic), 22–3
  Rhee's policy in south, 22–3, 25–6, 28,
    29–32, 36–7, 47–8, 56–7
  Moscow conference and (1945), 24–5
  KDP (Korean Democratic Party), 24–5
  RDC (Representative Democratic
    Council), 25–6, 27
  DNF (Democratic National Front), 26,
    28
  NSRRKI (National Society for the
    Rapid Realisation of Korean
    Independence), 28
  CC (Left-Right Coalition Committee),
    28–9
  visit of Limb, 29–30
  American aid for south, 31–2
  Joint Commission and, 26–7, 32–6
  American policy towards south, 35–7
  Soviet policy towards north, 37–40
  NKIPC (North Korean Interim People's
    Committee), 39
Korea, Democratic People's Republic of
  (North Korea)
  establishment of, 49–50
  character of, 50–1
  armed strength of, 51
  DFUF (Democratic Front for the
    Attainment of Unification of the
    Fatherland), 53–4
  American assessment of NKLP, 53–4
  relations with Soviet Union, 54–6
  start of Korean War and, 156–7, 162–3
  military defeat of, 187–201
  attitude regarding peace talks, 210–13
  nature of after 1953, 213–14
Korea, Republic of (South Korea)
  establishment of, 48
  character of, 56–68
  UN (United Nations) and, 59, 154–5
  guerrilla warfare against, 57
  Cheju rebellion and, 57

Yosu rebellion and, 57
  American policy towards (1948–50),
    57–68
  visit of Jessup to, 64
  KMAG and, 65–8
  Dulles's visit to, 158–9
  military reverses of, 159, 162
  formation of UN Command in, 169
  crossing the 38th parallel and, 187–93
  attitude regarding peace talks, 209, 213
  development of after 1953, 213–14
Kuomintang, *see* China *and* Taiwan
Kuril islands, 10, 80, 85

Lady, Harold, 64
Langdon, William F., 23–4, 27, 28
Lapham, Roger D., 107
Lee Bum Suk, 151
Leviero, Anthony, 195
Li Tsung-jen, General, 101, 102, 110
Liao, W. I., 114
Liao, W. K. 114
Lie, Trygve, 177
Limb, Byung Chic (B. C.), 29, 30, 151
Lincoln, Brigadier-General George, 14
Lloyd, Selwyn, 212

MacArthur, General Douglas
  end of Pacific war and, 12, 14, 21
  character of, 72–3, 175–6
  political ambitions of, 73
  Gascoigne's assessment of (1948), 73–4
  policies in Japan, Chapter 5 *passim*
  discussions with Kennan, 77–80
  views on a Japanese peace treaty, 78–80
  interview with Ward Price, 81
  preoccupation with Chinese
    communism, 83
  attitude to Soviet Union, 83–4
  relationship with Yoshida, 87–90
  attitude to Dulles, 91
  views over Taiwan, 113–17, 152–4
  immediate reactions to Korean war, 160,
    163–4
  Johnson's warning over instructions to,
    162
  appointed to head UN Command,
    169–70
  conflicts with Truman, 175, 180–1,
    207–8
  nature of 'court' of, 176
  military strategy of, 176–8
  visit to Taiwan, 179–80
  message to Veterans convention, 180–1
  Inchon landing and, 187–8
  British chiefs of staff and, 189–93, 207

meeting with Truman, 194–5
attitude to China, 196–201
Attlee's criticisms of, 206
final clash with Truman, 207–8
dismissal of, 208
Republican convention (1952) and, 208
MacDonald, Malcolm, 114
Maclean, Donald, 146, 157
Magruder, Major-General Carter B., 84
Makins, Sir Roger, 192
Malaya, xii, 112, 152, 167, 177
Malik, Jacob, 85, 139, 169, 182, 184, 209
*Manchester Guardian*, 32, 101
Manchuria, 7, 10–13, 19, 36, 38, 52, 100, 109, 120–1, 163, 189, 192
Mao Tse-tung, 8, 37, 99, 100, 103–5, 108, 111–12, 118, 119–20, 156, 161
Mare, Arthur de la, 27, 29–30
Marshall, General George, 12, 33, 99, 101, 104, 128, 129, 136, 140, 141, 188, 208
Martin, Edwin, 29
Masaryk, Jan, 133
Masaryk, Thomas, 130
MacDermot, D. F., 46
McCarthy, Senator Joseph, 188, 207
McNeill, Hector, 148 n43
Meiji constitution (1889), 50
Menon, Krishna, 211
Menon, Kumara P. S., 37, 45
Merchant, Livingston T., 118
Min Chong, 39
Molotov, Viacheslav, 33
Muccio, John J.
    appointed ambassador to ROK, 48
    character of, 48
    warns of DPRK strength, 51
    assessment of Rhee by, 56–7
    views of political situation in Korea (1949), 57, 61, 63, 158
    trenchant words to Rhee (Jan. 1950), 64
    reactions to start of Korean war, 159–60, 164
    views of MacArthur, 176, 194, 201 n2
Murphy, Robert, 138

NATO, 140–2
Nehru, Jawaharlal, 109, 185–6, 203 n47
Netherlands, 177, 193
*New York Times*, 112, 124 n68
New Zealand, 75, 93, 177
Nitze, Paul, 144, 181
Nomura Kichisaburo, Admiral, 6, 16 n27
Norstad, Lt. General Lauris, 118
North Korean Labour Party (NKLP), 53, 54

Okinawa, 13, 78, 80, 85, 88, 152
Oliver, R. T., 34

Pace, Frank, 194
Pai Chung-hsi, General, 110, 115
Pak Hon-yong, 8, 22, 39, 51, 68
Pakistan, 177, 193
Panikkar, K. M., 109, 186, 189, 192
Patterson, George S., 45, 48
Pauley, Edwin, 13
Peach, Major F. S. B., 154, 155
Philby, Kim, 146, 157
Philippines, 37, 45, 78, 88, 114, 119, 150, 152, 167, 177, 193
Poland, 10, 138
Potsdam conference (1945), 12, 13, 82, 116
Prague *coup*, (1948), 131–3
*Pravda*, 54, 165–6
Price, G. Ward, 81

Quirino, Elpidio, 60, 113

Radford, Admiral Arthur, 194
Rankin, Squadron Leader R. J., 154, 155
*Red Fleet*, 79
Rhee, Syngman
    early career of, 6
    developments in 1945 and, 22–3
    Hodge's relations with, 25–6, 28, 47
    rivalry with Kim Ku, 25
    Goodfellow and, 25, 41 n43
    and NSRRKI, 28
    political skills of, 29–30, 32, 36–7
    election as president of ROK, 48
    Muccio's view of, 56–7
    policy of (1948–50), 56–68
    incidents at Kaesong and Chunchon and, 60
    reaction to Connally's press interview, 62–3
    explanation of causes of inflation, 64
    growing authoritarianism of, 64, 157–8
    elections (May 1950) and, 65
    attitude to Chiang Kai-shek, 150–2
    meeting with Dulles (June 1950), 158–9
    reactions to North Korean advance, 162
    breakdown suffered by, 162
    crossing 38th parallel and, 183, 187–91
    British views of, 189–90
    attitude to peace talks (1951–3), 209, 213
    overthow of (1960), 214
Ridgway, General Matthew B., 207, 210
Roberts, Frank, 148 n43
Roberts, Brigadier-General W. L., 60, 65, 66, 165
Robertson, General Sir Brian, 135

Roosevelt, Franklin D., 9, 73, 98
Royall, Kenneth, 134
Rusk, Dean, 14, 62, 144, 153, 181, 192
Russia, Tsarist *see also* Soviet Union, 1
Russo-Japanese war (1904–5), 1, 10

Saito Makoto, Admiral, 4
Sakhalin, 10, 80, 86
Scandinavia, 142
Schaub, William F., 145
Schuman, Robert, 138
Sherman, Admiral Forrest P., 85, 118
Shigemitsu Mamoru, 6, 16 n27
Shin Ik Hi, 151
Shinwell, Emanuel, 192, 202 n5
Shtikov, General Terentyi, 26, 33, 36
Sihn, Captain, 151
Sino-Soviet treaty (1945), 99
   (1950), 119–21
Slessor, Air Chief Marshal Sir John, 144,
   190–1, 207, 208
Slim, Field Marshal Sir William, 190
Smith, Senator H. Alexander, 118
Smith, Kingsbury, 139
Smith, General Walter Bedell, 137
Sokolovsky, Marshal Vassily, 136
South Africa, Union of, 75, 177, 217
South Korean Labour Party (SKLP), 54,
   57
*Soviet Monitor*, 33, 120
Soviet Union
   policy regarding Korea (1945), 13, 19, 20
   trusteeship and, 23–5
   Moscow conference (Dec. 1945) and, 24
   Joint Commission and, 26–7, 32–6
   policy in north Korea (1945–8), 37–40
   withdrawal of forces from north Korea,
      39, 49
   relations with DPRK (1948–50), 49–56
   possible threat to Japan, 77–80, 83
   fear of Japanese revival, 82, 91–2
   Gascoigne's comments on, 91
   policy towards China (1945–8), 99–100
   Mao Tse-tung's attitude to, 103–4
   Acheson's view of Sino-Soviet relations,
      117–19
   Mao's visit to, 119–20
   Sino-Soviet agreement (1950), 120–1
   Chapter 6 *passim*
   and Czechoslovak crisis (1948), 130–3
   and Berlin blockade, 133–40
   American and British assessments of,
      142–5
   NSC 68 and, 145
   outbreak of Korean war and, 156–7
   Yugoslavia's attitude towards, 160–1

absence of from UN Security Council,
   160–1
reactions to war in Korea, 162, 164–9
return to UN Security Council, 181, 182
possibility of war with USA, 183, 195
Kennan's wish to foster contacts with,
   183–4
possible reoccupation of North Korea,
   191
British speculation on Sino-Soviet
   relations, 198
desire for settlement in Korea, 209
policy regarding Menon proposal,
   (1952), 211
Kim Il Sung's attitude towards, 213–14
Stalin, Joseph
   Kim Il Sung inspired by, 6
   views towards Korea (1945), 11
   Potsdam conference and, 12, 13
   division of Korea at 38th parallel and,
      14, 19–20
   attitude to CCP, 99–100, 119–21
   Mao Tse-tung's praise of, 103
   character and policies of, 127
   Berlin blockade and, 134–40
   possible attitude towards a war in Korea,
      51, 156–7
   response to Korean war, 164–5, 166
   Bevin's view of, 168
   death of, 213
Stevenson, Governor Adlai, 212, 216 n15
Stevenson, Sir Ralph, 111, 112
Stilwell, General Joseph W., 98
Strang, Sir William, 130, 135
Streat, Sir Raymond, 75–6
Strong, Robert C., 202 n12–18
Sun Li-jen, General, 111, 113, 152
Sun Yat-sen, 104, 113
Syria, 37, 44

Taft, Senator Robert A., 89, 118, 169, 212
Taiwan (Formosa)
   Kuomintang retreat to, 113
   relationship with Japan, 113–15
   autonomy movement in, 114
   MacArthur's attitude towards, 114–16
   US joint chiefs of staff and, 117–18
   Acheson's views on, 117–19
   Republican pressure for aid to, 118
   statements of Truman and Acheson
      regarding, 118–19
   links between Korea and, 150–2
   Rhee's views on possible capture of, 151
   MacArthur's warning over, 152
   change in American policy regarding,
      152–3

offer of military aid to ROK, 153
Truman's statement (June 1950), 153–4
views of Britain and India regarding, 167
Acheson's resentment at Bevin's reference to, 167
MacArthur's visit to, 179–80
suppression of dissent in, 179
Strong's criticisms of MacArthur over, 180, 202 n12–18
MacArthur's reiteration of importance of, 180
MacArthur's message to Veterans concerning, 180–1
Chou En-lai's strength of feeling over, 182
Kennan's views regarding, 183
Truman's discussions with MacArthur over, 195
Chinese wish to acquire, 209
POW issue and, 211
Tedder, Marshal of the RAF Lord, 191
Tehran conference (1943), 10
Terauchi Masatake, Field Marshal, 3
Thailand, 118, 177, 193
*The Economist*, 75
*The Times*, 198
Thurmond, Governor Strom, 146 n3
Tibet, 186
Tito, Marshal Joseph, 108
Truman, Harry S.
  succeeds to presidency, 11
  character and policies of, 11–12
  decision to use atomic bombs (1945), 13–14
  concern over Korea, 31
  determination to withdraw troops from Korea, 48
  approves economic aid to ROK, 48, 61
  Truman doctrine, 77, 128–9
  attitude to Japanese peace treaty, 88, 89
  policy towards China, 99
  opposition to communist participation in government of China, 101
  relationship with Acheson, 105–6
  ire at Chinese communists, 110
  appreciation of reasons for CCP victory in China, 117
  issues press statement over Taiwan (Jan. 1950), 118–19
  views on Soviet Union (1946), 127–8
  Berlin blockade and, 136
  NSC 68 and, 145
  statement (June 1950), 153–4
  views over Taiwan, 154
  response to North Korean advance, 160
  Webb's account of meeting, 161–2

condemnation of 'Munich-type' policy, 169
conflicts with MacArthur, 175, 180–1, 207–8
desire for British aid in Korea, 177
policy regarding Taiwan (June–Nov. 1950), 178
Nehru's doubts over, 186, 203 n47
decision to dismiss Johnson, 188
Wake island meeting and, 194–5
authorises release of account to Leviero, 195
no desire for conflict with China, 199
views Korean war as police action, 196
possible use of atomic weapons in Korea, 206
response to Chinese intervention, 199
hopes for contact with China (March 1951), 207
decline of popularity of, 208
supports voluntary return of POWs, 210
decides not to seek re-election, 212
Turkey, 31, 128, 143, 177, 193

UNCOK, *see* United Nations
UNCURK, *see* United Nations
United Nations
  involvement in Korea, 36, 43
  establishment of UNTCOK, 37, 43–4
  friction between Americans and UNTCOK, 44–6, 48
  divisions within UNTCOK, 45
  supervision of south Korean elections, 46
  report of UNTCOK on elections, 48
  recognises ROK, 49
  UNTCOK report on ROK (Oct. 1948), 48–9
  establishment of UNCOK, 49
  ambiguity over recognition of ROK, 49
  unhappy role of UNCOK, 49
  UNCOK on outbreak of Korean war, 154–6
  Soviet absence from Security Council, 160–1
  DPRK accused of aggression at, 161, 162
  establishment of UN Command in Korea, 169
  recommends military support for ROK, 177–8
  nature of operations in Korea, 178, 187
  possible involvement in Taiwan, 181
  British views on role of, 185
  British dissatisfaction with UNCOK, 185
  role of in a reunified Korea, 185

Slessor's comments on, 190–1
establishment of UNCURK, 193
UN forces cross 38th parallel, 195–6
UN forces in North Korea, 196
motion condemning Chinese aggression, 207
fears regarding MacArthur, 207–8
Chinese Communist desire for seat in, 209
Indian proposals regarding POWs, 211
UN forces in Korea, 217
UN casualties in Korea, 218
UNTCOK, *see* United Nations
United States of America
favours trusteeship in Korea, 10–11, 15
planning to end Pacific War, 11–13
policies of Roosevelt and Truman, 11–12
Potsdam conference and, 12
adoption of 38th parallel, 12–13, 14, 19
appointment of Hodge, 20–1
arrival of troops in Korea, 19
policy of military government, 21 ff.
Moscow conference and (Dec. 1945), 24–5
policy towards Joint Commission, 26–36
economic aid to Korea, 31
joint chiefs of staff assessment of Korea (Sept. 1947), 36
policy concerning UN in Korea, 37, 43–9
disaggreements over UNTCOK, 44–8
recognises ROK, 48
withdraws troops from ROK, 48
concern over North Korea, 57
policy towards ROK (1949–50), 59–61
vote over Korea aid bill, 61
statements of Truman, Acheson, and Connally, 61–3
role of KMAG, 65–7
initial aims in occupation of Japan, 72
role of MacArthur in Japan, 72–4
economic policy regarding Japan, 74–7
change in policy over Japan, 77–8
considers Japanese peace treaty, 78, 88–90
Kennan's visit to Japan, 77–80
policy towards Kuomintang China, 80–1, 98–102, 104
views on CCP, 80–1, 83, 103–4
policy over recognition of Chinese Communists, 104
exchanges with Britain over recognition, 106, 109–13
policy regarding Taiwan, 113–18
impact of Truman Doctrine, 128–9
policy towards Prague coup (1948), 132–3
policy concerning Berlin blockade, 133–40
construction of NATO, 140–2
policy over Taiwan (May–June 1950), 150–4
reactions to start of Korean War, 157–69
and UN Command in Korea, 169–70
Inchon landing and effects of, 187–8
crossing of 38th parallel and, 181–8
aims for unified Korea, 188–93
Wake island meeting, 194–5
conflicts between MacArthur and Truman, 180–1, 207–8
attitude towards possible Chinese action, 195–201
consequences of Chinese intervention and, 206
possible use of atomic weapon, 198, 206, 213
desire to condemn China in UN, 207
beginning of peace talks, 209
POW question and, 210–13
attitude to Rhee, 213, 214
termination of war, 213
continued involvement in Korea, 214

Vandenberg, Senator Arthur H., 61, 89, 101, 105–6, 128
Vandenberg, General Hoyt, 85
Voorhees, Tracy S., 116
Vyshinsky, Andrei, 82, 108

Wake island meeting (1950), 194–5
Wallace, Henry, 146 n3
*Washington Post*, 112, 124 n68
Webb, James E., 161
Whitney, General Courtney, 176, 194
Williams, George Z., 21
Williams, Jay Jerome, 6, 34
Willoughby, General Charles, 77, 92, 114, 176, 205 n110
Won Se-hun, 28

Yalta conference (1945), 10, 100
Yanaihara Tadao, 4
Yeh, George, 153
Yi dynasty (1392–1910), 2, 9, 22
Yo Un-hyong, 21, 26, 28
Yoshida Shigeru, 86–92
Younger, Kenneth, 162
Yuan Shik-k'ai, 2
Yugoslavia, 160–1, 163, 170

Zorin, Valerian, 132